AF600474

KNIGHTS IN ARMS

Prose Romance, Masculinity, and Eastern Mediterranean Trade in Early Modern England, 1565–1655

GORAN STANIVUKOVIC

Knights in Arms

Prose Romance, Masculinity, and Eastern Mediterranean Trade in Early Modern England, 1565–1655

UNIVERSITY OF TORONTO PRESS
Toronto Buffalo London

Toronto Buffalo London
www.utppublishing.com

ISBN 978-1-4426-4887-6

Library and Archives Canada Cataloguing in Publication

Stanivukovic, Goran V., author
Knights in arms : prose romance, masculinity, and Eastern Mediterranean trade in early modern England, 1565–1655 / Goran Stanivukovic.

Includes bibliographical references and index.
ISBN 978-1-4426-4887-6 (bound)

1. English prose literature–16th century–History and criticism. 2. English prose literature–17th century–History and criticism. 3. Romances, English–History and criticism. 4. Masculinity in literature. 5. Homosexuality in literature. 6. Commerce in literature. 7. Travel in literature. 8. Geography in literature. 9. Chivalry in literature. 10. Middle East–In literature. I. Title.

PR756.M36S73 2015 820.9'353 C2015-906755-3

This book has been published with the help of a grant from the Federation for the Humanities and Social Sciences, through the Awards to Scholarly Publications Program, using funds provided by the Social Sciences and Humanities Research Council of Canada.

University of Toronto Press acknowledges the financial assistance to its publishing program of the Canada Council for the Arts and the Ontario Arts Council, an agency of the Government of Ontario.

Canada Council for the Arts | Conseil des Arts du Canada

Funded by the Government of Canada | Financé par le gouvernement du Canada

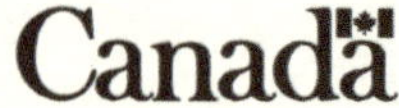

Contents

Acknowledgments

This book would not have been written without the short-term fellowships and grants from the Folger Shakespeare Library, the Huntington Library, the Newberry Library, the Harry Ransom Humanities Research Center at the University of Texas at Austin, the South Central Modern Languages Association, and the UCLA Center for Medieval and Renaissance Studies. Words of thanks are not enough to acknowledge the assistance I received from the staff of these libraries and archives; they generously shared their expertise with me at every step of my research. I am also indebted to the staff of the manuscripts and maps reading rooms in the British Library, and to the staff of the Bodleian Library for their help. I also wish to acknowledge the financial assistance from the Social Sciences and Humanities Research Council of Canada. I am particularly grateful to the Faculty of Graduate Studies and Research at Saint Mary's University for supporting my scholarship over the years. I am also happy to express my gratitude to the immensely helpful staff of the London Library. The Library of Congress proved yet again to be a resource of hidden treasures and a congenial writing space.

Suzanne Rancourt's interest in this project and her encouragement have made her an ideal editor to work with. My many thanks go to the editorial and production staff at the University of Toronto Press for their dedication to this project. I am especially grateful to Gillian Scobie for copy editing. My thanks go to the readers who read this book in draft and who made suggestions for improvements. Over the years, I have been fortunate to be supported by the generosity and insight of many friends and colleagues. They engaged me in discussions, invited me to give talks, and offered to co-organize conference panels with me;

they made suggestions for reading, questioned my claims, directed me to archival material I did not know about, pushed me to think in new directions, and generously and critically read drafts, and offered advice. Constance C. Relihan provided enthusiastic support and gave help at all stages of my work on this book. I remain indebted to her critical sensitivity and deep knowledge of romance writing. Lori Humphrey Newcomb has the talent to make many hours of talking about prose romances the most enjoyable time ever spent discussing these drawn-out fictions. Her enlightening ability to make powerful claims about the importance of fiction within early modern historiography and literary history, and her faith in this book, sustained me throughout my work on this project. Steve Mentz has been a source of insightful ideas about romance on many occasions, for which I thank him. I am grateful to Elissa Asp, Rebecca Bach, Reid Barbour, Gerd Bayer, Zorica Bečanović-Nikolić, Donald Beecher, Ronald Bond, Palmira Brummett, Sarah Carter, Basil Chiasson, Bradin Cormack, James Daybell, Mario DiGangi, Jonathan Ellis, Patrick Flanery, Stephen Guy-Bray, Teresa Heffernan, Elizabeth Hageman, Lorna Hutson, Ansgar Kelly, Veselin Kostić, Mary Ellen Lamb, Colin Lahive, Naomi Conn Liebler, Debra Ligorsky, Ivan Lupić, Melanie MacKenzie, Laurie Maguire, Robert Maslen, Carla Mazzio, Sara Malton, Marcus Nevitt, Tony Telford, Ian F. Moulton, Patricia Parker, Liz Pentland, Russell Perkin, Bryan Reynolds, Ana-María Sánchez Arce, Stuart Sillars, Peter Sillitoe, Alan Stewart, Tim Stretton, Valerie Traub, Daniel Vitkus, Andrew van der Vlies, Marcus Waithe, and Valerie Wayne. I wish to express my obligation to Will Flanagan from the Department of Geography at Saint Mary's University for producing the reference map of the Eastern Mediterranean.

This book is for my parents, who first introduced me to the Mediterranean.

An earlier version of some parts of the chapter, "Cruising the Eastern Mediterranean: The Knight, the Friend, the Favourite, and the Homoerotic Romance," was previously published as an essay in *Prose Fiction and Early Modern Sexualities in England*. I thank the Newberry Library for providing the images that appear in the pages of this book.

Illustrations

Reference map of the Eastern Mediterranean and romance writing, 1565–1655

Preface

This book argues that prose romances are expressive of three important cultural phenomena of the late sixteenth and early seventeenth centuries: the rise of overseas travel in the Eastern Mediterranean; the proliferation of travel literature and the fictions prompted by such travels; and the contacts between men from East and West engaged in trade. Because romance narratives are displaced in the East and because, as imaginary literature, romances engage with the wondrous and the faraway, prose romances create new literary means of conceptualizing other topics treated in the more factual travelogues: gender, sexuality, ethnicity, trade, and empire. The new openness towards the Eastern Mediterranean in late sixteenth-century England was not only a matter of overcoming isolationism or extending national interests in the political sphere of the Mediterranean. It represented a development in the complexity of England's relationship with Catholic Europe and the Ottoman Empire in the Eastern Mediterranean. It also complemented writing on English Protestant nationalism.

Among many fascinating features of romance, some of which have not yet been explored, their link of homosocial and homoerotic pleasure with attempts to eliminate that pleasure anticipates the complex intertwining and dynamic interaction that present-day queer theory pursues in its crucial and ever so important exploration of desire on the one hand, and compulsory heterosexuality and the enduring features of masculine domination, on the other. While differentiating the romances' fictionalization of male eroticism from the role of sex in early modern culture, and from modern models of male same-sex eroticism, I draw attention to the many ways in which the romances illuminate male sexuality against the ideals of dichotomized sexual difference and against the notion of male–male relations as always being framed by homosexuality. Desire "between men"[1] in romances takes more forms than even homosexual pleasure imagines itself to be against the heroically brash heterosexual norm and heterosexual lovemaking. The stories of erotic masculinity, of knights in arms when they are out of their armour, are not only fictions of the many unheroic ways that bring the knights together, but also narratives of the Eastern Mediterranean as a space that facilitates new bonds between men. In the Eastern Mediterranean, the new knights of the sixteenth and early seventeenth centuries – venturing merchants, young men in search of profit in trade, husbands looking to augment the wealth of their households – searched for glory and profit. Under the surface of chivalric narratives of romances another story unfolds, one in which territories of heroic valour become spaces of new trade. This book traces some of the narrative routes taken by chivalric fiction as it underpins fictions of trade, exchange, and contacts with the East, narratives that started to dominate romance writing from around 1565 until about 1655, the dates of the earliest and the latest texts discussed in this book. The progressive shift from romances' investment in chivalry to their growing interest in mercantilism shaped the ways in which the figure of the knight, the heroic male character, started to be re-envisaged in romances.

During the period covered by this book, prose romances became a "cultural reservoir"[2] of stories about masculinity. This took place at a time when heroic masculinity, familiar from medieval chivalric culture, was replaced with the romantic masculinity of Elizabethan England, and when England opened up trade and diplomacy in the Eastern Mediterranean. In the fictions written in the last few decades of the sixteenth century, we witness a progressive shift in emphasis from the militant and chivalric agency of men whose purpose is to prove their valour and fortitude in combat with other heroic men, to men whose agency's primary goal is courtship with women. Yet we also witness how, in these fictions of heteroerotic courtship, heroic men engage with other men, especially men from the East, in ways that complicate the heroic men's romantic endeavours. Arguing that "the prose fiction of the 1560s and 1570s" provides numerous examples of "the displacement of heroic masculinity from combat to textual exchange," that is from "the violence explicitly wreaked ... by men upon men, into vengeance visited by the narratives themselves upon their heroines," Lorna Hutson has illuminatingly documented the shift from the old ideal of chivalric or heroic masculinity to masculinity invested in the courtship of women and discourses of love.[3] However, heroic masculinity in the novellas discussed by Hutson is not only textually displaced in the heteroerotic narratives, but also in homosocial narratives in which heroic violence has metamorphosed into the strategy of negotiating the power of mercantile exchange between men. At such narrative moments in the mid-sixteenth century novella, negotiating economic advantage often means crafting rhetorical scenarios that also have sexual implications. Going beyond the decades explored by Hutson, we witness a further development and transformation of the narrative strategy of the displacement of heroic masculinity in texts that imagine that masculinity at the crossroads at which mercantilism and male sexuality intersect. Increasingly, in the prose fiction of the 1580s and 1590s, and progressively more so in the fiction of the early 1600s, chivalric agency is explored in the territories of the East where that agency is first tested in contacts and clashes with men from the East, before it is legitimized in courtship and marriage. This new kind of fiction, in which heroic men wreak violence against other, but foreign, heroic men has a different goal than the fiction of the preceding decades, namely that in these turn-of-the-century fictions, militant chivalry turned into a different strategy of engaging masculine agency in the service of the state: the pursuit of commercial interest and political power in the East. The joint effect of this cultural and social change meant that the knight became involved in different kinds of transactions with men from the East that were no longer fuelled only by the rhetoric of the holy war. Because prose romances are set in eastern territories far away from England and because they violate verisimilitude, their writers explore male subjectivity with the kind of permissiveness that was often limited in literature set at home. In cheap print popular literature, such as prose romances, the close relationship between language and materiality, and rhetoric and embodiment, reveal to the socially diverse classes of male and female readers possibilities of erotic experiences otherwise unavailable in early modern England.

Notable for their focus on the Eastern Mediterranean, the romances of Lady Mary Wroth, Emanuel Forde, Richard Johnson, Henry Robarts, Philip Sidney, Lawrence Twyne, Robert Parry, Diego Ortuñez Calahorra, Madeleine de Scudéry, the anonymous *Palladine of England, Palmendos, Amadis de Gaule, Palmerin D'Oliva, Palmerin of England, Oceander,* and several manuscript works, fictionalize masculinity within the arenas of travel, trade, and desire. These works reflect a fascination with the Eastern Mediterranean in early modern England. They are a reminder of the close link that exists between romance and the Mediterranean, a connection that reaches back in time to include the earliest romances of Hellenic antiquity as texts written early in the history of the novel.[4] The male characters, whose stories I explore in a range of archival texts about travel, geography, and commerce often embark on a chivalric voyage, or leave the paternal home to wander in the Eastern Mediterranean, and find themselves staying in the East. While most end up marrying a princess, usually from the East, before arriving at this idealized social and geographical destination, they become embroiled in complex situations involving merchants, other travelling knights, or threatening Saracens, that put masculine virtue to the test. Romance stories of mercantile exchange and contacts thus turn into stories of affective and erotic transactions between men from West and East. If homoerotic attachment between travelling knights put pressure on marriage, the homosocial bonding between merchant knights from the West and men from the East, or among knights-errant themselves, reveals how profoundly radical some of the romance narratives had become. The texts at the centre of this book imagine the Ottoman Mediterranean as a space of amorous, erotic, and commercial opportunity as much as a territory of danger and treacherous obstacles. They thus provoke the knight-errant to act in ways that some of his literary counterparts in drama do not.

This book is made up of two parts; the first part consists of three chapters, the second of two. The introduction, "Mapping Territories," covers the terminological ground, discussing the relationship between romance as a term in its historical context of late medieval and early modern writing and literature about travel and trade in the Eastern Mediterranean, which we can relate to romances both in terms of the themes covered in those treatises and in terms of the narrative strategies employed to explore those themes. The main argument here is that prose romances, travel and mercantile writing, and geographical treatises and maps of the 1580s and the first half of the 1600s share a growing interest in some of the same topics related to the Eastern Mediterranean as both a space of political rivalry and of cross-cultural exchanges. Helen Cooper's point that romance, being "a capacious term," has "an unnerving tendency to metamorphose from text to text or period to period,"[5] precisely captures the sense in which the rhetorical and conceptual structures and styles recognized in romances can also be found in other fields of knowledge and writing such as travel, mercantilism, and geography that constitute the discourses and narratives of the Eastern Mediterranean. In that sense, one could say that romance literature of the sixteenth and seventeenth centuries includes not just imaginative fiction but also writing about Mediterranean travel, trade, and geography. As Patricia Parker has argued, romance is neither a "fixed generic prescription" nor an "abstract transhistorical category" of escapist fiction, but a mode of writing distinguished by specific narrative strategies.[6] Expanding on Parker's line of argument, Barbara Fuchs makes the point that romance can be treated as either a genre or a literary strategy, but certainly as a resource in both fictional and non-fictional writing. In particular, she associates the mode of romance with the early modern literature of colonialism in the New World, thus creating a link between romance's investment in fantasy and the grand aspirations of imperial fictions.[7] The introduction also provides a methodological explanation for the adaptation of the critical strategy of "distant reading," adapted from Franco Moretti and employed in this book, not to assess the actual geography that frames fictional narratives, but to abstract the repeated references to some of the same geographical locales so that meanings about agency and the politics of fiction that shape it can be assessed.[8] The introduction ends with a brief critical overview of the definitions of the Eastern Mediterranean in early modern geographical writing and cartographic representations, and with an elucidation of the claim that romances were texts written by men for men at the time middle-class masculinity was shaped.

The first part, "The Knight and the Romance of Trade," takes as its subject the interweaving discourses of merchant empire, masculine agency, and romance geography in the Eastern Mediterranean. The principal text here is Richard Johnson's prose romance *The Seven Champions of Christendome* (Part I 1596, Part II 1597), a romance deeply engaged with the East and a fiction foregrounding the imaginary and conceptual commercial orientation of prose fiction with the subject of the trade with the East, most expressively embodied in the figure of the entrepreneurial knight. The first chapter in part I, "Purchasing Kingdoms in the Eastern Mediterranean," examines the rhetorical and conceptual similarities between the first part of Johnson's romance and early modern writing on trade in the East and the notion of empire, and introduces the concept of "merchant empire" as a critical alternative to imperialism as a political and ideological project that had not yet come into being. Arguing that Johnson's romance is a proto-imperial fiction, this chapter reads it as part of a larger body of writing in which the East is constructed as a mercantile opportunity for the West. The second chapter in part I, "The Knight on the Silk Road," reads the second part of Johnson's romance alongside early modern writing about the eastern trade, especially the Silk Road routes attached to the commercial roads within the Eastern Mediterranean. Between the sea ports of Northern Africa and Asia Minor, and the trading places in the strait of Hormuz in the Persian Gulf, the knights-errant of Johnson's romance and the long-distance travelling merchants of the travel accounts of the Mediterranean cross paths. In a unique way, then, the Silk Road, as Michael Murrin has also recently documented, became not only a powerful stimulus for the forced trade imagined along its territories, but also an inspiration for romance writing across Europe's linguistic and geographical boundaries.[9] In the third chapter of part I, "The Marriage of Merchant Kingdoms in Romances about Men," I discuss Emanuel Forde's *Montelyon*, and two anonymous romances, *The Famous Historie of Palladine of England* and *Oceander*. The authors of these romances create a double fiction of the Eastern Mediterranean, the Middle East, and Asia as extended territories connected with the Eastern Mediterranean. In these fictions, the heroic narratives of knights advancing to the far corners of the Eastern Mediterranean and beyond figure as both fictions of cross-ethnic marriage and as a pretext for the conceptual strategies for Western commercial enterprises in the Persian Gulf and the Indian Ocean.

Moving from heteroerotic to homosocial concerns, part II, "Intimacy, Sexuality, and the Queer Levant," explores a number of texts in which encounters between travelling and trading male characters within the Eastern Mediterranean are envisioned as opportunities for different kinds of bonding between men, which cut across class and ethnic boundaries. The knight-errant thus becomes both a humanist friend and a homoerotic playfellow, in the private space of the closet-tent shared with other knights; he is the submissive favourite in the course of commercial exchange with an eastern counterpart in the marketplace; and he seeks erotic pleasure from eastern youth in the baths of Northern Africa. In the world of "sex before sex,"[10] this part argues, the erotic body of the knight-errant of prose romances expands the capacity of writers' imagination to present embodiment, male agency, and fictional characters. By intercutting the stories of homosocial and commercial, homoerotic and heroic, playful and affective contacts between men from different religious and ethnic environments, romances fictionalize male sexuality *as* politics. The first chapter of part II, "Desire and Knightly Masculinity," concerns the construction of sexuality, especially male homoeroticism, in travel writing of the sixteenth and seventeenth centuries, which focuses in particular on the ethnographic, and specifically erotic, features of the Eastern Mediterranean. The "erotic ethnography" presented in the writing of Fynes Moryson, John Foxe, Bartholomeus Georgieuiz, William Parry, Robert Couverte, and Henry Timberlake provides us with an insight into the discourses and fictions about the sexual practices of Muslims in the Eastern Mediterranean. This writing circulated in England when romance writers were crafting their own fictional versions of homosocial interactions between men in the multi-ethnic world of the Eastern Mediterranean, as they imagined them in their romances. As this chapter shows, when read alongside the narratives of erotic ethnography, romance fiction like William Painter's *The Palace of Pleasure* (1567), the anonymous but influential *Amadis de Gaule* (1567), and the third part of the anonymous and equally popular *Palmerin of England* (1602) show the extent to which imaginative romance literature, much like travel writing, produced narratives in which episodes of commercial exchange and negotiation also become narratives of sexual transaction between men. The second chapter of part II, "Cruising the Eastern Mediterranean: The Knight, the Friend, the Favourite, and Homoerotic Romance," discusses the types that in romance fictions animate the narratives of sodomitic and homoerotic contacts between Eastern and Western men in the process of mercantile exchanges – sometimes with Eastern women as conduits for illicit pleasures between men. Some of the key texts discussed in this chapter are Philip Sidney's *The Countesse of Pembroke's Arcadia* (1598), the second part of the anonymous *Palmerin D'Oliva* (1597), the anonymous *Palmendos* (1589), the second part of Ortúñez de Calahorra's *The myrrour of knighthood* (1585), Robert Parry's *Moderatus* (1595), Lawrence Twyne's *The Patterne of Paineful Adventures* (1594), Lady Mary Wroth's *Urania* (1621), and Madeleine de Scudéry's *Ibrahim* (written in French in 1641, translated into English and printed in 1652).

The afterword, "Mediterranean Masculinities," provides a synthesis of the arguments about particularity in the construction of masculinity and male sexuality in Mediterranean romances. The narrative world of these romances is built not only on a seemingly endless sequence of heroic narratives in which male characters wreak violence on other men, but on equally prominent stories in which heroic violence in fact opens a space for imagining male sexuality in a range, and in different degrees, of male same-sex attachment and affect. At times astonishingly permissive and fluid, the presentation of male sexuality in Mediterranean romances provides us with an opportunity to expand the archive of texts about early modern male eroticism, because these fictions challenge the view of romances as texts that primarily celebrate heterosexual love and marriage, and the royalist cause.

Knights in Arms therefore moves freely, and critically, between queer early modern studies, gender and sexuality theory, narratology, historicism, and empire criticism. Read in these ways, romances work against the grain of the widespread cultural disparagement from humanists and Puritan clerics. Prose romances are lively texts, whose place in the history of English writing about subjectivity, travel, and empire is secured by their engaging and sometimes rhetorically polished stories deeply invested in erotic semantics, cross-cultural and cross-ethnic contacts, gender, and the complex politics of rule within the world of nascent global trade in the Mediterranean. If most non-canonical prose romances discussed throughout the following pages have not yet earned their place in the history of early modern English literature and in the critical body of writing about early modern masculinity and male sexuality, because they have appeared marginal to critics and are little-known texts, which most of them indeed are, it is my hope that they will earn their deserved place in the canon of early modern literature because they offer new insights into the rich and complex history of masculinity in the early modern period, history in which the Eastern Mediterranean was both a backdrop for, and a producer of, stories about masculinity.

KNIGHTS IN ARMS

Introduction: Mapping Territories

Critical Charting: "Romancy"

In the Epistle to the Reader in the 1653 edition of the prose romance *The famous History of PALMENDOS SON of the most Renowned Palmerin D'Oliva, Emperour of Constantinople, And the Heroick Queen of Tharsus,* the translator, Anthony Munday, or perhaps the printer, describes this work as the "Quintaessence of Romancy." In the following advertisement for the book, the term "Romancy" is defined in terms of its stylistic features: "any hath joined Art to abundance, and mingled mildnesse with Majesty, or hath raised his stile, without either losing himself, or straying from his subject, that is it which in truth we find no where better performed than in this History."[1] Most of the story of *PALMENDOS,* framed around the narratives of credit, debt, and friendship, is set in the Eastern Mediterranean. It involves Signor Traculento, an Italian merchant, and Palmendos, a wandering young knight, and it is concerned with Palmendos's romantic adventures in Asia Minor, culminating in his marriage, which takes place in Constantinople (Istanbul). The narrative takes the reader from the Aegean Sea, where Palmendos embarks on his voyage. It, then, takes the reader through Hellespont, Delphos, and the mountains of Arcadia in Greece, to Tharsus in Asia Minor and eventually to Constantinople, Palmendos's final destination.

As a term, "romance" is not exceptional, because it is mentioned in connection with late-medieval romances. For example, in the "Thornton" collection of romances in the Lincoln Cathedral Library, which collects fifteenth-century manuscript romances, the term "romance" appears as part of the rhetorical formula at the beginning of each text in this collection: "Here begynnes the Romance off Octovynne"

(*Octovynne* 98v–109v); "Here begynnes the Romance off Sir ysambrace" (*Sir Ysambrace* 109r–114v).[2] The word "romancy" reminds us that early modern writers recognized romance as a particular literary form; that they used it as a label to refer to that form; and that our modern usage of the term "romance" draws on that early notion of romance as it was developed in the English literature in the late medieval and the early modern period. In that early history of romance writing, the term referred to metrical chivalric romances. The term "romancy" testifies to an awareness of the generic specificity of this kind of text, whose rhetorical, stylistic, and narrative features identify it as a distinct category of writing. Since the French original, the mid-sixteenth-century romance *Amadis de Gaule*, was the original adapted in the English translation as *PALMENDOS*, which also influenced other English neochivalric romances of the sixteenth and seventeenth centuries, the association of that sea with romance writing is encoded philologically as well as culturally. In philological terms, the link, then, between romance writing and the Eastern Mediterranean is established in the process of transmitting it from one language to another and from the antecedent texts to their adapted translations in English. From a cultural perspective, the connection between the Eastern Mediterranean and prose romances is recognized in the analogies between the period's ways of thinking about the Eastern Mediterranean and the amorous stories set there.

References to the Eastern Mediterranean in prose romances of the late sixteenth and early seventeenth century are not merely ornaments, but a version of that space as debate in which different views on travel, politics, history, trade, identity, and gender are competing with each another. If Middle English romances "deliberately turn away from the adulterous love of their French courtly romance predecessors and focus instead on righting wrongs and re-establishing proper social order with families intact,"[3] their literary successors, sixteenth- and early seventeenth-century romances, trouble the idea of "proper" social order by displacing romance politics to the East. The Eastern Mediterranean encouraged the writers of romances to test the troubling of all kinds of order – gender, social, erotic – in part because the terms under which commercial exchanges and interactions within the Eastern Mediterranean were conducted required resorting to strategies that resisted circumspection. The palimpsests that form a body of writing about the Eastern Mediterranean resonate through romances, making them read less as "ornate and frivolous"[4] texts and more as stories of new social worlds. This is important for the discussion throughout the following pages because such an understanding of prose romances is grounded in the knowledge about the Eastern Mediterranean produced by other kinds of writing about that space: travel, geography, commerce. These palimpsests of the Eastern Mediterranean are the context within which I interpret prose romances. And I understand "context" to be, not a frame within which romances are slotted in without any contribution to the context, but what Terence Cave has described as "the coordinates that determine how a cultural artifact is positioned within the culture that produced it, what it is *doing* there."[5] The body of writing about the Eastern Mediterranean is made up of many reference points that connect it with romances. Therefore, when looking at geography, travel writing, and commercial treatises, interpreting the gender, social, and erotic "order" of romances means expanding our understanding of what romance writers may be doing when they turn to the Eastern Mediterranean as a space.

In the early modern period, romances were denounced by humanists like Roger Ascham, who dismissed those fictions (specifically *Morte d'Arthur*) because of their display of violence and bawdiness (of "open mans slaughter and bold bawdye")[6] and by Francis Meres, who suggested that Emanuel Forde's romance, *Ornatus and Artesia* (?1595), should be censored because, together with twenty-two other prose romances on his list, it is "no less hurtful to youth than the works of MACHIAVELLI."[7] Today scholarship on romances flourishes "because of their great success with readers, particularly those marked by their gender and class."[8] In recent years, criticism of prose romances has demonstrated that these fictions are a rich repository of discourses on genders, sexuality, social history, and royal politics. By engaging in detailed discussions of romances within these thematic fields, scholars have in turn expanded the boundaries of criticism about how masculine and feminine agency shaped discourses of the public and private, the historical and the intimate, in romances.

Since its inception in classical Greece, romance has been associated with travel. Thus, Heliodorus's *Aethiopica* is set in the mythical pastoral that descends to the seashores of the Mediterranean. And Aeneas's wanderings in the Mediterranean, as depicted in Virgil's *Aeneid*, provided a narrative model for the heroic dimension of sea wandering in romances. As Steve Mentz concludes, "prose romances derive from loss-wandering recovery narratives from Homer's *Odyssey* through the prose fiction of Byzantium, saints' lives, medieval biography, jestbook tales, chivalric legends, and Italian verse *romanzi*, among other forms."[9] Both *Aethiopica* and the *Odyssey* were only part of a large body of classical literature, including the heroic epic, where wandering on the sea and a quest for both land and identity make up the symbolic dimension of storytelling. Prose romances of the Eastern Mediterranean incorporate these influences, but their orientation towards that sea and the historical discourses that frame the writing about it set the body of romances examined in this book apart from other chivalric romances in the early modern period. Jennifer Fellows's brief but useful account of printed romances in the sixteenth century, for instance, lists only fifteenth- and sixteenth-century romances belonging to the group of heroic fictions modelled on French antecedents.[10]

By the time the sixteenth century has drawn to a close, which is when this book starts, prose romances have absorbed other discourses, especially of travel, geography, and trade. They have also become more distinctly politicized fictions so that their association with travel no longer makes them texts that present "the idealized picture of the self."[11] In the romance stories about the Eastern Mediterranean, that self is shaped in what one critic has called "the emotional geography"[12] of romances, referring to the power of the literary geography of the East to produce multifarious narratives of love and courtship. In this formulation, geography is understood to be a symbolic entity that engenders different affective responses in those who engage with it. Real or imagined geography in romances represents only one, important, feature of those fictions. Geography is important because it shapes the meaning of other constituent features of romance. Romance geography thus becomes a background against which stories of courtship, combat, and travel are narrated by writers with a particular gift for creating suspense styled for the exotic world of the East. Movement is one of the key features driving the narrative of romances forward in time and space. Early modern romances, like their influential medieval predecessors, are "stories of adventure in which the chief parts are played by knights, famous kings, or distressed ladies, acting most often under the impulse of love, religious faith, or, in many, mere desire for adventure."[13]

The following discussion is an attempt to go beyond the claim made by the medievalist Robert B. Burlin, who argues that romance is "historically attested as a generic term, in the medieval vernacular and for modern scholars."[14] From the formalist point of view, this may be true, in terms of romances' thematic engagement and orientation towards a specific historical world. But not all vernacular prose romances fall into the same category. For a modern scholar, an attempt to define prose romances that emerge from a specific historical, chronological and, in this case, geographical, context opens numerous possibilities for definition. In the flourishing scholarship on English medieval romance, scholars have not only grappled with definitions of romance as a literary form, but have made convincing arguments about the role romances played in voicing the national heroic spirit from Anglo-Saxon times to the late fifteenth century.[15] Extending this line of scholarship, my goal in this book is to contribute to the critical conversation about how the making of the commonwealth of trade in England continued beyond the medieval period, into the modernity of the sixteenth and the seventeenth centuries. I also wish to advance the point that a specific body of the prose romances of the Eastern Mediterranean contributed to the historical and cultural making of a nation and its subjects, and the imaginative literature that tells stories about characters whose fictional lives originated in the public and private concerns and fantasies, and political aspirations, of the historical moment that produced them.

There have been many attempts to understand early modern chivalric "romance" in multiple ways at different moments in the early modern period, which have been made differently by critics from different historical periods. For Northrop Frye, chivalric romance narrative "usually" presents "a hierarchical social order" that is rationalized through "the social structure of the feudal system," creating a fantasy of the historical feudal system in which "very few medieval barons resembled the knights of the Round Table."[16] Unlike Bishop Hurd, who saw the medieval baron metamorphosed into a giant of romance literature, Frye views romances as literature that engages in fantasy. For some medievalists a dragon belongs to folklore and imagination, and romances simultaneously fictionalize "deliberate departures from the natural world" and "are testimonies to some of the curious things which are to be found in remote regions."[17] The history and geography of the Eastern Mediterranean become the curiosity and the source of stories that fill the pages of prose romances set in this region. In the flourishing scholarship on romance, Jeff Dolven's book on the cognitive foundations of romance storytelling and on the ways in which the "preoccupation with understanding ... hard and elusive" things deeply imbricated the narratives of humanist romances, showing how the early modern readership of these stories comprehended the world in which they lived and learned, is a testimony to the discursive and conceptual depth of romances and to their potential to shape the world of thinking.[18]

When, in the 1590s, England began to lay plans for overseas commercial routes, thanks in large part to the noteworthy accounts of merchant–adventurers, such as Richard Hakluyt, Richard Hasleton, and Lewes Roberts, the spirit of internationalism that swept the country's restless entrepreneurs found a convenient literary outlet for its ideals in romances. Moreover, through the growing book trade, this historical moment found a way of promulgating and satisfying desires for both enterprise and adventure in the male audiences of romances. The roles of knight and merchant-adventurer overlapped and the Eastern Mediterranean became a place in which the knight-errant's agency transformed England's ambition to claim advantage and seize opportunities in the worlds previously occupied by other sea powers into fictions of masculinity at once romantic and pragmatic.

Distant Reading: Romances and Mediterranean Geography

From Hellenic to humanist romances, travel and courtship take place against the backdrop of Mediterranean geography. Scholars have searched for the best critical approaches to interpreting geography in romances, in particular for an explanatory framework that would illuminate the coexistence of fictive and real geography against which the romance plot is played out. For example, among the attempts to understand the significance of geography in the gendered fictions of romances, some critics have resorted to adjectival descriptions, such as "emotional geography,"[19] to suggest that the subjective interior and the geographical exterior in a romance coexist in a dichotomous relationship. Yet this kind of qualification prevents us from seeing the multiple ways in which geography itself is a signifying subject within the larger world of romance literature. Therefore I propose a different approach to romance geography, informed by Franco Moretti's quantitative approach to book history via three constructs – graphs, maps, and trees[20] – which arrives at a concise interpretation of literature through a process of "deliberate reduction and abstraction."[21] Asking what maps and geography can do that words cannot achieve, and reminding us that, like the map, narrative space is not linear but serial and spatial,[22] Moretti makes a provocative claim that literary cycles, periods, and genres do not explain everything in the history of literature, but that they do bring to light the "hidden tempo"[23] of other social realities that can be decoded through a different interpretive strategy of literary history. In literary history, the literary cycles of writing that share common features help align the cultural mapping of modern geography and the narrative mapping of literature, showing that a new grid of relations emerges between the cultural genres of the book and the map, and cultural history. Therefore, building on this conceptual basis, Moretti develops the method of "distant reading,"[24] where "distance" does not mean "obstacle" but encompasses "a specific form of knowledge" where a whole picture of geography is replaced with fewer elements – shapes, relations, structures, forms, models – and hence with "a sharper sense of their overall interconnection."[25] If we distance early modern maps from prose romances so that we do not seek to locate specific spaces where they might be in geography, which is a product of an interpretation of locations and of their exact locations, what emerges then is a critical matrix that shows why certain aspects of romances matter in literary history and why those aspects are crucial to an interpretation of romance narratives. Specifically, a distant reading of prose romances in relation to geography reveals correspondences between the ways in which geographers and romance writers conceptualized spaces of the Eastern Mediterranean as a common cultural story. Distant reading, Moretti elaborates, "is a condition of knowledge," allowing us "to focus on units that are much smaller or much larger than a text: devices, themes, tropes – or genres and systems."[26] One of the units "much larger" than a romance text is geography. The knowledge about the Eastern Mediterranean that geography shaped in the period is significant (it still remains unexplored) and the resonances of that knowledge are traceable in different kinds of writing. The conceptual reworking of geographical material in prose romances is especially revealing in discourses of eroticism and trade.

Moretti's critical strategy helps me avoid the traps of interpreting geography as allegory, unpacking the meaning of geography through endless explanatory possibilities. Renaissance maps of the Eastern Mediterranean zoom on the coasts, port towns, islands, and overland and sea routes that are the spaces and zones central to the ideology of commercial expansion in the early modern period. Those are also the spaces that constitute the geography of romances. In a distant reading, such maps may help explain why prose romances focus on the geography produced by the same expansionist and mercantile geography. The abstraction that a distant reading enables is not an end in itself; on the contrary, it is a way of expanding the field of critical interpretation. Distant reading of the flexibly imagined territories of the East helps me move between romances and geography as through a twinned field that produces a specific knowledge: of the restless Renaissance mind trying to imagine the curiosities of the Eastern

Mediterranean as best it could, reimagining the space along the way. Distant reading helps brings forward the importance of romances as works important for the study of England's opening to the international arena of activities and trade at the turn of the century. Distancing myself from the crowded space of maps and a focus on the overlapping elements in romances also allows me to think of using both geography and literature as ways of creating fantasies about places of common interest.

As in other texts that turn history into fiction, the historical setting is not a mere backdrop to literary stories. Writing about the relevance of the historical setting in the fictions penned by Philip Sidney, Thomas Deloney, and Thomas Nashe, Alex Davis argues that the historical setting can be "relevant ... productive of significance and thematic complexity," alerting us to the fact, too, that the "historical orientation of early prose fiction has largely escaped critical attention."[27] Although Davis's interest lies in recovering the history behind the thick layer of allegorical and stylistic presentation of it in the fictions about England, his warning that approaching historical settings as "essentially neutral" because writers often introduce them as part of the rhetorical formula of "once upon a time in ..." leads to unacknowledging the fact that specific historical moments motivate the narratives of romance fiction.[28] At the opening of his prose romance *Gwydonius, or the Card of Fancy* (1584), Robert Greene declares that "There dwelt in the city of Metelyne a certain duke called Cleropontes ...," inviting the reader to think about the romance in terms of the Eastern Mediterranean, specifically Greece.[29] A recent editor of this romance is prompted to state that the work is "Set in the Middle East of Robert Greene's imagination" and it "was meant to be exotic even when it first appeared."[30] This may be the case sometimes, but not always. History and imagination, as Alex Davis's book, *Renaissance Historical Fiction: Sidney, Deloney, Nashe*, convincingly documents, are constantly intertwined in romance narratives. Interpreted alongside a geographical account of the same region, the fictional geography *Gwydonius*, the Middle East of Greene's imagination acquires a new meaning where fictional and factual geography meet in compelling if, I argue, not surprising ways. In his account of travels in the Eastern Mediterranean, the Flemish cartographer and geographer Abraham Ortelius describes Greece:

> Sundry strange wonders haue bin said to bee in this countrie, as that the riuer *Melas* made white sheep to become black & that the river *Cephis* made

> the black ... and moreouer that the sea called *Euripus* did in 24 howers 7 times ebbe & flow. This noble countrie of *Greece* after all her flowrishing, lyeth now vnder the subiection and slauery of the Turk.[31]

For Ortelius, Greece is a country of wonders and marvels, which by implication should differentiate it from the West which identifies such wonders in territories beyond its frontiers. In Ortelius's version of Greece, the eastern part of the Mediterranean is not a space ruled by reason but one that is the subject to mysteries and strange occurrences, seemingly resulting from Greece's subjection to the Turks. To compare this version of wondrous Greece put forward by a famous cartographer, it is worth having a look at a different kind of representation of Greece in a map (Figure 1) published by Ferdinando Bertelli in 1564.

The details in this map reflect the authors' and publisher's concern with representing travel routes and places of use to those who travelled to the East by land and sea. This map represents the knowledge collected on the ground and intended for practical use, giving precedence to geographical knowledge over wonder. Yet Ortelius's map of Greece would have been closer to the idea of Greece one would have gotten from reading Robert Greene's romance, where it features as the main setting.

Greene's contemporary readers could easily have located Metelyne (Mytilene),[32] which appears in Ortelius's pocket-size atlas,[33] putting it in the specific context of geography, not safely if ambiguously only within literary imagination. Somewhere on the North African shore of the Mediterranean, where the Renaissance locates "Barbarie," Ortelius includes an Eastern Mediterranean country of "Biledulgerid," a land conjoined with "Barbaria," a territory populated by Muslims.[34] Given their mixture of fantasy and geography, it seems plausible to suggest that influential texts such as Ortelius's provided romance writers with set rhetorical and narrative formulas. In Ortelius, real-life experience and geographical knowledge are presented in such a way as to inspire thinking about Greece as a fantasy land as well, a land whose rivers have the power to change the colour of sheep's wool and whose seas go through seven tides in a day. This is romance history and romance geography, just as it is a text that blurs the boundary between geography and romance. The conceptual association of Ortelius's fictional Biledulgerid and the Barbary land of northern Africa in the Renaissance cultural imaginary places these two locations on the other side of Christian and, by implication, non-barbarian realms of Europe.

Figure 1. Map of Greece, *Totius Graeciae descriptione* (ca. 1564), derived from Nikolaos Sophianos's 1552 and Vincenzo Luchini's 1558 maps of Greece (The Newberry Library, Novacco 4F 359).

DES CRIPTIO
EVXINI PONTI PARS
THRA
CIA
PROPONTIS
PON
TVS. ET
BI THY NIA.
GALATIAE
MA
IOR
PARS
MYSIA MINOR
MYSIA MAIOR
TRIMENOTHVRITAE
MYSOMACEDONES
ASIA
PRO PRIA
GAEVM PELAGVS
ICARIVM PELAGVS
MYRTOVM MARE
CARIA
LY CIA
PAMPHYLIAE PARS
RHODVS
LYCIVM MARE
CRETICVM MARE
CRETA
LIBYCVM MARE
CARPATHIVM MARE
MILIARIA
STADIA

Thus Ortelius's idea of charting territories according to religious lines predates Edward Said's notion of "arbitrary" or "imaginative" geography based on the "our land – barbarian land" distinction.[35] Ortelius's version of this kind of fictional geography creates boundaries between the civilized and the barbarian. Yet those kinds of boundaries, as Said observes, do "not require that the barbarians acknowledge the distinction."[36] In the case of Ortelius, the distinction is implied for the sake of his readers, and for the users of his maps, in the West. Thus, already in Ortelius's version of Barbary, we witness what Said identifies as the main signifying features of such imaginary geography, whose "boundaries accompany the social, ethnic, and cultural [features] in expected ways."[37] Ortelius's approach to the Islamic Mediterranean in this instance, however, represents how the West saw the East in some of its most elaborate fantasies; how it projected its concern over the threat of the expansion of Islam in Europe and the fear that in mercantile competition with the Islamic world in the Eastern Mediterranean it was not the West but the East that had the advantage. But Ortelius's representation and articulation of the East is yet another reminder of the space geography and romance writing shared in the creative imagination and how fantasy takes over the realism of representation when the context so requires. Ortelius's representation of Greece is evidence that the Eastern Mediterranean is not, to echo Peter Burke, writing about early modern Europe, "a neutral geographical term,"[38] but a word capturing an ideological hierarchy between the Christian and the Muslim world. And this idea of ideological hierarchy exists, evidently, alongside consciousness of the Eastern Mediterranean as a collective and shared space between Christians and Muslims. Prose romances register this cultural condition in both the detailed and in the larger narratives of the East that fill their pages.

Chivalric prose narratives translate into fiction the belief in England that the Crusades are a materialization of the holy war, paying attention to the mapping of the Holy Land in their narratives. In that regard, the English simply follow European cartographers, who traditionally pointed out the importance of the Holy Land in their detailed descriptions and representations of places where Christian and Islamic forces had come into conflict. In a 1590 map of the Holy Land by Matteo Florimi, for example, one can clearly see the prominence of these biblical representations against a background of chivalric clashes between knights.

As its title suggests, Florimi's map "amplifies" the locations of the Holy Land by drawing the viewer's attention to a number of stock images that suggest Christian discourse on the holy war: a ship fires its cannons at another vessel (bottom-central detail) and soldiers are shown fighting with their lances to indicate places where Christian armies war with the Muslims. One detail, representing Galilea, depicts a clash between the Turkish king and the sultan of Damascus: "Here Saladine, the Turk, king of Babylon wins over the Sultan of Damascus."[39] This scene is meant to assure the Christian viewer that although the fate of the Holy Land is threatened by the infidel kings who fight for its territories, the Christian knight will defeat the threat in the end. The map also shows a mounted knight with a page walking behind him, locations identified with the apostles, Jerusalem, Bethlehem, Damascus, numerous fortified towns and bastions – and, among all this, a shepherd tending his flock. Pastoral Christian idyll has not been altogether disturbed by the chivalric activities against Muslims. The iconographic mixture of holy war narrative and pastoral romance makes us wonder at what point this map ceases to be simply a geographical presentation and becomes instead a pictorial rendition of romance narrative. We are reminded that maps, especially the early ones, are imaginative representations, incorporating cultural (and individual) prejudice, myths, and beliefs, as Jerry Brotton has recently proposed.[40] This allegory is characteristic of the "theological argument"[41] it encourages, for Florimi's map presents the Holy Land as a territory on the coast of the Eastern Mediterranean in which the clashes of the infidel armies ran parallel to the solitary paths of Christian crusaders, and in which fortifications and garrison towns represent both bulwarks against Islamic armies and places in which the knight of romances demonstrates his virtue in fighting the infidel. As Robert Schwoebel suggests, the medieval legends of the crusades, "and the new knowledge of the Levant were combined and adapted by these writers [of romances] to fit their didactic and moralistic purposes."[42] Maps of the Eastern Mediterranean help our definitions of prose romances as a literary genre because those maps contain depictions of places, routes, and sometimes people that are analogous to the imaginative stories in romances. The maps are like palimpsests whose charted territories come alive in romances. In that sense, maps and romances existed in the dialectical relationship of shared meaning within the market of literature and cartography.

Some travel accounts read like romance. Fynes Moryson, the author of one of the most popular and comprehensive travelogues about Europe and the Ottoman Empire in the seventeenth century, compares

Figure 2. Matteo Florimi, Map of the Holy Land, *Totius terre promissionis a dan usque Bersabee verissima et amplissima description*, ca. 1590 (The Newberry Library, Chicago, Novacco 4F 383).

Mons Galaad
MADIAN
Mons Nebo
IDVMEA
Scala miliarium
PETRA
DABIR
TRIBVS Gad
Tribus Ruben
Iordanis
MARE MORTVUM
Sodoma
Gomora
Terra Taphua
Tribus Effraim
TERSA
Mons Garisim
HIERVSALEM
BETHLEEM
Tribus Beniamin
MONS SEIR, SIVE SANIR
Mons Gaas
GAZER
TRIBVSIUDA
TRIBVS: SIMEON.
CEILA
ALBA SPECVLA
TERRA PHILISTEORVM.
MONS IARIN
ASDOD
ANTIPATRIDA
MARE MEDITERRANEVM

a group of armed horsemen that he encountered on his travels with characters in the second book of *Amadis de Gaule* (1595). The horsemen

> were armed with Launces, Shields, and short broad Swords, so as a man would haue said, they had been the Knights of *Amadis de Gaule*. Neither is it vnprobable, that those fictions came from the horsemen of *Asia*, since wee did see some mile from *Tripoli*, a Bridge called the Bridge of *Rodomont*, and a Fountaine neere *Scandarona*, called the Amazon Fountaine, and many like monuments in these parts.[43]

Moryson tells an interesting story on the one hand because his use of *Amadis de Gaule* as a shortcut to explain what he saw counts on his readers' familiarity with the French prose romance that would allow them to picture the group of soldiers. On the other hand, Moryson himself becomes a literary historiographer, that is, an archaeologist of literature, when he suggests that real place names of some of the eastern locations were taken from romances. Such instances in the writing about the Eastern Mediterranean are not merely background. They demand attention because they provide a different access to, as well as reviving, noncanonical works like *Amadis de Gaule*, giving that work attention and urging a modern critic to assess historical writing *as* romance narrative as well. These instances also provide the critical justification for the process of interpretation that regards a romance story as a kind of history of the Eastern Mediterranean. We might wish to pause at Moryson's use of the world "vnprobable" when he speculates about the source of romance stories. The word draws our attention to an awareness of the probable if not possible relationship between prose romances, between, that is, imaginative fiction, and its origins in real-life history. Analogy between history and romance for Moryson represents the line of thinking that helps him bridge fiction and the first-hand experience rendered in his travelogue.

Moments like those from Ortelius and Moryson occupy a role similar to what new historicists had once reserved for the historical anecdote, which "promised both an escape from conventional canonicity and a revival of the canon," except that the contextual material I use does not act as a "transgression against"[44] a canonical text. Encountering references to romances in the accounts of travel and geography helps rethink both the generic stability of their texts and the canonicity of romance literature. At which point, for example, does a travelogue or geographical account become a romance? When does romance stop, or start, being geography or travelogue? The historicist method I used in this book helps me rethink the archive of romances by incorporating in it a body of different texts and of geographical images. Discussing maps, geographical accounts of the lands and towns in the Eastern Mediterranean, and treatises of trade alongside imaginative literature, my goal is not only to illuminate the narratives of romances by reading them against the cultural and historical background that produced them, but also to explain different cultural narratives about the Eastern Mediterranean that circulated in the print market of prose in early modern England.

Thus, providing the geographical context for Mediterranean Greece, by discussing maps, helps critics assess the fictional geography of the Eastern Mediterranean and make that geography meaningful to modern readers of prose romances. As readers of literature we are accustomed to thinking of the romances' stories of courtship, distressed damsels, hermits, fairies, old royals, and wandering knights moving across large territories and in foreign lands. In classical romances, the mythical land of Arcadia often features as a pastoral land in which the improbabilities of romance writing take place. But the Renaissance did not treat Arcadia simply as a mythical backdrop for romance stories. It also represented it as a location that blended the geographical and the fictional. Claudio Duchetti's 1570 map of Greece (Figure 3), still in circulation at the end of the sixteenth century, is a case in point.

Duchetti's map presents Arcadia as a country in Morea, which was a sanjak, or administrative district, in Ottoman Greece.[45] He implies a conceptual link between the mythical country of romance and the early Christianity territory of the pre-Ottoman Eastern Mediterranean. Like romances set in this region, Duchetti's map preserves nostalgia for the world of early Christianity, long ago eclipsed by Ottoman rule, thus establishing a symbolic link between the past and the present. But by presenting Arcadia as the geographical Morea, Duchetti's map also suggests that Byzantine Mediterranean is a place in which telling stories of the past serves the needs and ambitions of men of the present day who travel to the Eastern Mediterranean for trade. The superimposition of the historical Morea over the mythical Arcadia thus invokes a close connection between romances and an existent Eastern Mediterranean, reminding us that "politics still intrude, even in Arcadia."[46] Since the Middle Ages, romances have been closely related to land ownership, inheritance, and gain, especially during the Crusades in the Holy Land,

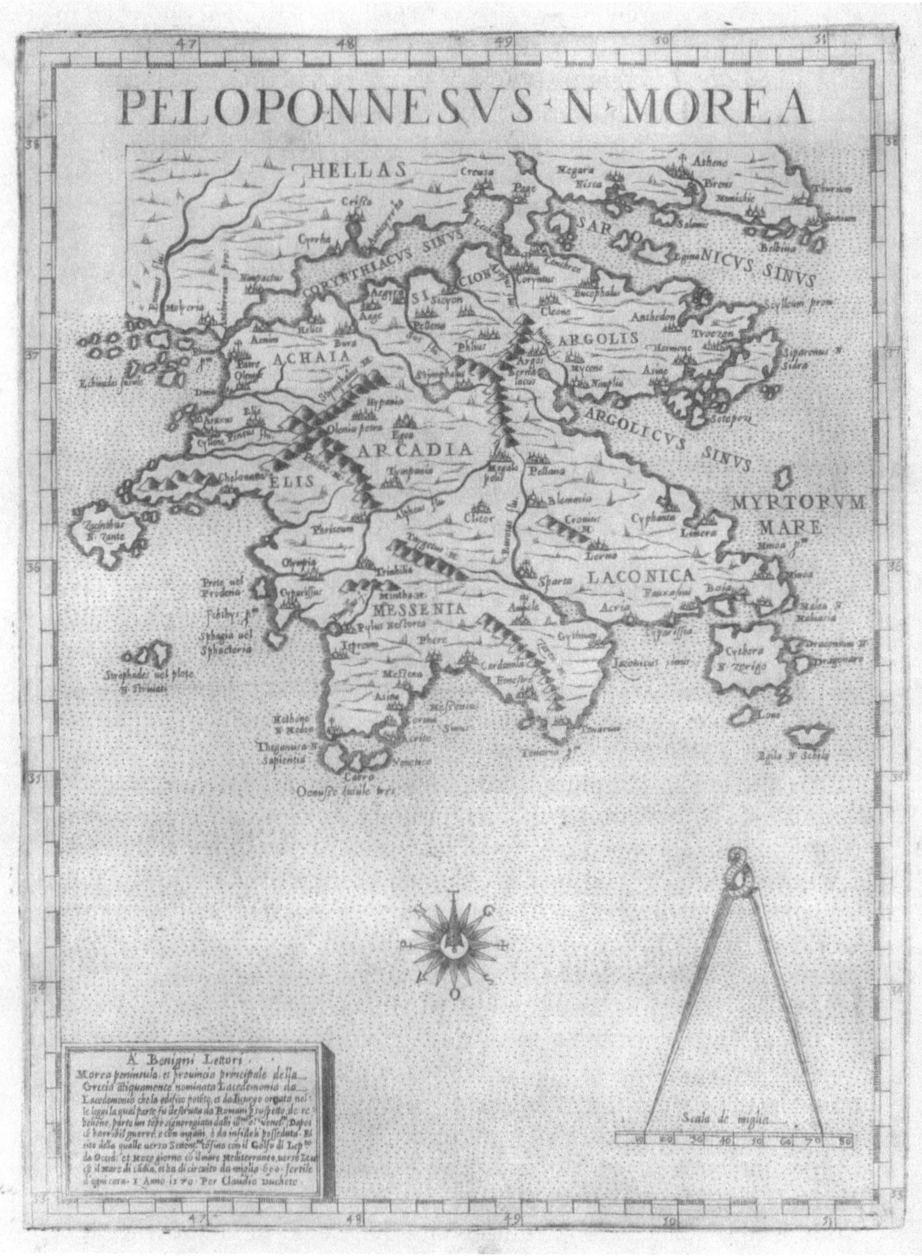

Figure 3. Claudio Duchetti, Arcadia, *Peloponnesus n[ominato]*, Morea, 1570 (The Newberry Library, Chicago Novacco 2F 193).

whose aim was not to liberate the Holy Land but, as Colin Imber states, "to end Ottoman rule in the Balkan peninsula."[47] In the sixteenth and seventeenth centuries, the issues of land claim and rule shifted to the Eastern Mediterranean, where England joined the commercial diplomacy with the Ottoman Empire as well as participating in efforts to defeat Ottoman military dominance in the Mediterranean.

Prose romances of the Eastern Mediterranean started to increase when the increase in trade and wealth accumulation became not only the preoccupation of Elizabethan and Jacobean politics, but also reflected a larger shift in society. With the relaxation, and waning, of the feudal system of land control and ownership came more liberty to acquire property and wealth, and for property and wealth to circulate, through growing overseas travel and trade. Since most of this travel took place in the Eastern Mediterranean, travel provided a discursive model for literary travels in that region that was told in the stories of prose romances. In the example of Philip Sidney's *Arcadia*, Richard McCoy demonstrates the depths to which history penetrates the fabric of romance mystery and the high level of fantasy. In addition, the Eastern Mediterranean helped generate romance stories because of the effect of the Reformation on Christian Europe. By splitting Europe in two, Andrew Hadfield argues, the Reformation made "a large number of areas [in East Christianity] dangerous or off limits to European travelers."[48] This encouraged narrative fantasies about that which could not be easily visited and described.

The clash between history and fiction, and evidence and imagination, was the subject of debate early in the history of critical reflection on romance writing. Thus, anticipating some of the concerns of this book, Richard Hurd, bishop of Worcester, highlighted, in his 1762 essay "Letters on Chivalry and Romance," the strong relationship between Renaissance romances, the militancy of chivalry, and the political power given to the knight-errant in these fictions. Concerned with how to interpret the anachronism of Edmund Spenser's *The Faerie Queene* (1590), Hurd suggests a way of reading romances, as texts that encode history. Thus, stating that "Giants were oppressive feudal Lords" which shade into "the Savages of Romances" where the "greater Lord was called a Giant, for his power,"[49] Hurd offers a model for the historical interpretation of these figures of literary fantasy. Most important, Hurd implicitly instructs his reader on how to enjoy reading romances. Having provided an example from Book III of John Milton's epic *Paradise Regained*, where Milton self-consciously emulates the story of the clashing armies from romance literature, Hurd offers the following explanation for a reading strategy:

> The classical reader is much scandalized on these occasions, and never fails to cry out on the impudence of these lying fablers. Yet if he did but reflect on the prodigious swarms which *Europe* sent out in the Crusades, and that the transactions of these days furnished the Romance-writers with their ideas and images, he would see that the marvelous in such stories was modest enough, and did not very much exceed the strict bounds of historical representation.[50]

Guiding the reader to interpret the story of romances against the background of the historical conditions that produced that fiction in the first place, Hurd is providing not just a formula for reading but, implicitly, a critical assessment of the historical anachronism of romances. Narrated events in the Eastern Mediterranean start to make more sense when read from the perspective of different discourses in the early modern period, that is, the interplay of historical and geographical knowledge and the knowledge gained from travel, than if they are read with the Eastern Mediterranean featuring only as an accidental backdrop to romance stories. Hurd is reviving his period's interest in the literature of Renaissance England, demonstrating that from the inception of that interest, post-Renaissance, critical intuition led critics to treat romances as narratives waiting to be read within the boundaries of history and politics. In our search for ways of reading romances, a search that has led critics to approach romances from many angles, reading romances as fictions of the Eastern Mediterranean where discourses of empire and mercantilism are subsumed by affective and erotic rhetoric extends romance scholarship to new realms of historicist interpretation and gender criticism.

Carpet Knights: Men and Prose Romances

The historical background for this reprise and metamorphosis of the knight-errant and his adventures is complex. Robert Ralph Bolgar reminds us that "The knight-errantry of the romances was a fictional and exaggerated derivative of a philosophical doctrine ... [according to which] the use of force is justified only when some villainy requires suppression."[51] Since, as Bolgar continues, "Heroes have never been independent of the social and cultural climate in which they come to flourish,"[52] the knight of prose romances of the Eastern Mediterranean then assumes a distinctive role deriving from the philosophy and the changing political values that occurred when Elizabethan and Jacobean England joined the arena of commerce and conflict in the Eastern Mediterranean. Therefore, this knight does not move "through the romances as through a political vacuum, a limbo symbolized by the ever present and boundaryless forest in which he seeks adventures equally isolated from the recognizable context of organized society,"[53] as Arthur B. Ferguson states in his study about the decline of English chivalry. What then is the Eastern Mediterranean in these romances? Where are the outer limits of its shores and how far does it stretch?

A widespread association of romances with women has prevented critics from exploring them as works for and about men.[54] Yet men read, owned, wrote, translated, and are the main protagonists of romances whose plots are shared between men and women. A view, for example, that Emanuel Forde's romances "were written chiefly to appeal to women and girls," can be countered, not only by the observation that male readers, too, could have found much to be interested in in the plots of Forde's romances brimming with the stories of travelling knights, cross-dressing knights, male friends (or sole warriors), and men from different and distant worlds crossing each other's paths. In fact, one might argue that romances, like novellas, were the kind of prose fiction that was closest in interest and narrative type to romances, as Lorna Hutson suggests:

> [and] served the "private causes" of their male readers by enabling them to inhabit the conceptual time/space of private affairs – that is, time/space of access between states of adolescence, manhood, and matrimony; between domestic interiors and community spaces such as the marketplace, the street, the church – in a new and effective way.[55]

Because romances fictionalized different strategies of men's success in the spheres of courtship, politics, travel, and, as I argue in these pages, overseas trade, and because they were composed of exemplary stories that were primarily meant to offer ethical models of social conduct based on temperance, one could say that romances were conduct books for young men in early modern England.[56]

Men dedicated romances to women, but romances were dedicated to men as well. The well-thumbed copy in the Huntington Library of *The Second Booke of Amadis de Gaule* (1595) bears several records that are testimony to its use and ownership by men, and to the translator's intention for it to serve men's reading. On one leaf a contemporary hand wrote, "Francis Hayes His Book" (B4^r); on another page, a certain "Richard Scotton" (L3^v) wrote his name. The dedicatory epistle implicates men as readers and owners of romances. In his dedication to "Gvalter Borovgh," the translator Anthony Munday, writing under the pseudonym Lazarus Pyott, recommends his book to a scholar's study on the rhetoric of humility topos:

> although it [this book] deserue no chiefe place in your studie, yet you may lay it vp in some [A3^v] corner thereof, vntill you best leasure will afoord you some idle time to peruse these abrupt lines of an vnlearned *Souldior*, who hath written plaine English, void of all eloquence.[57]

This passage is not only revealing about men as the target audience of romances, it also shows that romances in that period were thought of as light reading, as low-brow literature, and as rhetorically unpolished. (The view that romances are "void of eloquence" was not shared by all writers, as the earlier example of *PALMENDOS* shows.) Even in a book about women as readers of romances, Caroline Lucas nevertheless argues that romances "focused on the hero rather than the heroine, on adventure rather than love."[58] My book goes beyond Lucas's argument, and it is provoked in constructive ways by the assertion, like the one by Kathryn Schwarz about lesbianism in Sidney's *Arcadia*, that in such a story, "erotic exchange ... is never a transaction between men."[59] It is intended to forward an argument for romances as masculinist narratives that open up debates about masculinity and transactions between men in the shaping of discourses of empire, discourses that are closely linked with male agency. Romances usually narrate the passage of young men through treacherous and faraway territories, and as such they could be said to be developmental narratives, stories of male maturity. Since most of these young men mature into kings and rulers by the end of their passage, romances tell stories of the difficult and circuitous formation of patriarchy. If we do not study men and masculinity in literature whose narratives are about men's rites of passage, "how will we ever understand how and why patriarchy could endure?"[60]

The present book is less concerned with the reading of romances as queer texts or as works only about eroticism. Rather, the goal is to unravel and unsettle assumptions about masculinity as associated with courtship, marriage, and the reconstitution of royal rule. It also enhances our appreciation of the eroticism in romances by setting them within an integrated mercantile, historical, and geographical framework. The cohesive relationship between these discourses through which sex and gender in these romances are expressed makes these texts part of a significant body of works in the history of romance writing, what a critic has called "European erotic romance."[61] Approaching romances as deeply homosocial texts, my intention is to let prose romances speak in their own language of masculinity and to illuminate them on their own terms. This is especially important because most of the romances discussed in the following pages are texts that very few readers are familiar with; many have left the dust and darkness of the archive for the first time and deserve to have their own voices be heard accordingly.

The gendering of men, homosociality, male–male eroticism, and desire and emotion in prose romances have not been at the centre of gender and queer early modern criticism, even though some critical attention has been paid to individual texts. Yet in an age when the discourse of sexuality was not a separate area of knowledge, as the early modern period was, discovering sex between men and uncovering desire in the middle of heroic action alert us to the importance of the body and erotics as political signs within prose romances.

But the social conditions of chivalry, war, and wander, alone or with other men (and away from England), represent one set of circumstances that yield themselves to the scrutiny of masculinity and sexuality not only in opposition or resistance to the marriage and love-plot nature of romance but also, from the perspective of current criticism, sexuality as constructed in texts that are concerned with England directly. As a literary figure that comes at the end of a long history of romance writing, the knight-errant is stretched between "the myth of the reformed prodigal" of late fifteenth-century romances and "the world conqueror,"[62] so that his masculinity could be assessed in relation to two impulses that energize his existence in romances: wandering and empire-building.

Another set of reasons for a wide-ranging stories of male eroticism has to do with the nature of romances as fictions in which improbability and possibility, fantasy and politics, history and anachronism, mix and intertwine, providing multiple narrative scenarios and discursive strategies for toying with, probing into, and stretching ideas about masculinity and sexuality. To the extent that romances are meant to maintain the normative order and patriarchal system intact, not only do these texts complicate the process of courtship and trouble amorous fictions, they also blur the ending of romantic entanglement. A historicized understanding of discourses of eroticism that, for instance, enabled Valerie Traub to assess in detail "a genealogy of female homoerotic desire"[63] in the early modern period, is a critical strategy that I follow only in part in this book, because the erotic body of the knight-errant is a product of a new literary discourse that transforms predecessor heroic narratives into erotic stories. Romances present us with literary discourses of sex and sexuality, rather than reflecting actual sexual practices and sexual types that may have existed in early modern society. In their stories of the subjugation and assertion of masculinity, writers of romances make the knight's individual agency responsible for the fate of kingdoms they protect or purchase, and for the virtue their subjectivity is meant to uphold. These writers imagine a world in the process of establishing merchant empire that is not in conflict with the knights' private desires. They present the merchant empire as a facilitator of and a challenge to those desires at the point where ambition and virtue translated into love and desire shape "the sexual dimension of politics."[64] Within this dimension, the autonomy of identity and masculinity are possible only within the troubled and complex construction of merchant empire, which had a magnetic appeal to the early modern world. Among the most complicated and problematic acts of masculinity that a critic of romance literature grapples with is the interpretation of rape, murder, and different forms of violence exhibited by the knight, since those were markers of masculinity in the early modern period, as shown by Alexandra Shepard.[65] These acts overlay the discourses of merchant empire, not as substitutions, but as a parallel process of analogy and misogynistic aggression as a critique of merchant empire.

The emasculated knight, or "the carpet dancer" and the "carpet knight," as Emanuel Forde and Richard Johnson,[66] respectively, call their heroes, is not the knight of "anxious masculinity" registering "cultural tensions and contradictions" in the shaping of male subjectivity[67] within the patriarchal culture. The knight's fictionalized body teases out both the cultural and literary dynamics of gender construction[68] and the crossroads of chivalric revival that found one of its best outlets in prose romances, the commercialization of the early modern world, and the fantasies of profit in the emerging space of trade and travel in the Eastern Mediterranean. In the history of writing about early modern fiction and about the gender of sexuality, prose romances of the sixteenth and seventeenth century provide ample evidence for changing ideas about masculinity, men's intimacy, and affect, which change not only the picture of early modern manhood that we have, but also show how effectively romance adapted itself as a literary form that is ultimately about love and heroism at the time of the shift from the militant to the romantic concerns of men at the end of the sixteenth century.

What Is the Eastern Mediterranean?

The question "What is the Mediterranean?,"[69] and how to identify it, is not something asked only by present-day historiographers, it was also posed in the early modern period. David Abulafia argues that "the Mediterranean cannot simply be defined by its edges"[70] but also by its islands, and the cultures and states that have constituted it. Abulafia invites us to think about this sea in a flexible way as a geographical and historical construct, incorporating the sea, the hinterland, and the history that reverberates beyond its shores and waters. This is the meaning that the Mediterranean had in the early modern period.

Early modern writers, travellers, and geographers used the word "Mediterranean" in various ways. The body of water believed to lie in the middle of the earth is referred to in Christopher Marlowe's play, *The Jew of Malta*, where Barabas trades in "our Mediterranean sea" (1.1.46), alongside many merchant–adventurers. In his (proto)ethnographic treatise, *The Manners, Lawes, and Customes of All Nations* (1611), Ioannes Boemus refers to "the Mediterranean sea" which "deuideth Europe from Affric," and George Sandys describes "the *Mediterraneum*" in his travelogue, *A Relation of a Journey begun An.Dom: 1610* (1615).[71] In his illustrated atlas of the world, *An Epitome of Ortelius His Theatre of the World* (1602), Abraham Ortelius defines the Mediterranean as "the Midland" sea, which is also how the anonymous author of *Oceander* (1600) describes the setting of his romance ("the Mid-land sea").[72] The term used by both Ortelius and the author of *Oceander* suggests the common name for the Mediterranean used in the early modern period. In early modern England, the word "Mediterranean" was understood to refer to both the sea and the hinterland, though the precise denotation depended on whether the word was used as a noun or an adjective. Thomas Cooper, echoing Pliny, writes that if used as a noun (Substantium) "Mediterraneum" means "The middle of the land: land farthest from the sea," but when used as an adjective (Adiectiuum) it qualifies something "in the middle of the land," as in "Mediterraneum mare," meaning "The middle sea betweene Europe and Affrike."[73] Whereas in modern usage the term specifically refers to the body of water between Europe and Africa, in the early modern period, as Thomas Cooper suggests, the term encompassed both the sea and a landmass markedly remote from the sea. This double understanding of the Mediterranean as both a sea and a landmass, a conceptualization more flexible than the modern notion of the term, may explain why in prose romances the Mediterranean includes both the sea and its deep hinterland, such as the Persian Gulf and the port of Hormuz. As Jack Goody states, "[the] eastern Mediterranean always kept its commercial and intellectual links with the East and with central Asia."[74]

In a culture where increased sensitivity to language's potential for meaning coexisted with new perceptions of the Mediterranean as a place of global trade, these meanings intersected, broadening the ways in which the Mediterranean was understood as both a sea and as a land. Such an enriched understanding of the Mediterranean Sea and its shores extended to travel, geographical, and mercantile writings about the Eastern Mediterranean, creating a distinct poetics of the region. What appears to us today as remote, disparate, and widely scattered, once constituted a tightly knit Mediterranean world, as demonstrated by Fernand Braudel.[75] Braudel's approach to the Mediterranean was, however, largely West-oriented. He was primarily concerned with the European Mediterranean, emphasizing similarities between different lands within that European sphere. In contrast, the post-Braudelian studies of the Mediterranean have emphasized cross-cultural contacts and interactions, including diplomatic exchanges between the Western and Eastern Mediterranean. These new approaches diverge from Braudel's focus on the socioeconomic aspects of the Mediterranean, which largely ignored the Ottoman Mediterranean. In important respects, Braudel's idea of the Mediterranean is a product of his own time, foregrounding the similarities between different Mediterranean zones within a Eurocentric vision of the entire region in a way that seems analogous to the integration of African domains within European imperial control. The unitary term "Mediterranean," then, is retrospective: before the nineteenth century the Mediterranean was simply understood to be the centre of the known world and did not have to be named collectively.

The importance of the Mediterranean in connecting what now appear as distant parts of Europe is illustrated by the description in a cartouche of a 1595 Dutch map of the sea (Figure 4). Included in an atlas of the world's seas, the Mediterranean Sea is described as linking the Iberian Peninsula, France, and the British isles with the Atlantic Ocean.

Expanding land areas and shrinking the sea, Barentsz's map redraws the positioning of the territories of Europe before natural borders by making Britain an integral part of the Mediterranean zone. But it also draws attention to the prominence of the East in the Mediterranean region by magnifying "Barbaria," or the non-Christian Mediterranean. This presentation of the Islamic Mediterranean is further emphasized by an illustration representing some of the cities that were central to its political and cultural history – Oran, Algiers, Constantinople, Goletta, and Alexandria. A number of these cities feature as locales in prose and in dramatic romances. Although the map presents these cities as substantially similar to each other, as geographical emblems rather than actual places, this map reflects the political, ideological, and religious, features of the Mediterranean that marked its significance. It also draws attention to the involvement of other nations – Spain, France, and England – in shaping the representations and politics of the region. Symbolic connections between Britain and the Mediterranean draw our attention to the fact that the Sea was considered to be closer to the concerns of early modern Englishmen than it may initially appear to us. The Eastern Mediterranean of prose romances may be spatially removed from Britain, but conceptually, as suggested by Barentsz's map, it is as close to Britain as the political concerns fictionalized in romances.

This geographical notion of the Mediterranean as a network of shores, islands, and hinterland allows the Eastern Mediterranean of the prose romances and other "histories" to be connected to the Far East. It is not accurate to say that geography in the romances is mysterious; some of the places they mention – Illyria, Natolia, Lybia, Armenia – were once (and some still are) concrete geographical locations. Rather, geographical locations are collocated as signifiers of the political and historical situation within a seamless world of the Eastern Mediterranean. Such a vision of the world was in large part the product of the way maps presented the lands around the borders of the Mediterranean and its hinterland as borderless, undifferentiated. The knight-errant does not wander through mystical lands: he threads a geographical space that his period conceptualized as seamless and that the literature stylized as a propitious setting for transgression and trade.

The Mediterranean's constituent regions – once bounded by the deep commonalities of the sea, now pulled apart by the ruptures and disharmonies of history – have been aptly described by Iain Chambers as a geopolitical space of "an interrupted modernity."[76] Fictionalizing the agency of knight within the complex geopolitics of the mercantile

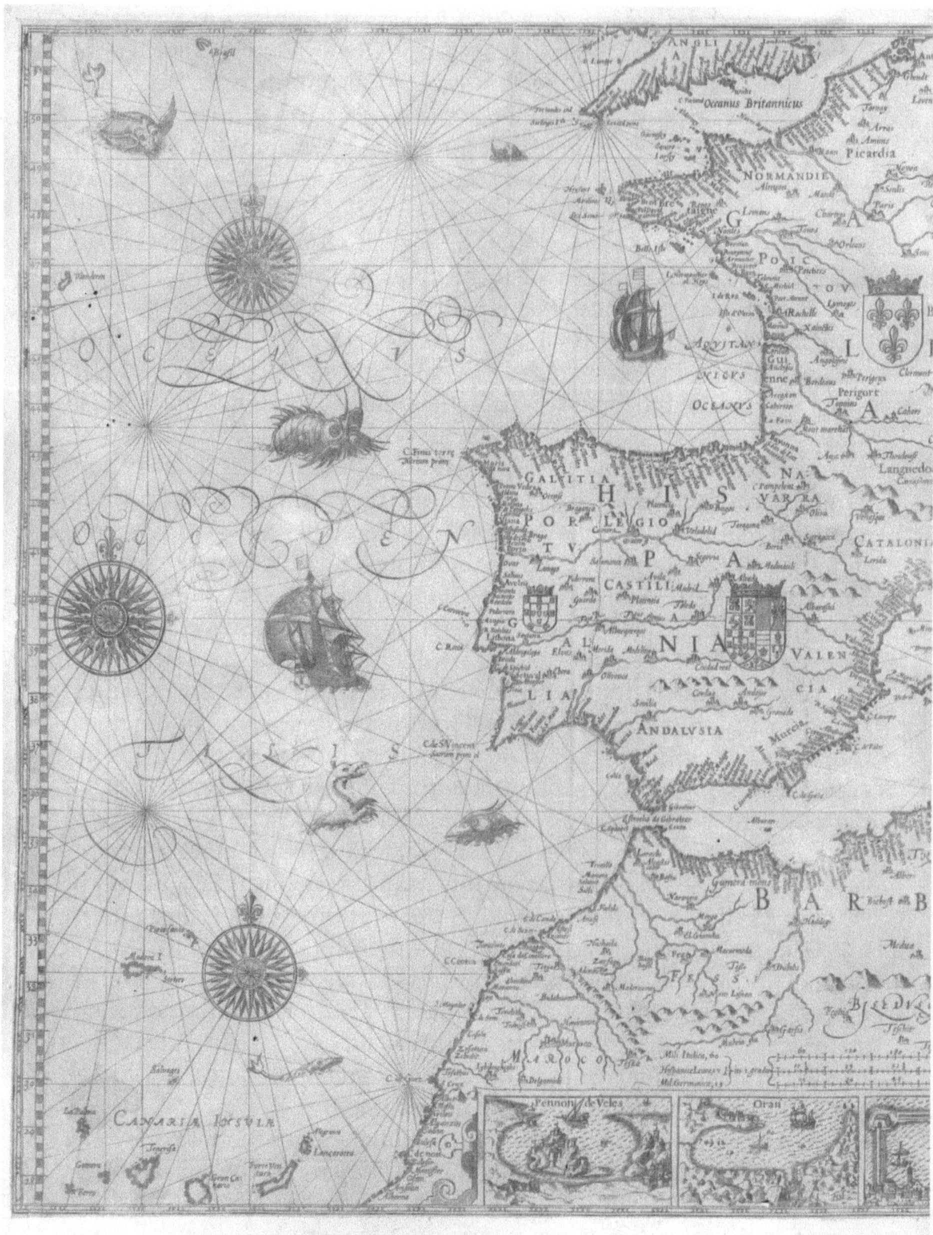

Figure 4. Willem Barentsz, The Mediterranean Sea, *Thalassographica Tabula totius Maris Mediterranei* (The Newberry Library, Novacco 4F 187).

Thalassographica Tabula totius Maris
Compascaerte
Constantinopolis
Goletta
Alexandria
Alger
POLONIA
BOHEMIA
AVSTRIA
HVNGARIA
SLAVONIA
WALACHIA
BVLGARIA
MOLDAVIA
HELVETIA
Savoie
Lombardia
PROVENCE
CORSICA
Mare Adriaticum
ITALIA
MARE TIRRENVM
SICILIA
Malta
MARE
MEDITERRA
BARCHA
TVNIS
Vienna
Cracow
Lublin
Villach
Tergwisch
Temeswar
Florentia
Loraine

Eastern Mediterranean at the moment of the historical shift from feudal to early modern conditions, romances of the sixteenth and the seventeenth century are even closer to modernity than their medieval antecedents.[77] With the decline of feudalism and chivalry, romances, too, assumed a different role. To regard early modern romances as belonging to a modern, progressive genre may thus seem to be at odds with literary history – especially since for a long time scholarship concerned itself with these texts' debts to their classical, medieval, and continental precursors and emphasized their apparent nostalgia for a lost age of chivalry. Yet a case can be made for treating romance depictions of chivalric pursuits in the Eastern Mediterranean as forward-oriented narratives, as exemplary texts that allegorize the pragmatic scenarios unfolding for English traders in this region. The knight-errant's bounty, a godly reward for his prudence, enables English visions of power and mercantile advantage in the Islamic Mediterranean. In that regard, Renaissance romances revise the feudal view of plenitude as a reward from God, adopting proto-capitalist, forward-oriented narratives in which the reward is measured in new trading routes, territories, and kingdoms. If feudal romances, with their fictions of knights' bravery, looked to the kingdom of God, these new Protestant romances embraced the kingdom of trade, centred on the Eastern Mediterranean.

Prose Romances: The Boundaries of Historicism

Critics writing after McCoy and Hurd have examined in detail the political and ethical concerns embedded in deep allegorical stories of romances. Blair Worden's dense interpretation of Sir Philip Sidney's *Arcadia*, for instance, shows that Sidney's romance is not only a mirror of most of the main political events of Elizabeth I's reign but that it "can help us understand [those] events."[78] Exploring in his fiction subjects that his contemporaries were dealing with less interestingly in their factual writing, Sidney, Worden argues, "made innovative contributions to the political and historical thought of his time."[79] Following up, more or less explicitly, on Sidney as the formative model of romance writing, the writers of prose romances that I interpret in this book give more meaning to the Eastern Mediterranean. Romance writers also fictionalize the Eastern Mediterranean in imaginative ways, ways that often exceed the experiential writing of a wide range of documents alongside, and against which prose romances are interpreted. Victoria Kahn has explored the contractual relationship between subjects encoded in romances published between the Civil War and the period just after the Restoration of monarchy in England, focusing on the various ways (e.g., gender, embodiment, marriage, violence, emotion) in which romances comment "on the contemporary crisis of political obligation."[80] Kathryn Schwarz has examined the legibility of lesbian desire in Sidney's *Arcadia*, locating gender and transactions between men within the politics of cross-dressing.[81] Continuing this line of criticism, which illuminates the gendered and affective relationships shaped within the social and political emulation of history in romances, Amelia Zurcher examines the allegorical, ethical, and political bases of the canonical *Arcadia* and several non-canonical romances.[82] And in her illuminating interpretation of the material basis of gift exchanges and ornamentation in romances, Patricia Fumerton demonstrates the extent to which the abundance of wealth and commodities resulting from England's trade with the East translated into the ornamental strangeness and stylistic opulence of romances, which she illustrates in her discussion of the gendered narrative of Edmund Spenser's romance epic, *The Faerie Queene*.[83]

Scholarship on medieval and early modern romances has been exceptionally vibrant in recent years. As feminism, queer theory, and postcolonial approaches to early modern texts shaped new arguments about body and identity in the early modern period, scholars have become increasingly drawn to these fascinating texts, in part because the core concerns of prose romances are gender, sex, desire, love, family, marriage, political rule, and reproduction. These concerns have been subjected to critical scrutiny in historicist and archival studies, demonstrating the level to which the feudal warrior ethic has met with resistance from the emerging bourgeois concern with family, sexual ethics, gender relationships, and wealth accumulation in a culture where the household has replaced the battlefield as a social ideal, as demonstrated by vernacular romances of the early modern period. The continuing scholarly interest in romances after the dominance of New Historicism has charted an exciting new kind of historicist engagement with early modern texts, which Denis Austin Britton has conveniently termed "historical formalism."[84] This historicist orientation in criticism takes as its subject literary form, and explores its features and transformation within a specific set of historical conditions within which the form in question (romance in this instance) flourished and which influenced the ways that form responds to the historical moment and reacts to the questions that it raises. The more that critical race studies and postcolonial approaches to early modern literature grew as fields of critical inquiry in early modern studies, the more these approaches discovered romances as a fertile body of texts to test its suppositions and discover new topics of inquiry. The meeting point of romance criticism and scholarship on race and colonialism has thus been one of the more invigorating and novel areas of critical examination in early modern studies. Britton has articulated this situation in a particularly eloquent way when he states that "A revival in studies of romance has uncovered its varied uses in early modern England, revealing its immense popularity (in spite of those who argued that it is a particularly wanton and Catholic genre) and the way in which its conventions spurred a reimagining of cross-cultural interactions."[85] At this post-historicism moment of historicist scholarship, when textual scholars and those interested in bibliography are working through the archive with effective tools of empirical research, critical orientation towards the formalist criticism of romance, coupled with an interest in the issues of race and proto-colonialism of the East, and complemented with queer theory, has imbued early modern literary studies with new critical vitality and analytical energy.

This criticism has shown the extent to which Fredric Jameson's notion of the "secularization of romance as a form"[86] is embodied in the rich body of romances produced in the early modern period, often especially because travel and trade have made it possible for some of the transactions between subjects, men and women, to be imagined in romances. This scholarship on romances has situated critical debates at the crossroads of politics, gender, and sexuality, leaving the critical stage open for further discussions on how masculinity is constructed within other spheres of knowledge and history that enabled romances. One of the main strands of historicist scholarship has been the exploration of a complex dynamic of "mutual constitution and transformation"[87] that characterizes the meeting point of discourses and material life. This cultural dynamic has been amply explored in the example of drama and has changed the study of prose fiction in exciting ways. Yet the relationship between cultural constructions of the Mediterranean and the role that the material history of the Mediterranean played in expanding the body of romance writing in early modern England has remained unexamined.

Geography, travel, and the politics of West–East relations in the Eastern Mediterranean are consequently treated in this book as historical codes, elements that make prose romance "possible," according to Jameson, "in the increasingly secularized and rational world that emerges from the collapse of feudalism."[88] Within that secularized world, the romance stock type, "miles christianus"[89] undergoes the transformation from a fighting soldier of a Christian army to a romantic knight-errant and to a wandering western youth whose masculinity and formative sexuality the Eastern Mediterranean puts to an unpredictable test.

The political Eastern Mediterranean of burgeoning commerce between England and the East is thus intricately linked with the erotic Eastern Mediterranean of pleasure and frustration. The historical background for this reprise and metamorphosis of the knight-errant and his adventures is complex. Bolgar reminds us that "The knight-errantry of the romances was a fictional and exaggerated derivative of a philosophical doctrine ... [according to which] the use of force is justified only when some villainy requires suppression."[90] Bolgar's assertion that "Heroes have never been independent of the social and cultural climate in which they come to flourish"[91] leaves it to critics to determine which specific historical backgrounds and political values give meaning to the knight's agency. In the prose romances with which this book is concerned, the political, commercial, and gendered discourses associated with the Eastern Mediterranean in romances and related writing represent the historical basis for the knight's role. Arthur B. Ferguson argues that the knight-errant moves "through the romances as through a political vacuum, a limbo symbolized by the ever present and boundaryless forest in which he seeks adventures equally isolated from the recognizable context of organized society."[92] Yet as I argue throughout the book, the knight-errant does not move through a political vacuum, but through the territories of the Eastern Mediterranean whose political, historical, and geographical importance for the opening up of the Elizabethan and Jacobean worlds to the navigation and commercial voyages in the Mediterranean these romances fictionalize.

The knight-errant's wandering is not without complications for a literary historian and critic. If one of the foundations of the logic of historicism is the argument that "the point from which the critic speaks is as unsettled by historicism as the object he or she interprets,"[93] as Paul Hamilton argues, I would like to invoke the earlier brief definitions of the Eastern Mediterranean as a fluid space of water and land that remains an object of political contention, especially today. My approach to the discourses of the Eastern Mediterranean in prose romances, which blends historicist, queer, gender, and mercantilist criticism, aims at "unsettling" the idea of the Eastern Mediterranean in prose romances as a space of exotic fiction about miracles and wonders.

Romance, because it is one of the oldest of literary genres, dating back to the Greek fictions written by Heliodorus, extending to medieval metrical romances, long prose experiments written in England by Sir Philip Sidney and Robert Greene from the 1570s onward, and the dramatic romances of Shakespeare's late period, remains one of the most resilient and absorptive of literary forms. Difficulties arising from the definition of the term romance result from the fact that, as Cooper points out, "It is much easier to recognize a text as a romance than reduce the term to a single meaning."[94] Therefore, attempting not to reduce my use of the term romance to a specific meaning, in this book I explore largely non-canonical, hitherto critically unexamined works of imaginative fiction, where a neoclassical revival of chivalric narratives mixes with historical material. Michael McKeon has suggested that the "modestly historicized" romance of the seventeenth century has become "anti-romance" because history has reduced the high level of fantasy and the prevalence of magic, which characterized earlier romances.[95] Although verisimilitude still remains compromised in the anti-romances that McKeon describes, romance now reveals a deeper level of complexity and ambition within itself: its stories are no longer grounded in the extravagancies of fantasy alone, but fictions inspired by the immediate historical and social movements that always touch romance.

One could argue, however, that anti-romance, in McKeon's sense, separates history from the fictional narratives of romances. But the historical framing of romances that is advanced in this book suggests the opposite. While I agree with McKeon that a new kind of romance writing emerged when history started to enter romances, it is also true that romance lubricated historical currents by staging scenarios of the historical future. This is not to say that history started to follow the narratives of romances, but that romances offered an alternative version of especially commercial and gendered history of the Eastern Mediterranean by assimilating cultural discourses and geographical knowledge about it. This historical knowledge, this new geographical empiricism, has entered the narrative and fictional tissue of romance, and has been transformed by that fiction just as it transformed the fiction itself and the category of romance.

Because history and the new knowledge gained from travel and geography helped the early modern writer shape new stories beyond the familiar model of the Greek pastoral narrative and of the medieval romances narrating the Crusades, both the familiar and lesser known prose romances examined in this book offer new opportunities to explore new ideas about agency and society. Prose romances that I examine are the works of prose fiction "suspended"[96] between novellas, expansive verse epics, and travel accounts with romance characteristics. In terms of their interlaced narrative structure and their focus on heroic masculinity and the erotic temptations that await travelling knights, English prose romances are closer to epic romance, such as Edmund Spenser's *The Faerie Queene,* not the metrical romance of the late medieval period. Yet prose romances differ from *The Faerie Queene,* not only because they are shorter prose works and cheap-print works of popular literature that ranked low in the period, but also because their narratives are set within the geographical boundaries of the Eastern Mediterranean, there is occasionally self-conscious acknowledgment of that geography, and because commercial contact between men from the West and the East is central to their narratives.

Spaces of Trade

The romantic knight and the merchant cross paths in the ports and on the sea in the Eastern Mediterranean of prose romances. The paths along which these two figures travel in prose romances are neither simple nor safe. The cultural background for their symbolic meeting in romances lies in part in the transformation of the ideas of masculinity, from heroic to romantic and from monkish to mercantile, as those ideas developed from the medieval to the early modern period. At this point my arguments extend, but also challenge, Deborah Kuller Shuger's assertion that "In northern Europe during the sixteenth century, Erasmian humanism and Protestantism conjointly discredited the two principal medieval types of Christian manhood: the monk and the knight."[97] The examples from romances discussed in this book, however, show that Shuger's assertion is only partially true because the knight, though discredited as a militant hero of the medieval fictions of the Crusades, resurfaces as a romantic knight in sixteenth-century romances. His manhood is both shaped and compromised by discourses of seduction, love, matrimony, and mercantilism under the rhetorical ruse of eroticism and heroism. Protestantism, which discredited the medieval knight as a militant man, accredited him as a pragmatic hero in romances of the East, where Protestantism inspired discourses and activities of trade and travel. Romances of the Eastern Mediterranean therefore show one of the directions romances took in their development as a literary genre in the early modern period.

Romances of the Eastern Mediterranean are cheap commodities on the market for literature about travel and trade, literature that also played a significant role in the shaping of ideas of gender in early modern England. The stories they tell are commodity discourses within pre-capitalist trade with the East. Bruce Robbins makes a claim for popular histories as commodities, although within a different cultural context and at a different historical moment such a consideration of the relationship of fiction and commodities encodes empire. His idea that books do not "take the existence of global capitalism for granted" but that they make "a forceful argument on capitalist's behalf"[98] could apply to romances of the Eastern Mediterranean, but only insofar as that empire is taken to be proleptic within the realm of literary imagination. In literature, such an empire could be constructed as something that has not yet come into being and that exists as an empire of trade, or merchant empire, where partners in trade, men from the West and from the East, are imagined as both rivals and equal partners, depending on individual texts. As improbable fictions, romances are not texts that offer concrete strategies to merchants on how to proceed with trade in the East.

Romances were related to masculinity in different ways during their cultural life in the early modern period. For instance, tracing the long history of printing Robert Greene's romance *Pandosto* (1588), Lori Humphrey Newcomb has demonstrated in compelling detail not only the endurance of Greene's romance as popular reading, but also that such cheap-print fictions were "a threat not only to masculinity but also to the economic and moral health of the nation."[99] Newcomb's detailed account of the commodification of *Pandosto,* from the first edition in 1588 until the eighteenth century, places the emphasis on the role that printing, book circulation, and textual interpretation had on the changing ideas about genders. However, in this book I want to show that a process opposite to Newcomb's also played a major role in the production of the ideas about gender, especially masculinity, namely the persistence of the Mediterranean romance on the marketplace of prose fiction. This is also the sign that romances were deeply involved in the formulation of discourses and ideas about mercantile masculinity that were imagined to augment the economic wealth of the nation and thus participate in maintaining the "moral health of the nation" as well.[100]

In that regard, authorship would have been seen as a facilitator of such national enterprises as travel to the East with the view of conceptualizing new mercantile opportunities.

Thus, if, as I propose in this book, we approach romances as texts whose focus is not on mercantile activities in the past, but on how such activities were perceived and represented in imaginative literature, then they are subjects of a work of cultural and intellectual history that touches on the history of ideas. Of particular interest to poststructuralist criticism is the fact that one of the fascinating characteristics of romance is that it is an absorptive genre. Romance is capable of simultaneously taking in and transforming a number of discourses – trade, masculinity, travel, sexuality – within the frame of a chivalric narrative. Trying to separate these discourses is to fail to capture the layered nature of these texts. My intention is not to imply that commercial activities, the sexual behaviour of individual knights, and desires written over the acts and travels of knights-errant must correlate in a straightforward manner to the actual or dominant conditions of trade, categories of sexuality, sexual acts, ideas about masculinity, or erotic concepts used in early modern English society. For example, critics have pointed out that there is "always considerable uncertainty about the erotic content of early modern friendship"[101] in England. By linking masculine social agency with the overlapping discourses of economic and contractual exchanges between men, and affect that brings men in the marketplace together, romances make both friendship and other forms of male alliances sites for exploring the valences of intimacy and desire that are not always sexual or coded as homosexual, or entirely bound up with anxiety – all of which increase the pleasure of reading eroticism in these texts that are consistently charged with desire. Prose romances thus urge us to relax the rigid dichotomy between literary representation and social behaviour or practice so we can see the possibilities that imaginative literature projects back into a culture and society as erotic fantasy.

Common to all prose romances discussed in this book is that in the process of reimagining the chivalric past they also orient the knights' energy and valour towards romantic pursuits and towards what could best be described as the emergence of a proto-imperial discourse of trade. The phrase "purchasing kingdoms," used at a crucial moment in Richard Johnson's prose romance, *The Seven Champions of Christendom* (1596/7) by the narrator, who is reflecting on the knights' aggressive actions and courtship adventures, gestures towards the idea of merchant empire before empire as a project came into being. Moments like this invite the critic to revisit the claim that "the impress of Empire upon English literature in the early-modern period was minimal, and mostly critical where it was discernible at all," by refining the use of the concept of empire, a concept that the early modern world was not unfamiliar with since "empire" was the vernacular correlative to the Roman term *imperium*.[102]

Geraldine Heng's book, *Empire of Magic: Medieval Romance and the Politics of Cultural Fantasy*, about the inscription of medieval Europe's earliest project of empire "in the Levantine colonization in Syria and Palestine," has prepared some of the critical territory that I am entering. Not only does her argument about the crossover between chivalric travel and imperial ambition foreground my point about the knight's agency within the merchant empire, but her point about the inseparability of pleasures "intimately" folded into and "imbricated" with "historical projects and agendas"[103] anticipates that aspect of my line of inquiry which argues that discourses of male erotics and masculinity are woven through the fictions of mercantilism and travel in the Eastern Mediterranean. Moments of such self-reflection on the part of the knight about his actions call for a new assessment of the knight's role in prose romances and for a reinterpretation of "the anachronism of knight-errantry in an increasingly commercialized world."[104] This line of criticism of romance is still developing and the goal of this book is to open a dialogue about one of the ways of reading romances. Listening to Northrop Frye's assertion that reality is "for romance ... an order of existence most readily associated with the word identity," one cannot help hearing in the phrase "purchasing kingdoms" the echo of the intertwining of at least two topics central to this book: mercantile mastery and masculine agency. Conjoining the merchant empire and the construction of masculinity and male erotic identity, this book expands the argument about Anglo-Ottoman trade and gender by looking at men, not women, as Bernadette Andrea does.[105]

This book focuses on the narratives of the Eastern Mediterranean in romances to unmask and carefully articulate the multiple ways in which masculinity was imagined in these fictions. This particular take on romances has been a neglected area of both criticism on romances and scholarship exploring the gendered construction of masculinity. Yet, the romances discussed in this book give enough textual evidence to trace the emergence of masculinity specifically connected with the formation of an empire of commerce and the discoveries of new markets for commodities coming from the East. The masculinities that thus emerge from the pages of romances set in the Ottoman Mediterranean are critically conceived within a particular set of historical and cultural circumstances created by travel and trade in – and geography of – the Eastern Mediterranean. Examining these specific agencies of mercantilist masculinity, the discussion in the following pages echoes what Elizabeth B. Bearden recommends, when she states that "identity in the early modern period should be conceived not in terms of individual agency, but rather as possible and adaptable within cultural situation, a distinction that calls for a more useful means of assessing identity that can perceive it in characters' responses to their environments."[106]

Romance and empire are predictable bedfellows. Joan Pong Linton's study of the interplay between popular romances and the colonial narratives of America also examines the crossover between colonial and gendered discourses. Linton's idea that the "desire for commercial mastery" produces fictions of gendered mastery in the treatment of women exchanged for commodities, and her claim that the contact between the colonizer and the New World subject is the point that "makes visible the fluidity of the English self," highlight in important ways the continuity of the kind of romance narrative built around some of the acts resulting from masculine dominance and the knight's role as a merchant that are fictionalized in romances of the Eastern Mediterranean.[107] Back in the Mediterranean, Benedict S. Robinson's account of the rewriting of medieval chivalric romance in the age of Shakespeare, Spenser, and Milton, that enabled "new ways of thinking about identity and difference" in the fictional encounters with Saracens, Moors, and Turks, cuts through the same generic and critical lands as my book.[108] Robinson's point, that the reader of romance is continuously invited "to imagine" the "possibility"[109] of arriving at the centre, which the reader never does, prompts productive thinking about how to conceptualize imagined mercantile goals set by the knight of romances, which I interpret.

If never arriving at the centre amounts to imagining possibility as a way of resisting the improbability of romance, then the knights traversing merchant empires could be said to be constantly imagining possibilities that are otherwise left unsaid, or fully narrated, in the endlessly interlaced narratives of romances.[110] These knights are the agents of fantasies – of mercantilist dreams turned into romance fictions – that were at the heart of the analogous texts about the Eastern Mediterranean, with which I frame romances, texts that reflected a habit of thinking about the Eastern Mediterranean and the possibilities it might yield to England. In the core chapter of the book, "Purchasing Kingdoms in the Eastern Mediterranean," I advance the idea of merchant empire produced by the overlapping realms of the romance fiction and mercantilist writing of the period, and show how it enables masculinity at a moment of the complex encounter with the Eastern Mediterranean, as a zone of England's new engagement with the world beyond its frontiers.

The period of romance writing that I am interested in falls almost entirely within the century of the growth of Eastern Mediterranean trade and the establishment of embassies in the Ottoman Empire, particularly in Aleppo, Smyrna (Izmir), and Constantinople (Istanbul). The social historian Ralph Davis captures the importance of England's trade with the Eastern Mediterranean well:

> The Levant trade [...] fulfilled all the dreams of the mercantilist; it balanced offering raw materials in exchange for English manufactures, employing large ships on a distant voyage, handled throughout by English merchants. The mercantilist and his dreams may be abstraction of the modern historian; the merchant was real, and for him, it appears, the Levant trade had great bounty to offer.[111]

The mercantilist and his dreams are equally an abstraction and a fiction of romance writers. Against the background of the historical situation that Davis describes, it is easy to see why mercantilism and the bounty of Levant trade became a staple of literature and why trade became a complex and controversial topic in prose romances, where chivalric valour and dreams of mercantilist success overlap with stories of pleasure and eroticism. Romances of the Eastern Mediterranean narrate imaginary scenarios of grappling with the vicissitudes of merchant empire by interrupting fictions of trade with erotic stories. The new mercantile class that emerged in England at this historical moment was preoccupied with civic ideals, with honour derived from social achievement, not from inherited right, including success in the domestic commercial market and on the overseas trading routes.

Mercantilism, however, is a problematic topic in the Renaissance, partially because, like economics, it did not have a "precise label."[112] Renaissance writing about mercantilism incorporates a variety of discourses, including travelogues. But romances add a fictional dimension to this body of texts, acting as powerful transmitters of mercantilist activities and further complicating the picture of mercantilist writing in the early modern period. If we view romances only as improbable fictions, the question to ask, then, is what to do with the narratives by merchants that use romances to reinforce the point, within texts like the one by Gerard de Malynes,[113] whom I shall discuss in chapter 2, in "The Giant, the Dragon, and Eastern Trade." The improbabilities of romance may be seen as an indirect attempt to mount a critique of the freedom and benefits of trade in a culture in which that trade is already defined in terms that sometimes portray it as an unheroic undertaking.

The capacity of romance to imagine Mediterranean trade against the background of the history and politics of the Eastern Mediterranean is an example of the crossover of politics and romances. The writers of royalist romances of the 1640s, as shown by Victoria Kahn, used romance plots to "stage and to deny any significance to the crisis of the civil war," making romances both "the contingent realm of fortune" and a "vehicle of consent, pleasure and virtue, destiny and choice."[114] The double role assigned to royalist romance is also the feature of those romances' predecessors, the turn of the century romances of the Eastern Mediterranean. These romances diagnose the benefits of Mediterranean trade and the pleasures gained in the contacts between men as agents in commercial exchange. Although prose romances valorize chivalric masculinity, they also critique it, rejecting the militant ethos by rerouting masculine agency to trade and homosociality. Prose romances that have been left out of the literary canon provide important views on early modern trade, Mediterranean politics, the changing meaning of masculinity in an age of commercial expansion and Mediterranean travel, and sexuality. By reading romances alongside a variety of texts about the Eastern Mediterranean – by reading, that is, history as literary narrative – I want to illustrate first that in a period when imaginative literature was not always privileged, separating fictional from non-fictional texts limits our understanding of how that period imagined the Eastern Mediterranean and what it understood literature to be.

Anglo-Ottoman Criticism and Romances

As suggested above, scholarship on Anglo-Ottoman contacts in the early modern period has shifted focus from those areas dominated by Spain and Italy to the Eastern Mediterranean controlled by the Ottoman Empire. Critics have demonstrated how the new "travel knowledge" became the source of new insights in England about the sea's eastern territories.[115]

They have also documented the multiple ways in which early modern England constructed, reported, feared, fantasized about, and transposed in literature its own contacts and interactions with the Ottoman Empire and with the religion and legends stemming from the Islamic world. In this respect, Matthew Dimmock's scholarship is particularly valuable because it richly documents the scope and nature of early English, and, more broadly, European, constructions of and fantasies about the mighty and threatening Ottomans.[116]

The complex and conflicting history of the Mediterranean, as the site of imperial history "from Alexander the Great to Suleiman the Great,"[117] as Daniel Vitkus perceptively observes, remains central to an understanding of the anachronisms of empire and the new mercantile pragmatism of the sixteenth century which engulfed both the ruling elite and the middle class in England. Writers of romances have absorbed the discourse of empire because the ancient empires took place within the space those writers' world claimed for itself: the Christian Mediterranean. At the same time, England, a relative latecomer to trading in the Eastern Mediterranean, searched for its role within that space of rivalry and competing interests. As Vitkus points out, "From a vantage point of awe and deference (and sometimes envy), English writers began to gather knowledge about the Mediterranean world from a position of inferiority, not power, and so a Saidian 'orientalist discourse' based on power and the control of knowledge was not possible."[118] The emphasis on "re-orienting the Renaissance"[119] by exploring cultural exchanges and knowledge transaction between the West and the Ottoman Empire and by memorializing English travellers and their experiences in the Orient,[120] has built a strong historical basis for further research, at the core of which are the ideas of contact and rivalry. Elizabethan commercial activities in the Levant were formalized when Queen Elizabeth signed a treaty charter with Amurath III (Sultan Murad) for five years and granted The Company of Merchants of the Levant and the Barbary (or Morocco) Company, charters after they were founded in 1581 and 1585, respectively. At that point "the English went to the Mediterranean to trade and pillage, not to seize and settle."[121] Distinguishing implicitly between two kinds of empire, the merchant empire, as I call it, based on trade and forceful acquisition of commercial interests and, as I argue later, routes; and colonialism, which resembles the nineteenth-century version of empire as claiming territories, settling, and establishing imperial laws and institutions, represents a helpful distinction for understanding the idea of merchant empire in this book.

The purpose of purchasing kingdoms, to echo Johnson's *The Seven Champions of Christendom*, is not to settle and stay, but to trade. And that trade in the Eastern Mediterranean of romances is often facilitated with violence, becoming forced trade. The idea of an exchange between the English and other western nations and the Ottomans coexisted with the various strategies of rivalling and weakening the Ottomans and of drawing profit from trading with them, and from the resources, including the markets, in their territories. Nabil Matar's juxtaposition of Britain's imperial ambitions in the Ottoman Empire as the testing ground for its subsequent colonization of the New World takes the discussion about Britain's engagement with the Mediterranean in a direction different from the one I am suggesting is the subject of prose romances.[122] But Matar's argument puts the writing about imperialism in a larger context of debate about the role of the English in the Mediterranean and the complex definition of early modern empire, charting a territory for specific and structurally different mimeses[123] of empire as a concept in imaginative literature. Cultural historians such as Jerry Brotton and Daniel Goffman have demonstrated that it is impossible to separate Renaissance Europe from the Ottoman Empire in discussions about global trade.[124] Prose romances add to our knowledge about these contacts by providing us with mimetic, literary versions of the story of these contacts and conflicts. One of the claims I make in this book is that ideas about early modern manhood presented in romances reveal in literature what often remains hidden in the social history about early modern empires and trade.

PART I

The Knight and the Romance of Trade

The four romances I discuss in this part – Richard Johnson's *The Seven Champions of Christendom* (1596/7), Emanuel Forde's *Montelyon* (?1599), and the anonymous *The famous, pleasant, and variable historie, of Palladine of England* (1588) and *Oceander* (1600) – assume a cultural awareness of the intersection between heroic and mercantile activities in the Islamic East, and of the dangers and profits ensuing from those activities. Each romance emphasizes actions along the trading routes mapped by the entrepreneurial spirit of Protestant England and Jacobean aspirations towards the establishment of harmony and equality between the trading kingdoms of the West and East. Each romance also stylizes its own version of the Islamic East.

Richard Johnson's *The Seven Champions of Christendom* was among the most popular romances of the 1590s, providing material for subsequent chapbook versions, including one that resembles a picture book.[1] I use it to frame most of the discussion in the following pages. After the success of part one of *Johnson's* romance in 1596, part two was published a mere year later. Both parts of this text, printed either separately or together, were reissued seven times between 1597 and 1635. Between1596 to 1640, this romance went through ten editions, sometimes, as in 1631, requiring more than one printing. Between 1640 and 1670, it was reprinted four more times, and in 1700 and 1720 two abridged editions were published in octavo format.[2] The romance also became a popular stage play by John Kirkman, printed in 1638, following its success on the stages of the Cockpit and the Red Bull theatres, possibly between 1618 and 1625.[3] Johnson's romance was still available in print in 1820.[4] Well into the twentieth century it continued to be adapted in the form of adventure stories for adolescent males.[5] We know very little about Johnson's life, except that he lived and worked in London. He was an apprentice in London in the early 1590s, around the time he would likely have been at work on *The Seven Champions*; in 1603, he became a freeman of modest means, though he never named his company.[6] Johnson's fiction clearly belongs to the corpus of romances set in the Ottoman Mediterranean. It is composed around the Eastern Mediterranean voyages of Christian princes from several countries, led by the English knight St George, and describes their marriages to eastern princesses, their conflicts with Muslims, and their attempts to convert Muslims to Christianity.

The Seven Champions of Christendom consists of two parts. The first part (1596) starts with a brief account of the legend about the origin of Britain ("Ille of *Brittaine*"), the foundation of London as a "new *Troy*," and the "wonderful and strange birth" of St George by "Kalyb the Lady of the Woods."[7] Thus, in an attempt to transpose the Virgilian myth of Aeneas's quest to found a new Troy onto the neo-chivalric fiction of St George as the English national saint, Johnson entrusts him with the mission to reclaim the fallen "Cittie of *Phrigia*" (the old Troy) for Christianity. This valiant mission becomes a pretext for a series of heroic battles against, and defeats of, Muslims holding power in Northern Africa and throughout the Eastern Mediterranean. Given the scale and significance of the cultural symbolism of St George's heroic mission, which was also intended to prevent Muslims from invading Europe, voiced as the narrator's fear that "the Prouinces of *Affrica* and *Asia*, had mustered vp their forces to the inuasion of *Europe*,"[8] St George is joined by knights from six other Christian countries: St Denis of France, St Anthony of Italy, St James of Spain, St Andrew of Scotland, St David of Wales, and St Patrick of Ireland. From Morocco to the Holy Land and Libya, from Sicily to Rhodes, and from Jerusalem to Tripoli and Cairo, the league of these Christian "knights at arms"[9] defeats one obstacle after another – giants, dragons, Amazonians, cannibals, tigers, lions, and infidels. They finally arrive in Egypt, where Johnson finishes the first part of his romance. In the second part (1597), Johnson pushes the geographical boundaries of his fiction further into the East. The same cohort of knights continues to win one battle after another, against their Muslim opponents in Syria, Persia, Babylon, Armenia, Thrace, Hormuz, and Damascus. The second part concludes with the knight's "triumphs, tilts, and tournaments solemnly held in Constantinople by the Grecian Emperour."[10] In this formulation, the Elizabethan London of chivalric jousting, veiled as Byzantine Constantinople, erases the line between Christian past and present. The narrative recovers the past of old Christianity in the East for the present time of Queen Elizabeth I's reign, a national icon glorified throughout Johnson's romance. In turn, this juxtaposition of Constantinople and London solidified in the minds of Johnson's readers another purpose of the knights' adventure – to celebrate the growing fame and power of London as the new Troy.

Johnson's deep engagement with the East makes him one of the first major fiction writers of "orientalist" themes among his contemporaries. His fictional reinvention of the story of St George belongs to the orientalist turn in romance writing in the last decade of the sixteenth century and the first half of the seventeenth century. This orientalism is not only evident in Johnson's consistent subordination of the values of the East to those of the West, it is also shown, indirectly, through the legend of St George's birth in Cappadocia (in central-eastern Turkey). Johnson could also have got the idea of St George as the main character in a chivalric romance from some of the contemporary writing about St George as a "valiant knight," as Peter Heylyn refers to this saint.[11] And in *Saint George for England* (1601), a compilation of fictional accounts about the saint, the Flemish merchant–adventurer Gerard de Malynes establishes a more direct link between St George's mission as a Christian knight and his heroic adventures in the East, where he fights infidels. Writing about this champion of Elizabeth I, de Malynes says:

> The invented historie of *S. George* … howsoever heretofore abused, may conveniently be applied to these our dayes of her Maiesties most happy government, wherin the beames o the Orientall starre of Gods most holy word appeare unto us most splendent and transparent, to the singular comfort of all faithfull. For whereas vnder the person of the noble champion Saint GEORGE our Saviour Christ was prefigured, deliuering the Virgin … from the dragon or diuels power.[12]

Both a panegyric to the Queen and her government, and to the heroic valour of the national saint, de Malynes's account resonates with irony, as he tells his readers that the history of St George is both invented and likely absurd. By the seventeenth century, so ironic an attitude towards the legend of St George was not uncommon, and de Malynes wrote his history in that vein. But Johnson's achievement as a romance writer does not lie in merely rendering the improbabilities of his main hero's heroic acts as entertainment and light reading for a growing number of readers of romances. Rather, Johnson takes the invented history of

St George both to write his own elaborate and allegorical version of the praise of Queen Elizabeth and to imagine fictional versions of other historical opportunities waiting to be grasped by the ambitious men of his time. If we take de Malyne's remark that St George "as he is commonly described ... is to be counted rather Symbolicall, than *Historicall*"[13] as advice to his readers to interpret St George's character as a fictional and symbolic, not historical, character, then we can also imagine Johnson writing his version of the history of St George in that vein. In Johnson's romance, St George's actions are to be taken as symbolic agency, veiling a story of developing Elizabethan involvement with the East and of the period's attempt to conceptualize the ways of succeeding in its ambitions to reclaim the East through trade. The East of Johnson's romance is not merely a geographical backdrop against which his narrator celebrates the absurdities of chivalric quests, it also animates the structures and habits of social thinking about the East as both a rival and an opportunity. The East of *The Seven Champions* is thus both a fictional construct and a historico-political reality, alive in western social and cultural imagination.

Johnson's romance narrates a series of victories by St George in the Barbary lands. St George is the appointed "chiefe Generall, and principall leader" of this military "consort of Christendome,"[14] which includes the six other knights, mentioned earlier. The seven champions are engaged in "attempts that appertained either to the benefit of Christendome, or the furtherance of their fortunate proceedings."[15] Johnson's narrative focuses on St George's seven-year imprisonment by the Persians, his successful effort to free himself, his quest for the Egyptian princess Sabra, who has been abducted by the Moroccan King Almidor, the liberation of Sabra and the killing of Almidor, and St George's marriage to Sabra. The chivalric voyages described here take place in kingdoms between Morocco and Persia. The knights' task is to "preuent the inuasion of Christendome, the ruines of Europe, and the intended ouerthrow of all Christina Prouinces" by "the bloody minded Infidel"; and they are known for their fearless "Conquering fortunes."[16] The conflicts start to unfold when Almidor informs Sabra's father, the King of Egypt, that St George, having heard of Sabra's unparalleled beauty, has set out to court her. The king is less than sympathetic to the suit: "Now by *Mahomet*, *Apollo*, and *Termagaunt*, three Gods we *Egiptians* commonly adore ... this damned Christian shal not gaine the conquest of my daughters loue."[17] The nationalist fervour of Johnson's romance cuts across a number of cultural boundaries in its account of religious conflict, colonialism, and sexual relations.

Johnson's work is at the centre of romance writing in which cultural and specifically mercantile interests are explored through writing about amorous conquest and eroticism. For example, typologically close to Johnson's work is *The Three Kings' Sons*, an early sixteenth-century French romance translated into English later in that century and so entitled in the British Library's Harley manuscripts collection. Surviving in a single copy, this romance delineates the arduous voyages and inter-ethnic marriages of the three princes: Philip of France, Humphrey of England, and David of Scotland. There must be some doubt as to whether Johnson was familiar with this romance, since its elaborate illuminations and the manuscript form suggest that it was probably intended for private use in a noble household.[18] But the translation of *The Three Kings' Sons* around the time of *The Seven Champions* helps us to consider Johnson's romance in the context of other romances with similar concerns and to think of both texts as part of a budding archive of literature in which cross-racial dynastic marriage in the East is connected with the opening up of commercial traffic within and beyond the Eastern Mediterranean. Individual autonomy and agency that are encouraged and to a large extent produced by the new proto-capitalist world of expanding markets in the East at the end of the sixteenth century get their literary correlative in the heroic agency of the knight-errant within the Eastern Mediterranean.

The close connection between the knight-errant and the Eastern Mediterranean of prose romances requires a new conception of chivalry and a new idea of the East in the Eastern Mediterranean and a conception of the role of love within that space. The complaint of the narrator in Johnson's romance, immediately after the marriage of Sabra and St George, that the champions have wasted too much time on amorous dalliance in Asia:

> Come they from Europe to fight in cotes of steele, and will they lye distraught in tents of loue? Come they to Asia to purchase Kingdomes, and by bludy war to ruinate countreys, [and] will they yeeld their victories to so foule disgrace? O shame and great dishonour to Christendome! O spot to Knighthood and true Chiualrie.[19]

at once illuminates the purpose of the knights' love conquest, as a way of conquering kingdoms, and critiques that enterprise as dishonourable on both religious grounds and at the level of the knight's social status. Purchased kingdoms, merchant empire enforced by the commercial and proto-imperial aims, shapes their own fictional and conceptual world of romance. Within the stories of merchant empire, the Eastern Mediterranean is no longer just geography but is reimagined as space within which the turbulent and unfolding and "never complete" process of the empire of trade shapes literature "with its imaginative and material results."[20] In the Eastern Mediterranean of merchant empire, writers of romances reimagine heroic virtue, rule of the land, political power, and desire in ways that now reflect the affective need and cultural demand of early modern mercantile England and its ambitious factors and nobility, looking beyond the frontiers of the English kingdom for glory and profit.

Early modern fictions about commerce presented trade as a pacifying activity that can help curb warring tendencies among nations and even lead to friendship, as suggested by Anthony Munday, a translator of many romances of the Eastern Mediterranean:

> Of such honor (amongst all nations) hath the trade of Merchandizing been ever acco[*m*]pted that Commerce (ever in the hottest flames of Warre against one another) could finde no better, or fayrer meanes to unite them in amitie, and to ioyne the[*m*] (as it were in wedlock) then by commerce and Negotiation. This is that chayne which bindes kingdoms in Leagues, begets loue betweene princess farre remoued asunder, and teacheth nations, different in qualitie, in colour, in religion, to deale faithfully together as brethren.[21]

This call to the brotherhood of trading nations and their heroes, coming from a soldier, John Reynard, "the gonner,"[22] places the idea of empires in romances in a new light. Giving up war for commerce as a way of binding kingdoms reflects the shift from militant to commercial masculinity that occurred towards the end of the sixteenth century. Yet romances often push in a different direction, where, in the context of war between kingdoms, masculine violence becomes a mechanism for creating the circumstances for trade.

1 Purchasing Kingdoms in the Eastern Mediterranean

In *The Seven Champions*, St George, the English knight, marries the Egyptian princess Sabra, his victory prize for having saved her from being raped by the giant Osmond. In the kingdoms of Egypt and Persia, which he now rules, St George has "established good and Christian laws" and has given his fellow knights the titles of the "pettie kings"[23] of Egypt, Persia, and Morocco, thus consolidating English rule in the kingdoms and territories of a vast swathe of the Eastern Mediterranean. The matrimonial union, this cross-ethnic and cross-religious bond, crowns a series of wondrous chivalric adventures that resonate with symbolism, conjoining religious and imperial rule by the English in Islamic Mediterranean and the territories associated with it. Like the Egyptian princes, the prospective mercantile bounty of the Eastern Mediterranean becomes a victory prize for the knight-errant as he moves eastward, overcoming obstacles along the way in repeated demonstrations of his military prowess and valour. The dual price of Sabra and the Eastern Mediterranean is a reminder of the global dimension of Anglo–Mediterranean politics in territories beyond England; ambitions that come into sharper focus immediately after the marriage of Sabra and St George. Johnson's romance begs the question of what it means for an English knight to fight in the Eastern Mediterranean and set up a royal household there.

Writers of romances employ the terms "kingdoms" and "empires" to imagine territories that cannot be integrated into the commonwealth of England.[24] Since England's fully developed commercial empire only took shape after the Restoration, late sixteenth- and early seventeenth-century romances present us with an unformed idea of empire. This concept has more to do with the creation of new commercial frontiers than with the possession of territories, which is how, in the strictest sense, imperialism was structured later in the seventeenth century. The wonders and challenges created for the knight-errant in romances are not mere obstacles raised to test his valour and challenge his heroic masculinity: they are, rather, stepping-stones towards forced possession of the lands of the East. In this context, the cross-racial and cross-religious marriage of Sabra and St George suggests the expansion and claim of a commercial territory by England. Because early modern marriage was understood as a political and economic institution, a kind of social contract that assumed husband's sovereignty over wife, marriage became a crucial political and ideological tool in the Elizabethan and Jacobean politics of territorial rule and claim in discourses that involved women as subjects, within and outside England. The assumed mutuality of marriage did not preclude inequality and subjection of the wife, or, symbolically, the land that came with her, in romances. The analogy between marriage and land sovereignty fictionalized in the episode of Sabra and St George, "was to naturalize and romanticize absolute sovereignty by making it seem that the subject, like the wife, was both naturally inferior and had consented to such inferior status out of affection,"[25] as Victoria Kahn observes. Kahn's point is a reminder that the process that she described in detail in her reading of late seventeenth-century romances was already in place in their sixteenth-century antecedents narrating the politics of marriage and empire in the Eastern Mediterranean.

The analogy between marriage and claim to land is one aspect of the layered discourses about the relationship between the knight and empire, between heroic masculinity and mercantile ambition. The kingdoms through which the knights-errant wander, fight the infidel, defeat dragons, and claim territories as reward for victories, however, are nor subjected to jurisdiction. Rather, the meaning of these imagined territories in romances is fluid and open to negotiation. In *The Seven Champions*, for example, the Eastern kingdoms should not be seen as implying claims to territory. They are a fictional embodiment of the "glorious and vertuous enterpryses" acclaimed by Richard Eden, the translator of *De orbe novo* by Pietro Martire d'Anghiera (Peter Martyr of Angleria),[26] representing both a symbolic reward for the knight and new opportunities for heightened commercial activity. For Eden, virtue and glory no longer derive from heroic actions alone, but from the ability to gain advantage, and to triumph, in other enterprises of interest to Christianity.

In a dense and illuminating study of the intersection between the common law, jurisdiction, and literary nationalism, Bradin Cormack argues for "productive flexibility"[27] in using the Roman concept of *imperium* to discuss empire in early modern English literature. He does so in part because, as David Armitage has also shown, *imperium* captures the fluidity of ideas about political authority at a moment when the historical empire is only beginning to emerge. In Cormack's analysis, empire as *imperium* designates a jurisdictional claim to another territory or sea trade; it is *dominium*, Cormack suggests, that implies territorial possession and thus conquest. While jurisdictional ground for territorial claims could take different forms, involving land, borders, or seas, Cormack argues that this process of the formation of empire was concomitant with the rise of the common law in early modern England. Thus *dominium* became a notion flexible enough to be reimagined in different forms within literature, one of which, as I will argue further, is found in the cross-racial and cross-religious marriage with which romances often end, a transactional contract in which the female body embodies the territory, the *dominion* to which England extends its rule. In prose romances the concept of empire is less connected with the idea of political authority than with notions of speculative virtue and prudent agency which clear the way for England's enterprising activities in the Eastern Mediterranean.

In romances this flexible notion of empire augments the idea of "supreme and extensive territory (especially an aggregate of many separate states),"[28] because it intersects with an equally expanding concept of "emporium" as a place of trade. In romances, emporium becomes a succession of eastern kingdoms and lands as spaces for trade and exchange rather than territories subject to the rule of a single emperor sitting in a centre of power.[29] Thus the definition recorded by the *Oxford English Dictionary* (*OED*) for the early modern period not only frames but also limits the literary version of empire as it was increasingly fictionalized in early modern romances.

Romance writers' engagement with the Eastern Mediterranean and the eastern territories beyond, and the marriage plot within the discourse of the East, are an important context for the notion of power over land and the idea of frontiers. Since romances fictionalize dynamics between the West and eastern kingdoms before English overseas colonies (except Ireland) came into being, they are, to borrow from the language of contemporary postcolonial theory, pre-subaltern texts. The Barbarian enemy, who features as an obstacle to the knight, is neither socially subordinate to his Christian counterpart nor inferior in power. Rather, the infidel is the knight-errant's obverse other – inferior by virtue of his religion, but a mighty opposite in terms of his military strength. This balance of heroic might is important not only because the knight must be faced with an equal force for his victory to be adequately earned and celebrated, but also because the victory prize itself then gains in worth. Against the historical background of the Islamic dominance of the Eastern Mediterranean, the neo-chivalric romances of the Elizabethan and Jacobean periods idealize Christian victories as signs of power over the Barbarian and legitimize newly won control of territories and trade routes in the East.

In romances and works narrating travel and trade in the Eastern Mediterranean the conceptual framework of "the Mediterranean empire" emerges as a new notion. It is connected with the development of more organized commercial shipping and trade in the Mediterranean, which replaced the "scattered English mercantile" colonies of the medieval period.[30] Within these new historical conditions, the medieval tradition of Arthurian romances, which continued to circulate in large numbers in England at the end of the sixteenth century, was no longer sufficient to respond to the realities of overseas trade, or to the imaginative prospects opened up by the voyages of the merchant.[31] Romances arising from the proliferation of mercantile discourses and activities in the sixteenth and seventeenth centuries reveal a transformation of romance as a historical project. Thus, as Geraldine Heng argues, from the early history of romance writing in England, the Arthurian version of the genre, "collaborates with medieval Europe's earliest project of overseas empire."[32] But if the first Levantine "crusader colonies," in Syria and Palestine, imagined in the Arthurian romances, were western cultural and historical projects arising from the chivalric and religious endeavours of the First Crusade, the Renaissance successors of these medieval fictions conceptualize the Levant as something other than the territories of heroic spectacle and triumph over Islam.

Early modern Christian anxiety over Islam's aggressive expansion in Europe not only produced, as Daniel Vitkus argues, "the denial or the radical distortion of what Islam really was" but that "perceived threat"[33] was also used to fictionalize other discourses as a way of resisting Islam and asserting Christian power over the seas and territories of the Eastern Mediterranean. Johnson's response to the Islamic threat prepares the ground for the champions' progress in the East:

> true reports [of Islamic invasion] had blazed abroad to every Princes eare, the bloody resolution of the Pagans, and how the Provinces of Africa and Asia, had mustred up their forces to the invasion of Europe: all Christian Kings then at the intreaty of the Champions, appointed mighty armies of well approved Souldiers, both by sea and land, to intercept the Infidels wicked intentions.[34]

The point at which the process of intercepting the pagan enemy turned into the project of purchasing kingdoms is the point at which the narratives of defence and merchant empire intersect through the knight's double agency as a defender and conqueror.

Johnson's romance is potentially revealing of the desire to claim territories by resorting to anachronism, a mode of narrating history that some critics of romances used to denounce them. A few lines after his narrator has voiced anxiety over the Islamic invasion of Europe, he digresses by giving us an account of war preparation across Europe:

> This honourable warre so fired the hearts of many youthfull Gentlemen, and so incouraged the minds of every common Souldier, that some mortgaged their lands, and at their owne proper charges furnished themselves: some sold their Patrimonies to serve in these honourable warres: and other some forsook Parents, Kindred, Wife, Children, Friends, and acquaintance, and without constraint of pressing, offered themselves to follow so noble a Generall, as the renowned Champion of England ... To be briefe, one might behold the streets of every Towne and City throughout all the Dominions of Europe, beautified with troops of souldiers, which thirsted after nothing but Fame and Honour.[35]

History mixes with the fiction of self-congratulatory nationalism, as knights are preparing, as they did, for the war against the infidel, and as Johnson is imagining St George to be just the perfect kind of general for this pan-European army. But this account ultimately raises another question: how to interpret this anachronistic passage that reads like something out of the crusades in the Holy Land.

The nature of anachronism as a narrative trope and strategy may be an answer to this question. Writing about anachronism as a way of reading Renaissance history and literature, Margreta de Grazia has argued that "anachronism is a later phenomenon ... coinciding with the formation of the disciplinary divisions"[36] in modern times; it is not something that bothered the early moderns as much as it does modern critics.

The point of de Grazia's argument that is relevant for my analysis is the suggestion that anachronism may become discourse through which imperialism speaks in the new language of another period. De Grazia illustrates this by interpreting Lorenzo Valla's disputation about the origins of Roman empire from the account of the *Donation of Constantine*.[37] The historical and cognitive distance from which Valla examines the rhetoric of the *Donation* reveals that anachronism is a way of writing about imperialism, of constructing an empire in discourse. From our historical and cognitive distance, then, we may approach the anachronism in Johnson's romance as a way of preparing for a forceful taking over of Islamic lands, not to liberate them for Christianity but to prepare them for commerce and profit.

The strategically important and symbolically powerful position of the Ottoman Empire, between the centres of growing Asian trade and the dynamic and rich mercantile exchanges of the Western Mediterranean, places the Eastern Mediterranean at the heart of the commercial route connecting the Mediterranean region with the markets of the East. In prose romances, the Eastern Mediterranean is thus the living scene in which the valorous deeds of the knight merge seamlessly with the analogous projections of his entrepreneurial efficacy beyond the Ottoman Empire.

Romances of the Eastern Mediterranean served the ideology of robust mercantile expansion by imagining both actions and rhetorical skills by which overseas markets could be claimed for the sovereign at home. Empire as imagined in prose romances is a hybrid product of philological heritage and contemporary travels. This notion of empire in the Eastern Mediterranean begins to crystallize at the time of England's economic rivalry with Spain and Portugal. The idea of connecting the Mediterranean with trade in the Indian Ocean became crucial to England's role and presence in the Mediterranean, an idea that first acquired shape in Richard Hakluyt's developing notion of empire. In his writing, Hakluyt the Elder elucidated the concept of empire, an unstable term during the reign of Elizabeth I, as having more to do with securing markets for trade and exchange with the Ottomans than with conquering and claiming territories.

In the treatise *The decades of the newe worlde of west India* (1555), written in Latin by Pietro Martire d'Anghiera and translated into English by Richard Eden, empire is conceptualized as an intellectual framework formulated ("delivered") by "learned men" to describe the establishment of governments in newly discovered overseas lands. But in contrast to his call for exploiting every bit of land in search of resources and commodities for trade, Pietro d'Anghiera urges England to be more docile. This is how Eden translates d'Anghiera's lines describing the way the Spanish and the Portuguese "subject[ed] in obedience" and "prescribed lawes" in their western plantations, and addressing England: "Be not indocible [unteachable] like Tygers and dragons, and such other monsters noyous [vexatious] to man kynde."[38] And when Pietro d'Anghiera refers to "the lawes of the empire and other princes Lawes,"[39] he does not equate the laws of newly discovered lands with the royal laws of the land, even if he endorses the legal foundations of empire. Read alongside Hakluyt's words of warning, the empire of trade forged with force in Johnson's romance does not come across as a social ideal Hakluyt envisaged.

Similarly, Richard Hakluyt speculated that the legal foundations of empire were not a product of legislative planning.[40] Rather, empire comes out of something at once more banal and more integral to the psyche: idleness and the lack of heroic challenge, which may lead to thoughts of something worse. So conquest, Hakluyt contends, "be also caried to kepe men occupied from worse cogitations, and to raise their myndes to courage and highe enterprises and to make them lesse careless for the better shonnynge of common daungers in such cases arisinge."[41] If conquest is an effective purgative remedy for undesirable thoughts at home, it is also meant to encourage valour in useful enterprises. These early notions of empire and conquest were the result of speculation by learned men, ambitious entrepreneurs, and adventurers, and were inspired by their observations of the early growth of the Spanish and Portuguese empires in the 1590s. But the early modern concept of empire in England was transformed into something more pragmatic: it became a way of looking at overseas lands as commercial territories, as trading routes, and as locations in which trade could occur.

Writing about empire in the sixteenth century from the point of view of Ottoman diplomatic and mercantile history, and not from my own perspective within an English (or pan-European) archive of printed literature about the Eastern Mediterranean, Palmira Brummett summarizes the issue:

> Conquest was determined not in terms of chunks of territory but in terms of routes defended ... Frontiers then were large and porous, the borders of one empire melding into those of another with many independent and semi-independent governors in between ... Sixteenth-century monarchs were not preoccupied with drawing boundaries so much as they were

> with the controlling of agricultural and mineral resources ... and demanding the submission of subordinates and opponents.[42]

Brummett's argument sheds important light on how the early modern reader might have interpreted the repeated victories of the romance knight as he moved from one territory to another in the Eastern Mediterranean. In romances the ideas of defended routes and the frontiers of kingdoms melding into one another extend to the notion of symbolic empires and territories of the East through which the knight advances.

Prose romances are proto-imperial and proto-orientalist texts, in that they do not propagate or imagine the colonization of foreign territories. Rather, they narrate fictional scenarios of heroic success and masculine virtue within a web of lands that straddle the imaginative and the geographic, the chivalric and the mercantile. Joan Pong Linton has argued that prose fictions did not engage with the Eastern Mediterranean but were invested in allegorical formulations of the colonial projects in the New World. Unlike "romances of empire," such as Thomas Deloney's *Jack of Newberry* (1597), which Linton identifies as texts envisioning specific bourgeois and masculine projects in the new American colonies, the romances of the Eastern Mediterranean are less invested in such specific middle-class enterprises and are oriented instead towards exemplary stories of mercantile success.

A distinction, therefore, can be made between the link between empire and the epic, and between merchant empire and prose romance of the Eastern Mediterranean. This distinction provides an important corrective to the overarching arguments made by postcolonial criticism about English imperialism in the early modern period and its fictionalization in literature. Postcolonial criticism has frequently claimed to discern imperialist tendencies manifested in early modern English literature, as if sixteenth-century England was an already established empire, already involved in colonies in North America and Asia. In some ways, postcolonial early modern criticism treated Elizabethan England as if it were imperial Spain or Portugal. Elizabethan England was in fact a small country at the northwestern corner of Europe beginning to undergo a major social transformation from a feudal to a proto-capitalist society and beginning to develop traffic and trade in the Eastern Mediterranean.

Thus, as romance literature moves from the Middle Ages, where the knight's status was more clearly defined in terms of "military function"[43] and in his successful courtship of a damsel, in the early modern period the status of the anachronistic figure of the knight and his role in romance is much less certain. The knight's role is circumscribed by the social and political contexts of the middle-class concerns of the household. And both the practice of and the writing about travel and trade in the Eastern Mediterranean also changed the nature of romance writing. The medieval idea of "love service"[44] which linked knightly prowess to earning the love of a woman metamorphosed in early modern romances into love, not exclusively and exactly as service to women but to an affect that facilitated homosocial as well as political bonds upon which merchant empire and commercial exchange depend for their success. Narratives of matrimony in prose romances are not "the subservient obverse of imperial conquest narratives";[45] they are the result of the completion of the process of "purchasing kingdoms."[46] The emphasis on marriage and the new household in the endings of romances is meant to eradicate, if only obliquely, the difference between West and East, not to subjugate eastern kingdoms to western laws.

The multifarious meanings attached to the notion of empire as an enterprise that Elizabethan England pursued with force compelled early modern masculinity to assume an equally robust and militant stance, for which the most suitable literary expression was the knight-errant. And so the main hero of early modern romances is not the knight as such, but the forceful and highly individual ego that corresponds to the task of building a new mercantile world on behalf of a western kingdom.

Masculinity and Merchant Empires

The complexity and flexibility of the concepts of empire and imperialism within the debate of their use in the romances of the Eastern Mediterranean shift the direction of those debates towards the economic basis of that empire in ways that are different, and, I would say, defused, compared to the epic. Barbara Fuchs has thus cautioned against conflating imperial projects with the purpose of prose romances: "Although it might seem ideally suited to the enterprise of empire, it is also possible to read romance as the deflation of epic purpose and imperial conquest."[47] I read prose romances not as a deflation of epic purpose and imperial conquest but more as works in which masculinity is expressed through the combined discourses of mercantile travel and the homosocial agency of the knight within, what I have already termed the merchant empire, as an imagined possibility of commercial success, imagined in fiction that is.

Moving away from imperialism understood as territorial claim to merchant empire understood as imagining success on and along trading routes in the East, that is, from the ideology of subjection to that of economic speculation, connects merchant empire with "men's economic agency."[48] Alexandra Shephard's analysis of "the language of social description" of manhood and male agency, which linked manhood to a man's patriarchal role within the household, has revealed numerous ways in which men departed from socially scripted "evaluative schemes."[49] From the household as a micro-commonwealth, that is, the state as a larger structure upon which the household was modelled, to merchant empire as an extension to the state's power and men's rule, early modern masculinity occupies a hierarchy of connected social spaces. Because the language of merchant empire, like the rhetoric of imperialism and colonialism, had not yet fully developed in England in the early modern period, especially when it came to the territories of the East,[50] so the masculinity that drives empire in general needed to be rendered in a number of discursive ways. Within the space of merchant empire, masculinity is expressed "sometimes explicitly, and often by implication, but it is always there."[51] The meaning of private and public male selfhood emerges equally from the narratives of masculine agency as from the contexts that enable that agency. Historical context is not always just a background that helps define a subject, masculinity in this instance. That context also implicitly tells the story of masculinity, because it is there in the close proximity of fiction, with which that context shares the historical time, topic, and themes that generated the discourse of romance and which are encoded in the language of the genre. A distant reading of romances is at once a distant reading of masculinity within them and of the expression of knightly masculine agency and the role of the knight as a creator of merchant empire.

How then do empires of the East and the kingdoms that constitute it create this mercantile knightly masculinity in romances? And what stories do texts about the Eastern Mediterranean tell about merchant empires and the men who create them? In "The Authors Induction to the Christian Reader unto the Historie of the Turkes," his preface to *The general historie of the Turkes* (1603), Richard Knolles laments the "long and still declining state of the Christian commonweale, with the utter ruine and subuersion of the Empire of the East" and "the unspeakable ruine and destruction of the Christian Religion and State: especially in Asia and Affricke, with some good part of Europe also," now absorbed in the "great Mahometane Monarchie."[52] Knolles's complaint is intended to present the decline of the old Christian lands in pre-Islamic Asia Minor as a grievous blow to Christianity in the Levant and to portray the Ottomans as a cause of this great misfortune. Historically, however, the decisive blow the Ottomans dealt was to an already declining and dysfunctional Byzantine Empire, torn by its own internal frictions and reduced wealth, influence, and power.[53] Similarly, in an anonymous petition by Christians living under the Ottomans, the Eastern Mediterranean is imagined as the ruined garden of Christ:

> In the Emperie of *Greece*, Kingdomes of *Epyrus*, *Lystria*, *Crete*, *Cyprus*, and other the Mediterranean Nations, CHRIST had ... his beloued Vineyard, planted, tended, wel dressed, compassed about. But now the Turke (like wilde Boares are entred, the Vineyard is wasted ...) is drunke with Christian blood and there is no Christianitie left, no outward Church.[54]

In this formulation, Christ's sacrifice becomes a metaphor for the suffering of all Christians living under Ottoman rule in the Eastern Mediterranean. The idea of sacrifice prevails in "histories" of the Eastern Mediterranean, narratives in which there is much concern for the metaphor of the holy war and the allegory of the re-conquest of old Christian lands. The symbolic redemption of Christian faith threatened by Islam in the Near East often takes the form of a conflict between a Christian knight and a non-Christian infidel. Knolles's words are an implicit invitation to the knight to act, to assert his physical capacity in reclaiming kingdoms of the East and display his heroic masculinity against Muslims.

This occurs in a romance published around the same time as Knolles's book. In *Sir Bevis of Hampton*, the 1585 English version of a fifteenth-century French romance, the hero, who for Christ's love wears "a crown of thorne," kills a Saracen who has insulted Christ's name. He commits the murder on Christmas Day, so that "men see without doubt, / Whether he wer stronger in heauen, or all the Mahounds [Mahometans] you can name."[55] The knight's murder of the Saracen, a symbolic defeat of Islam by a Christian hero, is a leitmotif that in later romances comes to define the knight's wanderings in the Eastern Mediterranean. This social performance of masculine selfhood is the precondition for the purchasing of kingdoms. Unlike late medieval romances where the romances' version of masculine identity presents "the tension between self and society in the process of internalization by which men incorporate the constructions of community into their own identities,"[56] the public and heroic masculinity of the early modern knight fulfills ideological aspiration and literary fantasy in consonance, not in tension, with society. The dependence of knightly masculinity on Muslim men to produce a story of power and success, not anxiety, is deeply embedded in the discourses about men in prose romances of the East. The Ottomans may incur cultural anxiety in the realm of politics, but they do not cause it at the narrative level of masculine confrontation with Christian knights. As a literary phenomenon, knightly masculinity is a source of unending success of men from the West in the kingdoms of the East. As reading material, prose romances offered a version of heroic masculinity and fortitude that was more complicated, more deeply imbricated with ideological currents and social aspirations than just having "an aura of aesthetic anachronism" about them, as chivalric masculinity has in stage drama, certainly in Shakespeare's plays.[57] During the chivalric revival that swept Elizabethan England, "romantic chivalry was not more than theatrical sentimentality" in the drama of Shakespeare and his contemporaries.[58] But the fictional revival of chivalry in prose romances may be said to be a reaction against the excessive sentimentality of chivalric masculinity in drama by rehabilitating some of its political and ideological power in romances in which the politics and ideology of the present times were extended, resisted, critiqued, and complicated, but not mocked.

The knight in Asia Minor exercises his masculinity precisely in the service of commercial kingdoms. Some of the Eastern Mediterranean locations that feature as settings in romances, such as Phrygia, Galatia, Bithynia, Lydia, Lycia, and Cappadocia, are also listed in the short entry on Natolia (Asia Minor) in Abraham Ortelius's annotated atlas of the world, *Theatrum Orbis Terrarum* (1570). In the 1606 expanded English translation of Ortelius's work, Willian Bedwell, the first English orientalist and "the father of Arabic studies in England,"[59] expanded Ortelius's original entry in Latin with his own impressions of Asia Minor. Bedwell refers to "the miserable estate and condition of [those] countries, [and] the maner of life and customes which the people there do now at this day use."[60] Here Bedwell echoes the cliché of western representations of Asia Minor as depleted and impoverished by the Ottomans, even if on the same page he draws his readers' attention to Paphlagonia's "the mines of Copper and Brasse" and the wealth accumulated through high taxes collected in gold by Paphlagonia's King Ismael. Bedwell's gloss sheds some useful light on romances. Read alongside his fiction of the Levant, the frequent romance references to

Natolia seem more than a mere residue from classical romances and other texts in which this country features. Rather, Natolia seems to have a strategic function as an actual place.

In her book on trade and diplomacy in the sixteenth-century Ottoman Empire and the Eastern Mediterranean, Palmira Brummett argues that the Ottoman trade in copper, found in abundance in Anatolia (the Natolia of romances) was "crucial ... for an understanding of the mechanisms of trade"[61] in luxury resources, spices, and silk between the Levant and the Indian subcontinent. The Ottomans used copper as both a trade good and a trade currency in their transactions with the Europeans, who valued it highly, and in India, where this sought-after metal could be exchanged for spices and silk. Intended for merchants who, as he knew, sought out Ortelius for reliable information on eastern trade, Bedwell's additions to Ortelius thus contribute to a panoply of English-language texts, from maps to travel accounts and romances, that was beginning to shape language and thinking about English trade as an activity that both rivalled and capitalized on the efforts of established trading powers in the Mediterranean.[62] Bedwell's gloss also sheds light on how empire and trade were conceptualized as ways of appropriating trading territory and securing commercial routes and markets in and beyond the Eastern Mediterranean before the English voyages of discovery in the Americas. Ortelius's descriptive summary of Natolia and Bedwell's information about its supplies of copper and brass imply that the Eastern Mediterranean was thought of, not as space that could be claimed politically as a territory, but as an area whose resources could be exploited. Access to these territories of the East provided an opportunity for early modern men to assert and prove the attributes of worth, esteem, and authority on which male social status depended in the early modern period. Romances participated in creating the divergent meanings of manhood in the early modern period by offering stories in which those meanings existed in tension with each other along the lines of virtue and men's social role.

Masculine Virtue in Romances of the East

In romances trading kingdoms are also territories in which the knight's exercise of virtue, in its humanist sense as *vir virtutis*, a virtuous man, is at once presented as a precondition for success in commercial undertakings and critiqued as the social and personal engine that drives such undertakings. Quentin Skinner defines *vir virtutis* as a man's use of his skills to overcome obstacles and attain his goal, especially in the face of unpredictability.[63] The connection between virtue and manhood is the basis for any subsequent stylization and fictionalization of masculinity in early modern literature. Conceptualized as the ability to employ skill, virtue is a feature of manliness, with which it is etymologically connected through the root *vir* (man). Margaret Tyler, the English translator of *The mirrour of princeely deedes and knighthood* (?1578), from Diego Ortúñez de Calahorra's series of popular chivalric romances, *Espejo de cavalleros*, captures the sense in which the heroic and virtuous actions ("princely deedes") of the knight-errant are offered to her English readers as models for successful enterprises:

> So Gentle Reader if my trauaile in Englishing this Author, may bring thee to a liking of the vertues herein commended, and by example thereof in thy princes & countries quarrel to hazard thy person & purchase good name, as for hope of well deseruing my selfe that may, I neither bend my selfe therto nor yet feare the speech of people if I be found backward.[64]

In translating this Iberian romance, Tyler conceptualizes virtue as a trait of selfhood that prompts heroic deeds, recommended in a series of actions that nourish and preserve the culture of lineage and win fame for the valorous knight.

Virtue and valour are repeatedly conjoined in writing about heroic actions and travels in the East. Giovanni Botero, a Renaissance Italian poet and diplomat, describes "true *Valour*" as consisting

> partly in judicious apprehension, (whereby both convenient opportunities are discerned and entertained, and all difficulties discovered and prevented); and partly in the forward resolution of the minde: by conjunction of which two Vertues, great enterprises are undertaken with good successe; dangers almost inevitable made light, and weighty attempts brought to happy conclusions.[65]

Botero's view of virtue helps us see what early modern readers would look for in the fictions of their time. Advised to seek examples that illustrate "resolution of the minde," the humanist reader would recognize in the knight-errant's readiness to counter dangers the kind of virtue recommended for the successful completion of a "great enterprise." Similarly, the virtuous ability to render dangers "light" as being "weighty attempts" for "happy conclusions" is a skill applicable to all manner of "great enterprises," not least those concerning foreign territory.

The general advice to "purchase good name," which is how Tyler formulates the romance capacity to give instances of heroic deeds, represents the cognitive frame for the knight's assertion of his masculinity and virtue in the East. It does so in a way that fictionalizes Botero's idea of virtue in the great enterprises in the East. This is promoted, in his text, mixing discourses of travel and ethnography with the mode of romance, as an invitation to men to undertake them. Botero's notion of valour is presented in the context of his discussion of the geography, cultures, and religions of kingdoms stretching from Bohemia to the Ottoman Mediterranean. This connection between a theory of valour and the application of that theory in travel and geography makes Botero's text even closer to romances set in the same territories.

Judging by the number of English translations and editions of Botero's treatises on travel in southeast Europe and the Middle East, his writing was popular in England. In *Relations from the most famous kingdoms* (1630) Botero links valour to perilous travels through a series of kingdoms in northern Africa and the Middle East, using narratives that resemble the stories of the knight-errant's heroic passages in romances. At the heart of both the humanist idea of *vir virtutis* and Botero's rendering of the concept of valour as men's judicious agency leading to success, is prudence, the ability to predict and fashion future successes on the basis of present experience and prior profitable actions. In the early modern period, prudence was understood to be

> that virtue by which we take counsel, we iudge & com[m]and all things to be done which do appertaine & conduct the life of man unto a good end ... The virtue of Prudence instructeth us to prouide for things to come, to order things present, and to remember things past.[66]

The prudent knight who devises heroic and persuasive strategies for overcoming errors and obstacles on his travels is also the knight who, in doing so, helps to establish the conditions for a successful commonwealth of trade.

Writers of romances, however, do not embrace the idea and rhetoric of prudence uncritically in their narrative of merchant empire and the knight's role in it. By complicating and compromising the valorous knight's masculinity along the ways of mercantile routes and by employing erotic writing to divert the knight from his chivalrous quest, romance writers make their narratives open to scepticism and the possibility of practical success at all times. The criticism of the knight's prudent actions in romances could also be seen as romances' clear orientation towards civic topics which, unlike faith, are the subject of scepticism and the endless "possibility of practical certainty."[67] It is in part for this reason, too, that romances were vehemently attacked by the preachers and the humanists. The association of romances with improbability is tested and challenged if we read them both alongside and against the historical discourses intended for raising awareness in the culture about the probability, and attractions, of trade and profit in the East. At the point where the cultural and the fictional discourse of "purchasing kingdoms" intersects we can also see how that probability and improbability can be said to have shaped the modes of turning fantasies of the Eastern Mediterranean into texts. David Armitage has persuasively argued that it was not the Protestant impulse for conquest, but the zest for commercial gain and mercantile competition with the older overseas empires of the West that impelled Renaissance England to expand its interests in the Mediterranean and contemplate further overseas expansion.[68] The repetitive nature of the knight's adventure, together with the repetition of the same geographical locations, consolidates the idea of the Eastern Mediterranean as a place in which the English knight is bound to achieve victory. This in turn creates a mental map of territories in which the fashioning of the prudent knight is put to profitable use for the commonwealth; it imprints on the reader's imagination the notion that the East is a location where heroic virtue acquires a new meaning associated with trade.

To understand how the notions of virtue and valour in early modern writing specifically connect with the early modern ideas of empire with which they sometimes intersected in the past, we need to recover the ideas built into the exemplary narratives of heroic agency in romances. In seeking to do so, I am extending my earlier argument that the Eastern Mediterranean of romances is a hybrid of literature and history, not simply a reflection of one or the other influence. Ideas about the East and its conquest have had an enduring life in Western literature. The notion of empire first began to be shaped in classical literature, most expressly in Xenophon's treatise on the household (*Oeconomica*), Cicero's *On Duties* (*De officiis*) and Horace's collection of fictional *Epistles* to young men (*Epistularum*). As works with a pedagogical purpose, these texts offered differing models of exemplary behaviour but also imbued the humanist curriculum with varied notions of the East. Xenophon, for instance, uses the Persian skill in warfare as a model for successful household management.

Horace's *Epistles*, to adduce another example, illustrate the relationship between moral teaching through the use of classical *exempla* and masculine virtue as it was displayed in eastern travels. Thomas Drant, the first English translator of the *Epistles* (1567), drew his readers' attention to the "moral precepts, full of pretye speaches, full of Iudgement" (Ciiij^{v}) expressed by Horace.[69] Influenced by Horace's own desire for travel, the *Epistles* not only introduced to humanist education models of epistolary writing interwoven with ethical precepts, they also offered formulas for epistles in travel and prose literature, and showed how writers might delineate the relation between the West and the East.[70] Some of the discursive similarities between Horace's text and romances raise questions about the extent to which the classical text helped shape, not only the story-telling strategies of romances, but the ideological spirit of these fictions. In addition to references to the islands and territories of the Eastern Mediterranean, Horace's epistles also refer to Sicilian tyrants (II), Tiberius's conquest of the East (III), Calabria and Cappadocia (IV), Armenia (III), and "the wealth of Arabia" (XI). It may well be due to Horace that the English Renaissance "revived the image of fabulous eastern wealth."[71] Despite Horace's warning, "fuge magna" ("flee grandeur") or "flye great doings" [D8^{v}], in Drant's translation), the western knight and his monarch remain enamoured of the wealth and victories waiting in the East.[72] *The Seven Champions* repeatedly returns to the images of grandeur, that is, heroic deeds that involve using force, in Barbary, the knights' indulgence in it, and its importation to London.

Similarly, in Geoffrey Fenton's translation of Francesco Guicciardini's collection of historical fictions about the fall of Constantinople, the Bishop of Ossimo appeals to the French king to embark on a territorial expansion into the Eastern Mediterranean, which, he says, would curb the Ottoman invasion. Citing the conquest under Alexander the Great and Julius Caesar, Ossimo urges his Christian prince

> to turne his armes against the *Lutherans* and Infidels, with great glorie, and with more occasion of greater conquests, the which I know not why they should not be also desired *Afrike*, in *Greece*, or in *Levant*, although it were easie to amplifie his dominion amongst the Christians, as many [...] do vainly imagine.[73]

Fenton projects an empire in the Ottoman Mediterranean precisely where Johnson and other romance writers set their fictions of matrimonial conquest. His idea is to expand ("amplifie") the Christian realm between the territories of Africa and the Levant. In these "great conquests" he sees "great glorie" for Christendom. The heroic enterprise imagined here correlates with the narrative designs of romances that seek to find valour and virtue at the heart of the modern knight's actions in the East. Page after page, the narrator in Johnson's romance guides the reader to imagine such speculative "occasions for greater conquest," as displays of the knight's ability to clear territories for trade couched in the language of heroic spectacle. The next section discusses the interweaving of the heroic and mercantile paths of the seven knights.

The Knight and "our Barberie Merchants"

In the first part of *The Seven Champions,* Almidor, the Black King of Morocco, offers to St George concrete enrichment of England:

> let my life be ransomed, and thou shalt yearely receaue ten tunnes of tried gold, a hundred webs of wouen silke, the which our *Indian* maides shall sit and spinne with siluer wheeles: a hundred Argases of spices and refined suger, shal be yearely paid thee by our *Barberie* Marchants: a hundred waggons likewise richly laden with Pearle and Jasper stones, which by our cunning Lapidistes shall be yearelie chosen foorth and brought thee home to *England,* to make that blessed countrie the richest land within the Dominions of *Europe.*[74]

The geographical coordinates of this passage locate the knight's heroic actions within the territories of both actual and probable trade with the East, from India to the Barbary lands of the Eastern Mediterranean. The reference to "Argases" (argosies) laden with spices and sugar from the East connect the Eastern Mediterranean with the world of Asian trade, via the reference to argosies, small fast ships built in Ragusa (Dubrovnik), in the southeast Adriatic Sea, that sailed across the Mediterranean and as far as Ferrol, a port on the Atlantic coast of Spain, and England.[75] In this instance the prospect of England becoming "the richest land" in Europe is offered to the reader as a direct consequence of commercial activity connecting India with the Eastern Mediterranean. At the heart of this activity is trade in silk and gems, commodities that were among England's main imports from the East. Johnson's romance ponders another mercantile probability, in which England's material enrichment comes from an exchange of precious commodities within the well-mapped and increasingly well-known territory of the Eastern Mediterranean, with its links to the markets of Asia. This imagined narrative push to link the Eastern Mediterranean with the Indian Ocean through trade in commodities heralds what David Abulafia has called "the fifth Mediterranean." Abulafia refers to the eagerness of the West, especially England and France, in the nineteenth and twentieth centuries, "to create an effective link between the Red Sea and the Mediterranean," and, thus, with the Indian Ocean beyond.[76] But the commercial link between the Mediterranean and the Red Sea that facilitated the flow of commodities from the Far East and the Mediterranean had already been conceptualized in the early modern period. At one point, the narrator in Johnson's narrative draws the reader's attention to a merchant who sets up a table "richly furnished with all rich and costly wares, as Cloth of Gold, Siluer, [and] Silke,"[77] commodities that pour into England from the Eastern Mediterranean. Yet what sort of transaction does Johnson's fiction imagine, at this point, when Almidor promises to St George (and to Elizabeth's England) a flow of Levantine merchandise?

Johnson's fiction of eastern trade, formulated in Almidor's ornamented and persuasive rhetoric, has equivalents in contemporary writing about international trade. In *The glory of England* (1618), a largely fictional comparative survey of the mercantile empires from which English trade is supposed to draw benefits, Thomas Gainsford's description of the origins of traffic and trade in the East indeed bears a resemblance to Johnson's fiction. In chapter 4, "The Empire of Persia," Gainsford describes Persia as a mediator in western trade in commodities from India. At this point Gainsford's account turns into a story about the young and energetic Sheikh Ismail (*Xequesmaell*), nicknamed Sophy:

> Thus then from *India* to *Arabic* East & West, and from the *Caspian* to the *Persian Gulph* (where the great *Euphrates* emptieth his streams, and vnder whose shores is that famous *Ormus* cited where they [the Persians] fish for pearle, and trauell six weeks together, from *Damascus* to *Cairo* to the same, with 6. or 700, camels and asses in company, to carry their prouision, for feare of the theeues of *Arabia*) preuaileth this Emperour [Sophy], possessing withal diuers cities on this side of *Ganges*, as intermingled with the *Portugals*: so that in India at this instant you haue many ports and

> harbours of fortification lying intricately diuiuided [*sic*] betweene *Turkes, Persians, Spanyards,* and the *Indians* themselues.[78]

This passage is a representative example of the complex intertwining of discourses about the East in travel literature, romances, and treatises on global trade and mercantile politics. Gainsford's description of the whole web of Sophy's influence, together with the details of the routes taken by the great Persian caravans, gives a vivid sense of power relations in the Mediterranean and of the concomitant flow of commodities across this region, from as far afield as India. These commercial flows determined the relationship of the Eastern Mediterranean with the mercantile routes in the Middle East and from there to India. The list of trading nations for Muslims – Persia, Spain, and India – summarizes exactly the important powers that dominated the Mediterranean trade and which England had to overcome to claim status in that trade. Like Johnson's fiction, Gainsford's text is conceived as a likely scenario of mercantile success for an entrepreneurial English merchant–knight. Gainsford fictionalizes for the English reader some of the realities of eastern trade, bringing that trade closer to England and encouraging the reader to see how probable success would be if such enterprises were embarked upon by Englishmen. Sophy in Gainsford's account is only another literary version of Sophy, the Persian emperor with whom the Portuguese negotiated conditions of trade at Hormuz and throughout the Persian Gulf as they expanded towards India and the East.[79]

When Gainsford turns Sophy into a fictional character and endows him with language, detailing for the English reader the routes and structures of Portuguese trade, we see how the historical narrative of a power centred on commerce and transmitted to literature through the tradition of travel writing becomes an exemplary fiction of English trade in the East – a role mediated in Gainsford's text by the Persians and already taken up by the Portuguese in the Persian Gulf. Gainsford fiction, then, is a story of competition with the trading Portuguese. The Persians, who act as middleman between East and West in the transport of commodities on behalf of the Portuguese, resemble Johnson's "Barberie merchants" with their pearl-laden carts. In his fiction of the Sophy of Persia, the title accorded Sophy by Pires, Gainsford imagines Persians as the facilitators of trade with the Portuguese; and with the English too his fiction gestures towards a complex flow of luxuries, notably pearls, silk, and other Indian goods, originating from the East and making their way to both Portugal and England via Persia. Gainsford expands the interest of early modern English literature in the narratives of Persia as a resource for romance writing.

This new interest in Persia included both fiction and drama, such as "the romance play," *The Warres of Cyrus*, published in 1595.[80] If in 1590s drama Persia was of interest to English dramatists because it was seen as at once "barbarian" and "civil,"[81] for writers of prose romance Persia conjured the discourse of eastern trade and commercial routes. Persia became important for Mediterranean traffic and trade because it was both a mid-point of trade, with Asia itself a source of commodities of particular interest for England, notably carpets, which were traded on markets in the Ottoman Empire, and other commodities such as silk. This trade was so important that in 1589, a merchant recorded that "[c]ertain notes of consideration to be had for Persia, tending 'to diverse good purposes," and recommended that the ambassador who was to be sent to "deal" with "the Sophy of Persia" was "to be a learned man, bred up in court."[82] The cultural symbolism of Persia that resonates through romances, in which the land features as a central location, thus connects the world of expanding international trade with the imaginary domain of popular fiction, which offers its readers a version of glory and success. It is through the discourse of Persia, then, that early modern English mercantilist and romance writing voiced the enterprising ambitions that were increasing in the sixteenth century, particularly in response to Portuguese and Venetian trading in Hormuz.

Romances depicting victories in the East, culminating in the knight's enthronement in an eastern kingdom, conceptualize success and ambition in eastern markets against the background of Spain and Portugal's commercial dominance over the English in the Persian Gulf and the East Indies. At the turn of the century, the continuing rivalry between England and Spain threatened the expansion of English trade in the territories controlled by the Iberians. In 1601, on behalf of English merchants, Hakluyt informed the newly founded East India Company about the state of Spanish trade in the East Indies, "Proveing in whate partes of the same Indies the Spanish King hath Souerig*n*tie and in what other partes he hath no coller to barr other Christian Princes &c fro*m* trade."[83] It appears that Hakluyt is anxious for the English to enter the arena of eastern trade as soon as possible. Offering a detailed list of the locales of Spanish trade, including "Ormuz" in the "mouth of the *Persian* gulfe,"[84] the ambitious Hakluyt encouraged mercantile competition with the Spanish, arguing that "the Spanish had no exclusive claim to many places where the Company wanted to trade."[85] However, the Privy Council "turned the Company away, fearing that its effort to expand trade to the East would inevitably alarm the Spanish."[86] Given this turn of events, the English commercial presence in the Persian Gulf remained hypothetical. But against the background of this probability, romances created their own versions of English mercantile expansion in the East, their imagining of English ambition and the urge to expand advances and heroic victories in the East.

Read along with Gainsford's fiction, then, the trajectory of Johnson's knights from the shores of Egypt to victorious battles in Persia hints at the trials and triumphs of English merchants as they travel from the Far East to the ports in the Eastern Mediterranean and from there to Europe. The knight in Henry Robarts's romance, *Honours Conquest*, who on "the third day" of his travels "had sight of a mightie conuoy of Cammils, being at least sixe thousand, with their Merchants, which came from India, bound into Egypt,"[87] meets a caravan travelling the same route as the merchants in Gainsford's fiction. The route of Robarts's fictional knight also intersects with one of the busiest trading routes in the East, a road from India to the Eastern Mediterranean, which had grown in importance since the Middle Ages.[88]

In both Johnson's romance and Gainsford's geographical survey, the desire to chart new trading routes and establish merchant empires in the East is framed within nationalist stories of arduous travel. In both fictions, successes and chivalric victories are imagined to take place along the commercial paths already dominated by the Portuguese, who, as Richard Eden reports, "sayled where antiquitie denyed passage, beyond all Africa and into the Indian seas." There, Eden continues, John the Second, the grand nephew of the Portuguese King, Don Henrico, "sent also expert and cunning traueylers into Aegypt, and the redde sea coastes to espye what way the Portugales might looke for beyond the Cape of good hope to Calecut in India: the which viage in his sonne Emanuell his tyme, was prosperously taken in hand by Vasques Gama [Vasco de Gama]."[89] The Portuguese of Eden's history of travel in the East and West Indies sail and trade between Calcutta and Egypt – in that respect his text intersects with Gainsford's – and Johnson's merchant–knights cover the territories between Egypt and the Ottoman parts east of it. In their heroic victories they travel in the trading lands unclaimed by the Portuguese. The desired goal of the arduous journeys in the East, full of difficult victories and conquests, makes these travels "as plausible as any other journey, if our passengers may returne with plenty of silver, silkes, and pearle" (iiii^{r}). Silver, silk, and pearls, some of the new luxuries of nascent capitalism, are among the commodities that start to bring wealth to the London of Johnson's narratives when the champions return from their eastern adventures. The eastern booty acquired by the Portuguese features as talismans of conquest and reasons for inner satisfaction. For as Eden says: "Desire of rule breedeth victories, victories come by co[n]quests, conquests are furthered by traueyle, trayele can not bee maynteyned without great wealth, wealth maketh all traueyle pleasant."[90] The rhetorical emphasis of Eden's language on the benefit and pleasure of conquest whose end is acquiring wealth would not have escaped the early modern reader. The emphasis in this anadiplosis, in which the last word of one clause is repeated at the beginning of the next – victory, conquest, travel, wealth – creates a sense of urgency and force precisely by putting stress on the words that circumscribe the new ideology of travel-as-conquest leading to wealth. In the larger context of Eden's writing, focused on the East and the opportunity of trade therein, a specific dimension, and vehemence, is added to this rhetorical climax. In conjoining pleasure and wealth, Eden is urging his reader to undertake eastern travels as a way of accumulating wealth and bringing fame and pleasure to England.

The trading routes for silver, silk, and pearls left their traces on the narratives of sixteenth-century romances. They are listed among the most noteworthy of the exotic imports that arrived to England from Mediterranean port cities.[91] For nearly the whole of the seventeenth century, raw silk was one of the major imports by the English Levant Company, which had traded in the Eastern Mediterranean since the late sixteenth century.[92] The company also imported woven Persian silks as a marker of status and wealth and a sign of profitable trade with the East. Thus, silk found its way into romances. In a way, then, one of the last legs of the Silk Road became the territory for imagined scenarios of successful English trade with the East – the successes being seen as chivalric victories in the lands around the Mediterranean ports from which silk was sent to England and Europe.

Although some critics have agreed that Spanish imperial conquests in Latin America were adopted by the English as models for their own colonial enterprises, Lorna Hutson has cautioned against treating English emulation of the Iberian romances as fictions about English colonization, because neither "the precise nature ... nor the specific humanist mode" of this emulation in "literary stylization and simultaneous deprecation" have been fully recognized yet.[93] This literary absorption,

Hutson contends, took place in the context of the Anglo-Spanish political rivalries of the sixteenth century and within the humanist discourse of instruction about timely and pragmatic agency. The philosophical ideas of Aristotle's theory of prudence from the *Nicomachean Ethics* "as the form of activity of judgment,"[94] as summarized by Victoria Kahn, can provide a critical tool in dealing with the problem of how romances might have been read and understood. Fifteenth-century Italian humanists, working through and commenting on Aristotle's ideas of ethics and rhetoric, started to understand prudence as "the precondition" of both artistic and ethical decorum. Rhetoric thus helps translate prudence as an act of judgment into an activity that is both ethical and rhetorical, leading the reader to *know* the text as practical, and encouraging a certain action after the reader has applied judgment to select and discriminate ideas leading to practice.[95] This closely echoes Hutson's argument about the Iberian romances as prudential fictions, if approached through the humanist theory of prudence. It might be a stretch to argue that chivalric romances were read as models of specific actions, which in an age of chivalry used for ceremonial purposes only would have been superfluous. But it might be possible that romances featuring men as primary agents in the fictions of travel and trade offered possibilities for imagining the ways in which manhood could still be presented in narrative and rhetorical terms, that is, as powerful, in the kind of literature that also fictionalizes it as romantic.

Under the growing influence of writing about travel and trade in the Eastern Mediterranean, telling stories about the East as a territory for trade and exchange became one of the staple features of romance writing at the turn of the seventeenth century. As Michael Murrin has argued persuasively, "a new kind of heroic narrative that developed in response to travels into Asia" demonstrated that "merchants – not knights – were the *real* heroes behind" the narratives of chivalric romances set in Asia.[96] The conceptual proximity of Asia to the Eastern Mediterranean in romances was made possible by the still prevailing view, as Murrin argues, that "Europe was but a peninsula of Asia," something the Europeans discovered in the middle of the thirteenth century.[97] Evidently, Johnson picked up on this new trend and, as I show in the next chapter, he devoted a significant number of pages in his romance to the seven knights' adventures on the threshold of the Silk Road. His fiction made the reality of commercial travel on this busy artery of trade the subject of some of the most suspenseful and complex writing in his romance.

2 The Knight on the Silk Road

The Seven Champions starts with a reference to the destruction of Troy (which Johnson calls "Phrigia")[1] and Aeneas's departure from his burned and ruined homeland. This situates the romance in the interstices between discourses of imperial nationalism and heroic masculinity embedded in the myth of the foundation of Britain as the new Troy. Already on the first page, this myth turns into a celebration of the London of "sumptuous buildings" and "valiant and courageous Knights."[2] Urban wealth and military chivalry may look like an uneasy pairing, but it is in moments like this that the courage of the knight-errant and the victory of English mercantilism meet in an image of sumptuousness brought to England and enabled by the knight's role in the East.

The London depicted in the opening of Johnson's romance will be conjured again at the start of the second part of *The Seven Champions*, but this time the splendid grandeur of its buildings is complemented with the luxuries from the East, both being constituents of the idea of London's rise as a city of trade and wealth, a growing and prosperous capital in northwestern Christendom. Just as Johnson imagines London profiting from the knights' adventures in the East, so Richard Hakluyt proposes that "the inriching of the citie of London" is a benefit to the commonwealth, a boon provided by the use of "some effectual means" employed also in "the furthering of the navigation" and the "trade into the Levant."[3] If Hakluyt suggests that one of the "effectual means" of enriching the commonwealth, and thus London, lies in the expanding commercial links with the Levant, Johnson solidifies that meaning by yoking merchant kingdoms with dynastic marriage.

Writing about the impact of colony on the metropolis, Andrew Hadfield argues that "the identity of 'home' has changed beyond recognition" under the influence of colony.[4] Although it is hard to know where "home" is (and what it means) in the shifting geography of the Eastern Mediterranean of romances, London remains the place where the West intersects with the East in these capacious narratives. In both Hakluyt's and Johnson's writing, London is not a metropolis "irrevocably"[5] left behind in the colonial project, but a city to which the merchant–knight returns to celebrate the gains of his trading and commercial adventures.

The valiant knights in *The Seven Champions* have returned home, "having brought into subiection al the Easterne Parts"; their Eastern wives now "trip up ... and down" the streets of London like "the *Grecian* Queenes" and their chivalric husbands are emasculated by the "silken snares of loue" – all of which makes London look more like a "paradise for heauenlye Angels than, a place for earthly inhabitants."[6] The language of prosperity inspired by the power acquired through trade luxuries from the Levant is here presented under the stylistic guise of the emasculating effect of love and the East. At the point when Johnson's narrative focuses on London and the luxury goods found there, the fiction of the splendour of urban capitalism intersects with the inflated language of Protestant patriotism. This discourse is best expressed by Robert Greene in *The Spanish Masquerado* (1589): "the Lord our mercifull God maketh England like Eden, a second Paradise."[7] It is the wealth arriving from the East, not just the Tudor Reformation, that makes England like a new Eden among nations. Invested in writing a chivalric fiction structured around an endless number of episodes involving the knight's victories in the East and of commodities on their way to the Mediterranean and from there to England, Johnson was no doubt aware of the difficulties as well as the benefits of these commercial and political undertakings, fictionalized in literature and reported in history. These episodes occupy more narrative space than those of moralizing generalizations but they are not interlaced with the heroic narrative in Johnson's romance. It may be, then, that Johnson's preoccupation is with heroism as a language through which aggressive mercantile pragmatism expresses itself, not with the pious moralism that so often fills the pages of sixteenth-century chivalric romances. Just as commercial traffic, trade, and rivalry in the Eastern Mediterranean was a recent social phenomenon for which English writers tried to find the language to talk about in different works of non-imaginative literature, so that subject matter looked for the ways of expression in imaginative literature increasingly interested in the Eastern Mediterranean.

A telling episode, which captures the difficulties experienced by the English in the shadow of Spanish trade in the Gulf, involves Piero Priuli, the Venetian ambassador to Spain. In his dispatch of 12 March 1611, Priuli records that Anthony Sherley, an envoy sent by Shah Abbas to the Christian rulers of Europe, had to wait for an audience with the Spanish king, whereas the Persian ambassador was received immediately. According to Priuli, this was because the Persian emissary brought an "offer to send all merchandise from Ormuz (Hormuz) to Lisbon – which would be a great gain to the Spanish Crown – on condition that the Spanish King Philip III would attack the Turk. He has brought two hundred bales of silk, as a sample." In return for this favour, Philip III demanded that the Persians "establish a route [for silk trade] ... that will suit him best" and that will "cause some injury to the market of Venice, where that silk usually arrives from Syria."[8] Commodities from the East are seen here to be a powerful weapon in the diplomatic game being played by the West and East to weaken Turkey's dominance of the traffic in luxuries from the hinterland of the Eastern Mediterranean to the markets of the West. Returning to *The Seven Champions*, we see that, in gaining control of the land between Persia and Syria, Johnson's knight comes to dominate the very trade route that Philip III had asked the Persians to establish. Thus the dragon and the giant who, in Johnson's fiction, upset the equilibrium of trade between kingdoms in this hinterland of the Eastern Mediterranean, do not merely represent a challenge to the knight's heroic masculinity and an opportunity to satisfy the contemporary reader's nostalgia for the fiction of chivalric jousting from the past, but also serve to draw attention to the new roles that heroic, aggressive masculinity has acquired in the fictions of prudential agency.

Some critics have interpreted romances as narratives of cross-cultural encounters, "religious identities in a state of war" and "paradigm[s] for thinking about a crisis of identity and narrative in the early modern period."[9] Yet Johnson's romance seems to trouble such assertions, since it could be said to be doing just the opposite of presenting a crisis of early modern identity. Into the fictionalized world of religions in conflict, Johnson is inscribing the kind of chivalric agency that is ruthless and romantic at the same time, unstoppably aggressive in clearing the land of the infidel which makes "portly manhood"[10] triumph in the knight's heart and expressively romantic in courting eastern princesses. Johnson creates an image of manhood that differs from the idea that the self-government expected of manhood should be the only basis of "man's claims to authority."[11] The knight who could not govern his temperance might not be able to govern the household, but in romances the intemperance of the knight-errant, his aggressive masculinity, becomes the precondition for successful trade and fierce competition with his rivals.

The Giant, the Dragon, and Eastern Trade

The surge of English prose romances and the translations of their Iberian precursors reflected the burst of Elizabethan nationalism inspired by the opening of Mediterranean trade. Gerard de Malynes wrote enthusiastically of the link between Elizabethan nationalist politics and national legends, providing a profitable context for our reading of prose romances. He begins *Saint George for England* (1601) by reminding readers that the allegorical fiction of St George celebrates Queen Elizabeth's reign because, however abused the saint's history was, his deeds demonstrate the "pure doctrine of IESUS CHRIST" that she had forged, in a confirmation of the tenets of the Tudor Reformation.[12] But he goes on to argue that the religious enlightenment depends on the commonwealth's equality in trade and commerce with other countries, which is "brought to confusion and utter destruction by the means of [the] Dragon."[13] At this crucial point in de Malynes's treatise, the Dragon, the central topos in the allegorical representation of St George, has come to signify both an obstacle to trade and a force disrupting the balance in trade between commonwealths: "The Dragon bringeth inequality in a commonwealth ... and depriveth the Prince ... of his treasure and ready money."[14] De Malynes's dragon is persistently associated with Islam, and "infected" and "pathologized" throughout his treatise. The dragon is also presented as both an enemy of Christianity and a threat to the health of transnational trade, on which England's honour, De Malynes tells us, depends.[15] Eliminating the dragon not only means restoring equality and wealth in the kingdom, by ridding the mercantile body of trade of Islamic infection, but, in doing so, also claims for England the power of restoring the balance in trade between commonwealths. Johnson's romance, narrating the heroic victories of St George against error and obstacles – and against the fictional Dragon that disrupts trade and commonwealth – offers us a key to unpacking the allegorical incredulities of romance writing within the context of Eastern Mediterranean commerce. The romance knight does not travel through the Eastern Mediterranean simply to prove his valour, but to bring peace to the commonwealth so that traffic and trade can develop uninterruptedly, and every member of the commonwealth can, in Johnson's words, "live contentedly and proportionably in his vocation."[16] The peace that the knight brings to the kingdoms of the East does not merely confirm the ethical dimension of his heroic acts; it is necessary for the equality between kingdoms upon which trade is based.

Like dragons, giants also complicate trade. When in *Historie of Palmendos* (1589), a French romance translated by Anthony Munday and set "in Europe and the Mediterranean Sea, very near the Isle of Delphos" (C1^r), the giant Baledon threatens the life of a merchant on Delphos who had been rescued by Palmendos as the hero sailed through the Aegean Sea on his way to Persia (E1^r–E3^v), we are reminded of the threat to trade in the Eastern Mediterranean posed by the Muslim pirates prowling western trade routes to the Levant.[17] Seen in the context of de Malynes's text about trade and romance, this episode comes to look like a palimpsest of multiple discourses involving travel, heroic masculinity, and the politics of Mediterranean trade. Palmendos's killing of Beledon eradicates an obstacle on the mercantile routes leading from Persia through the Aegean Sea, where the giant is defeated. The title of this work states that Munday translated it from the French, even though the version on which the French translation was based was originally written in Portuguese by Francisco de Morães. Perhaps it was the printer, John Charlewood, who added the title page to Munday's translation. Thus the Iberian connection of this romance may not have been lost on the readers of this period, a time when Anglo–Iberian trade and political contacts and conflicts were at their peak. Arthur B. Ferguson sums it up eloquently when he says that romances "served more than we are always willing to admit as the mirror and model of social realism, however much they might deviate from actual practice. In the romances, especially, we may see reflected not what the knight was, but what contemporaries, himself included, thought he should be."[18] By imagining those victories in the East, Johnson participates in both Reformation debates about cross-religious contacts and Elizabethan promotion of the East as mercantile opportunity, as the empire of imagination.

Knightly Masculinity and the Silk Trade

The knights who married "Greek" princesses in *The Seven Champions* and who are now dressed in the silk robes of eastern rulers remind the reader not only of the victories in the East and the rewards they brought, but also of the romance's connection with the Silk Road and the markets of northern and western Europe. As Michael Murrin has demonstrated, the network of roads taken by the characters in prose fiction corresponds to the geography of complex routes that were being established as the search for Asian silk increased in the West.[19] The European market for raw silk from Persia was largely a royal monopoly at the turn of the sixteenth century; it grew under King James I, who encouraged trade with Spain.[20] Social historians can be of service to literary critics of romances here, because their findings help us understand that repeated references to silk in romances are not mere conventions and stylistic ornaments but carriers of meaning in a narrative underpinned by material culture. Writing about the relationship between England and the Eastern Mediterranean in the early modern period, Ralph Davis has offered evidence to support the argument that the robust growth in the import of raw silk bears some relevance to the emphasis on laying claim to the silk trading routes in prose romances. Davis shows that by the 1620s, raw silk had become "the largest of English raw material imports," so that "[b]y James I's time a silk industry of some size existed in England, and it continued to grow rapidly for nearly two hundred years."[21] And just around the time when the silk trade in England was peaking, the Levantine politics centring on that trade had begun to turn to the advantage of the English. When the Venetian ambassador to Constantinople, Zorzi Giustinian, informs the Venetian senate that, as part of his wars against the Turks, the King of Persia promises to secure Babylon and occupy Aleppo using the money from the silk trade, and then to "give the same silk to the English there, and to smooth the way to the treaty represents that by diverting the silk trade they [the Persians] will deprive the Sultan of a large sum of money ... with so much advantage to Christendom," we witness how the silk trade and the profits it generates help to constitute a political scenario that may come to favour the English. And this is the case even if the English, as Giustinian suggests, "do not think these advantages outweigh the other considerations, especially as they know full well that the King of Persia has made the same offers to Spain, where they were not accepted."[22] Giustinian's dispatch narrates a scenario that is not too remote from the capture of silk markets and trade routes depicted in Johnson's romance. Indeed, by the early 1630s the English (and the Dutch) had succeeded in pushing out the Venetians as the preeminent traders in silk in Hormuz, a key point of entry to the routes leading to India, and positioned themselves as the dominant power in cloth and silk trade in Hormuz and the Persian Gulf, much to the grief of the King of Persia.[23] Patricia Fumerton has provided an extensive account of the ways in which the merchants of the East India Company in Hormuz exercised brutality in getting rid of those they considered pagans, who stood in the way of the Company's intentions for "splitting up" Hormuz with the Persians, attacking the trading settlements of the Spanish and the Portuguese there, and in the long run controlling the trade to and from India via the Strait of Hormuz.[24] While Johnson's romance is not allegorizing these real events, it imagines the fictional scenarios of English heroic power required to achieve advantage in Hormuz, by making the knight do the fighting and removing the infidel from the path of that success and through an intricate and difficult diplomacy with the Persians.

The Silk Road starts on the Mediterranean coast in the ports of Antioch and Alexandria and then diverges in two main directions, one leading inland through Samarkand, to the northeast of the Eastern Mediterranean, the other passing through Persia and India in the direction of China. Since the latter arm of the road involved less travel for the English, English merchant-adventurers preferred to use this route than to travel via Samarkand. In the sixteenth century the Silk Road had yet not become a commercial path well-trodden by caravan carts and merchant adventurers; but the printed and oral accounts of the difficulty, danger, scenic grandeur, and rich commodities of travels along that route "greatly added to its romance,"[25] adding another narrative layer to the literary romances of the late Middle Ages and Renaissance. The journey of silk to the Eastern Mediterranean was, as Fernand Braudel suggests, "jealously guarded" and had taken centuries to reach from China. The Sassanid Persians, living between China and the Eastern Mediterranean, kept "a vigilant watch" on it "in both directions."[26] Passing through their territories was often fraught with difficulties, so strategems were needed to avoid their vigilant watch of the silk trade. The knight-errant's heroic passage from the Eastern Mediterranean and back, through Persia and the lands beyond it, fictionalizes both the difficulty and the success of the endeavour to bring silk to the shores of the Eastern Mediterranean.

This cross-fertilization of the cultural, the historic, and the literary illustrates the capacity of romances to take in material from a variety of genres and to assimilate the ever-changing currents of politics and ideology. So it was that the Silk Road found its way into late medieval romances, most notably in *Le livre du trésor* (The book of treasure) by

Brunetto Latini, a work that most likely benefited from Marco Polo's travel accounts. *Le livre du trésor* influenced Dante, and possibly even Boccaccio.[27] John Mandeville's fictions of the East, which intermingle realism and fancy, are evidence that the fascination with the Silk Road was as much a matter of imagination as trade. Even if, as some critics have argued, Mandeville did not travel to the East, his narrative is animated by the authentic details and a familiarity with the fictions of the East that had come from trade in that region.[28] England received the first contemporary account of the Silk Road in the sixteenth century. This was most likely a compilation of other accounts that circulated in the period, mixed with reflections on the travelling experience, by Anthony Jenkinson, a London merchant known to have visited Bukhara, an important town on the Silk Road.[29] What stimulated the romancing of the movements of the silk trade through Egypt, Syria, and the lands from Asia to the Mediterranean and the European West, was the very complexity of these movements. They have not yet been worked out in modern historical scholarship, "and they probably never will be."[30] This enduring uncertainty makes it easy to imagine how the obscure intricacies of the silk routes would have given rise to many fantasies about such enterprises. Donald F. Lach identifies particular uncertainties about the routes between Egypt and Syria. These two locations constitute the boundaries of the chivalric travels of Johnson's champions, who move within a seamless and fluid mercantile geography that connects Europe with Asia.

The silk trade route from China and India to Europe led through the Persian Gulf and its seaports, particularly the Strait of Hormuz, and thence overland through the Middle East and through the Ottoman dominions to the shores of the Eastern Mediterranean. Silk was the most important of all the goods arriving in England from the Levant,[31] becoming the "first fruit ... of the Persian trade."[32] The trade in Persian silk, monopolized by the Ottomans, who imposed various "export prohibitions"[33] on English merchants, became the focus of the encounters of English merchants with traders from the Levant and the Far East. The routes of the silk trade also intersected with the battlefields during the Ottoman–Persian wars in the sixteenth and early seventeenth centuries.[34] Turkish monopolization of the trading routes in the Eastern Mediterranean was such a problem for the English that, as Richmond Barbour argues, they contemplated avoiding the Eastern Mediterranean and developing new mercantile paths through Arabia to the markets of India.[35] Against this background, we could view the knight-errant's penetration into the kingdoms of the East in *The Seven Champions*. The Persia–Egypt link in Johnson's romance represents an imagined version of the economic history in which silk from India was transported via the Persian Gulf and Aleppo, and onward to the Eastern Mediterranean port outlets, rather than through Anatolia. This route was intended to circumvent the Ottomans, who had by then occupied Persia, establishing themselves as middlemen in the silk trade and imposing high taxes for the transportation of silk through Anatolia.[36]

In the travel account entitled *A Relation of a Journey begun An. Dom: 1610*, which is a work that combines romance fiction, ethnographic accounts, myth, and Eastern Mediterranean travelogue, George Sandys makes an observation that hints at just this flow of merchandise from India to England through Persia and Arabia. Describing how the Moors of Egypt trade with the Indians he says: "In Cities the best of them [the Moors] exercise merchandize: rich by mean of their trafficke with the *Indians*; yet that decayed since our East-Indian voyages; insomuch, as Spices brought out of the *Levant* heretofore, are now with profit brought thither by our Merchants."[37] Sandys comments on the decline of the Moor as an intermediary merchant between India and England, because of the success of the East India Company, founded in 1601, but his account also registers, retrospectively, what the structure of such trade looks like. That Johnson's romance, an antecedent to Sandys's travelogue, charts the same travelling trajectory as Sandys, starting from the West (Sandys sets off from France) and venturing through the Holy Land (digressing and pausing in Jerusalem), the Ottoman Empire, Egypt, and Persia, is less important for this contact, because with some variations this was a common route taken by western travellers in the Levant. What is more important is that Johnson's romance fictionalizes the trajectory and structure of trade that would dwindle for the Muslims in the next decade, an occurrence from which the English would profit.

Behind the silk robes of the western knights and of their princesses lies more than just the metaphor of emasculation. Parts of Johnson's romance integrate fictions of the adventures of the knights in Persia at a moment when silk trade from China and India, via Persia, is rapidly increasing in Europe. The silk for the "mantles of silk," worn by Sabra, St George's princess, was, Johnson tells the reader, fetched "from the furthest borders of *India*," where "the skill of *Indian* weavers" embroidered it "with the most richest ornament that ever mortal eye behelde,"[38] representing the Sun and Moon at its centre. The reader is led to think of the nuptials in Constantinople on the shores of the Eastern Mediterranean not only as a symbolic connection between the West and the East, but as an act that connects the Mediterranean with Indian silk trade in the most profitable way, with England imagined as the chief benefactor. At this point Johnson's romance becomes a literary expression of the period's investment in the East as a source of commodities. Like other such fictions, then, Johnson's romance of the East connected the market for eastern luxuries with the low-end print market for fiction. In doing so, it erased, if only symbolically, the distinction between the marketplace for luxury goods and the market for popular literature.[39] Romances easily absorbed this cultural erasure.[40]

Scattered throughout *The Seven Champions*, frequent references to romances are a constant reminder of the long association of the silk trade with the East and by extension the importance of the East in conceptualizing the narrative space of English prose romances. Sabra is dressed in "*Arabian* silke";[41] Rossalinde, a Thracian damsel, dressed as a page, wears a head dress adorned "most cunningly with a silken list"[42] and carries a "Poniarde ... beautified with tassels of vnwoven silk."[43] Johnson's sharp eye for detail, his attentiveness to the political dynamics of England and the East in the 1590s, and the passion with which he makes the heroic and romantic threads of his narrative gesture towards a mercantile strategy, make him unusually attuned to the changes prose romances were undergoing at the close of the sixteenth century. By making the knight-errant's agency dependent upon his ability to win advantage in the East and by making him rule the East through heroic victories and marriage, Johnson makes his knight bring "distant parts of Europe and the Mediterranean world closer together"[44] at the point when England is shaping its mercantile identity in the East.

If the connection between the knight and the fictions of commercial trade drifts in and out of the discourses of heroic travels and romantic conquests in the East, that connection is explicitly and sharply expressed in mercantile writing that is particularly concerned with England's robust entry into the space of commerce in the Eastern Mediterranean. In an allegory of St George written by Gerard de Malynes, the legendary patron is imagined assuring "Equalitie concerning the trafficke and negotiation betweext his dominions and other countries in the trade of merchandize."[45] Associating England's legendary hero with a prudent merchant trading in overseas markets, de Malynes re-imagines English chivalry as international commerce within the very same spaces of the Eastern Mediterranean in which Johnson fictionalizes merchant empires and in which England asserts his presence. In Johnson's romance and in other fictions enabled by the discourses of Levantine trade, the Eastern Mediterranean becomes the subject matter central to the idea of the East, and, more broadly, in English writing about the Muslim world in the early modern period. In an emphatic formulation, "India, Persia, and the Ottoman Empire materialized Europeans. That is, they provided much of the *matter* (fibres, textiles, dyes) that shaped European bodies."[46] These three locales are also the termini on the routes taken by Johnson's knights. It is in these spaces that the bodies of Christian knights, including the St George of *The Seven Champions*, undergo a transformation from militant English men to rulers dressed in silk, to fulfilled or mourning lovers. The first part of *The Seven Champions* ends with a celebration of imperial victories and the promise of more to come, symbolically burying, with Sabra's entombment, the romantic sentimentalism that inspired St George's quest. Once so absorbed in his love of Sabra that in Persian captivity he was "carving her picture with the nayles of his fingers upon the wals of the dungeon,"[47] St George has become "the bourgeois national hero"[48] with international aspirations.

The second part of Johnson's romance begins with the summary of St George's and other knights' conquest of the East and a celebration of this conquest in London. The reader is reminded that the Christian knights "had brought into subiection al the Easterne Parts, and by dint of bloodie warres yoaked the stubborne Infidels euen to the furthest boundes of *India* ... and they returned with the conquest of Imperiall Diadems."[49] India is the easternmost boundary of the mercantile geography in Johnson's romance, a destination that the knights do not reach but where silk, which has started to dominate the world of commodities in *The Seven Champions*, originates. The historical arc of eastern trade that spans the territories between India, Syria, Persia, and Egypt turns into the fictional trajectory along which Johnson's knight defeats the dragons that threaten the equality between the trading kingdoms along the Eastern trading route.

The juxtaposition of the battlefield ("champions fields") and the "heaps of sun burnt mosse" in "the confines of *Africa*"[50] with the soft "beds of silk," and with their "silken curtens and curious canopies"[51] in London posits the two termini that mark the knights' adventures in Johnson's romance. Between the emasculating comfort of London and the military glory in the near East, the knights in *The Seven Champions* signal the change that heroic masculinity has undergone at the end of the sixteenth century, as the concern of fiction shifted from heroic to romantic masculinity, from the battlefield to the household. While, as Lorna Hutson has persuasively argued, this shift characterizes the representation of masculinity in sixteenth-century fiction, *The Seven Champions* resists a challenge to heroic masculinity by treating women as mere conduits for men's heroic ambitions in the East.[52] But St George's marriage to Sabra and his establishment of a court in Constantinople suggests that his ruling authority in the Eastern Mediterranean is a result not of a violent conquest and territorial possession but of heroic efficacy leading to marriage with the woman who metonymically and symbolically confirms his victory and subjugation of the Muslim world in the Eastern Mediterranean.

At the beginning of the first chapter in the second part, Sabra, who brought Egypt into St George's fold, dies after falling from her horse during a hunt: "being careless of her selfe thorough the ouer swiftness of her Steede, shee slipped beside her saddle, and so fell directly upon a thornie brake of brambles, the prickes whereof more sharpe than spikes of steele entered to euerie part of her delicate body."[53] But Sabra's death is a narrative ploy that advances the plot deeper into the East. Thirty days after Sabra's death, St George, dressed as a pilgrim, leaves London for Jerusalem, entrusting the King of England with his sons. The knight-errant's return to the East claims that territory for Christianity, and for England.

Johnson's interest in both the East and marriage, and that of other romances, is both an attempt to connect discourses of trade and politics with those of love and affect. How these two discourses produce romance fictions of trade in the Eastern Mediterranean and the new masculinity associated with that region is one of the most provocative aspects of Johnson's romance. Stories of a simultaneous claim on the kingdoms of trade and on eastern princesses as a symbolic embodiment of land in the context of historical events in the regions turned into romance literature is one way of finding a critical approach to these romances. Lois Potter has rightly claimed that how early modern romances "were read must always be a puzzle," offering as a clue samples of the traces of reading, in the form of marginalia in a selection of seventeenth-century romances, where a contemporary hand marked passages of political discourses, suggesting that such material traces that serve as evidence of reading are also indicators that some modern readers did not read romances as escapist literary fantasies but as realistic genres "from which much can be learned."[54] The copies of *The Seven Champions* that I have examined do not bear specific traces of reading.

But the fact that Johnson's romance was heavily sought after and that its aesthetic appeal lies more in the ways Johnson fictionalizes politics than in stylistic artifice and compositional strategies, suggests that *The Seven Champions* was read for lively stories whose subject matter was not entirely removed from the reality of the growing knowledge of, and interest in, the Mediterranean at the end of the sixteenth century.

The last pages of Johnson's romance echo in fiction the anxieties about the Elizabethan expansion of English power, the dominance of the Ottoman Empire in the Eastern Mediterranean, and the capability of the non-Christian cultures of Asia Minor and Ottoman Africa to interfere with the eastern trading routes. The Levantine realms of this romance, as the champions' report to the King of England suggest, are gifts to "the omnipotent God of New Jerusalem,"[55] and to Queen Elizabeth I in the city of London. In the years when ideas about English imperialism began to take shape and King James I launched his peace-making diplomacy in Europe (in part also to assuage western Christendom's fears over Turkish expansion on the continent), *The Seven Champions of Christendom* would reappear in many new editions (1608, 1612, and 1623, and one each year for a period after James's death in 1626). The popularity of Johnson's romance in the decades during which England solidified its commercial presence in the East and during which the romance genre emerged as one of the most popular kinds of prose, shaping, testing, and troubling romantic subjectivity, suggests that it was one of the most popular of romances to bring together mimetic, heroic, and, as we shall see, erotic energies in the process of creating a literary version of romantic masculinity. It is in marriage that these energies will display their full force in contesting romance as a way of harmonizing politics and bringing peace and harmony to the state. Romance's pronounced interest in courtship and marriage suggests the domesticating of heroic masculinity and of countering masculine aggression.

3 The Marriage of Merchant Kingdoms in Romances about Men

Two models of marriage existed in England towards the end of the sixteenth century and in the early seventeenth century. Arranged marriage was an older model based on a "strenuous dependency in all household management decision-making and subordination of wife to husband as his 'chattel' (subject to his will in all matters)."[1] Within this model, male authority was "tempered by the mutual duties of Christian marriage," becoming "a clear enough guide" to the roles of husband and wife within marriage and a husband's efficient management of the household.[2] The augmentation of the husband's estate was his primary economic preoccupation within the household, especially among the nobility and gentry.[3] The problems this aspect of marriage raises is vividly fictionalized in romances of the turn of the century, especially in the knight's efforts to purchase kingdoms as a way of increasing his estate and extending his estate's domain outside its boundaries. A new model, the companionate marriage, was based on mutuality and free choice of a mate. Since household management within marriage based on conjugal love was conceptualized on the model of the royal household, it reflected the preoccupation of the state as well as being a private affective unit. Negotiating the space between the public and the private aspects of marriage based on conjugal love, the romances of the sixteenth and seventeenth centuries do not merely mirror the social situation, despite the fact that the quest for a mate is at the core of their narratives. Rather, they turn around the idea of the royal household as the model of the household within marriage by making the household acquired through marriage in the East a model for the royal household in its quest to expand its economic rule and trading spaces outside the boundaries of the royal household at home. The important aspect of marriage as an "economic and social partnership"[4] to which a husband would contribute, particularly by working towards augmenting the household estate, acquires a new dimension in romances in the narratives in which the knight, a future husband, turns his absence for the purpose of acquiring property into a strategy of acquiring mercantile kingdoms overseas.

Companionate marriage also constituted the basis of "the contracted reproductive household unit,"[5] making this kind of relationship of each new couple in conflict with the first model not only on ideological grounds, because it did not subordinate a wife completely to her husband's rule, but also because the model for the lineal family based on affective equality and emotional contract was based on the bonds of kinship and "contracted undertakings between non-kin male 'friends.'"[6] A specific form of male friendship thus became a model for a reproductive union that, in turn, complicated the degree and nature of emotion, and intimacy that existed within the relationship, because it transferred its value from an all-male social institution onto a male–female bond. In the new model of marriage, as in the male–male unit founded on the principles of the oaths of friendship, male friends and non-kin partners were brought together not only by emotions but also by a desire to "optimize the social and economic possibilities for their own 'domestic' unit."[7] The male–male model of a familial unit was based on a specific kind of relationship between chivalric knights, and, as Alan Bray has documented, it reaches deep into the past of heroic bonds of "sworn brotherhood," practised in some parts of Europe in the early Middle Ages, and in England and Ireland in the sixteenth and seventeenth centuries.[8] Any meaning we attach to marriage and intimacy in romances should be conditioned by the proximity of male friendship and economics, and therefore by a certain level of homosocial intimacy that accompanied friendship between male characters. At the same time, any such meaning should also be offset by economic concerns.

The extent to which models of arranged and companionate marriage coexisted is still one of the great debates among social historians. Social historians also struggle to understand how these two models worked simultaneously and, indeed, how each of them, separately, was understood and practised.[9] However, these models created a social environment that opened up the institution of marriage to debate, scrutiny, and even new fictions. To that extent, romances are not only part of the cultural debates and fantasies about marriage, they extend those debates in realms that are not altogether beyond the social boundaries within which marriage was organized, experienced, and contested.[10]

The problems companionate marriage raise resonate through the pages of prose romances. They are crucial to the narrative and plot of these romances and they are cross-over discourses of courtship and merchant empire. The desire that drives the knight to court and to marry an eastern princess suggests not only romances' concern with love and marriage, but also shows that what is proven to be beneficial erotically can also be beneficial politically and economically in West–East contacts. In turn, the plots and narratives of romances acquire additional erotic charge from the secrecy that is part of the friendship culture upon which marriage was modelled. Marriage in prose romances of the Eastern Mediterranean is not merely the end of the knight's quest for a woman with whom to establish a household; it has to be offset against the consequences of knightly violence that accompany the establishment of merchant empires and the moral problems arising from an enforced merchant empire. Companionate marriage and the lineal family are neither easily achieved nor are they established on clear grounds of intimacy and economic interest at the end of romances. The passionate and aggressive pursuit of merchant empire and the overcoming of the obstacles that stand in the way of this new social passion of the knight trouble any closure of the romance.

These two models of marriage – arranged marriage and marriage based on the free choice of a partner – are subjected to fictional scrutiny in romances, and their boundaries teased by the unbridled desire of the knight to acquire both mercantile kingdoms and a woman for a dynastic marriage, and by the part other men play in that quest. Within this marriage economy, commercial and affective, public and erotic concerns expand the idea of marriage of romances, making it an institution that accommodates competing desires and social interests.

Trading in Arabia

While Johnson's romance imagines the kingdoms and commercial routes between the Aegean Sea and Persia, Emanuel Forde's *Montelyon, Knight of the Oracle* (1633) displaces the knight's heroic adventures even further into the East, as far as Assyria and Arabia. Although the oldest extant copy of this romance is dated 1633, which is the first of twelve known editions in the seventeenth century, it was probably published in 1599.[11] Now almost forgotten, *Montelyon* was once a very popular romance, and Ernest Baker even suggests that only Sir Philip Sidney "ran [Forde] close in sustained popularity": "none of the early novelists or romancers had anything like such a hold on generation of readers."[12] That Forde inspired writers for well over a century after his disappearance from the literary scene late in the sixteenth century is suggested by the number of reprints and abridgements of *Montelyon* in the seventeenth century, including an almanac version of it published under the same title by John Phillips, one of John Milton's nephews. In verses "In Praise of the Author," appended to the 1640 edition of *Montelyon*, one R.K. thanks Forde for "offring at free cost, / His Talent for our hearts delight."[13] After the second edition in 1640, *Montelyon* went through a number of reprints and abridgements in the seventeenth century.

Like Johnson's *The Seven Champions*, Forde's romance is set entirely in the Islamic Eastern Mediterranean and its Arabian peninsula. The titular hero's adventures begin in Assyria, take him to Persia, and end in Arabia. Montelyon travels through some of the same territories and along some of the same roads taken by Johnson's champions, and some of his adventures resemble those of Johnson's knights. But *Montelyon* has no connection with the West. Even the title hero, according to the Hesperian oracle, is a non-Christian from an eastern background, "begotten in Persia, born in Arabia and brought up in Assyria."[14] Montelyon was abandoned in infancy and has been travelling on a quest for a land to rule since early youth. This reversal of religious origins, upon which the meaning of the heroic action depends, makes Forde's fiction a rare instance of a romance in which the main hero is a knight-errant of eastern descent. What example was the early modern reader likely to have drawn from reading a fiction celebrating the victories of an eastern knight?

When the Arabian hermit warns Montelyon that "the most inhuman and wicked" giants dwell near the desert of Arabia, readers may expect to be entertained by the knight's "straunge adventures" involving the giants, but they are also invited to connect both the giants and the knight's effort to rid Arabia of them to other texts that tell of obstacles and other heroic efforts in the same land and along the same network of roads.[15] Both the network of sea and land in the symbolic geography of Forde's romance, and some of the specific geographical locations, such as Persia and Arabia, are precisely the regions through which products of the East and trade with the East reached Mediterranean shores. Alfred C. Wood argues that the first trading routes, which started in the East and led to the Levant, passed through the Caspian to the Black Sea, via Persia and Aleppo, or across the Red Sea to Alexandria.[16]

It is along the same sea and land routes that the old medieval trading roads are re-imagined as sites in which the victories of the eastern knight Montelyon are transfigured in exemplary narratives of success and peace in the lands of trade. Forde imagines this geographical trajectory at a moment when, at the height of Elizabeth's reign, her merchant–adventurers were encouraged to resume trade with the Levant and indeed to extend it.[17] It is in this context that we should view the fact that, in *Montelyon* and his other romances, Forde's sympathy lies with the merchant rather than the lower classes.[18]

What then is the reader to make of the curious episode in the middle of the romance in which Montelyon, halfway between Assyria and Persia, kills three Arabian giants (chapter 23)? And why is Montelyon's earlier liberation of Philotheta from the dragons made secondary to the hero's search for Constantia, daughter of the King of Persia, to whom he is engaged?[19] The threat to maidens by giants overlays the narrative of the quest for harmony and advantage announced by the dynastic marriage to Constantia, rendering unwed maidens prey to giants' aggression and presenting giants as a threat to those kingdoms that have not secured peace through marriage. Male aggression and wars in romances have been interpreted as instances of the display of unruly masculine energy that has not yet been tempered through experience and prudent argumentation, and as situations in which the knight has yet to prove his knighthood and chivalry. Yet, regarded in the context of romances' orientation towards the East and the Renaissance (and specifically English) interest in the geography of the trade areas of the East, repetitions of these clichés also appear to stylize the masculine efforts required to eliminate obstacles along the trading routes projected for entrepreneurial Englishmen. The temperate knight who defeats Arabian giants restores a peace required for the equality of trade, just as his defeat of the usurping Persians in a long war with the Armenians establishes harmony among the kingdoms in the East.[20] The giants symbolize both the aggressive competitors in that trade and the obstacles to the flow of commerce along the trade road.

The conceptual framework has already been set for some of the mercantile adventures and challenges awaiting the English merchants who will join the East India Company in the late seventeenth century. The Company merchants would have to negotiate their way out of difficult commercial encounters with the Turks, while at the same time ensuring the transportation of English cloth to the Persian Gulf and through Arabia, "bartering it in Persia for raw silk."[21] The English often discouraged the Persians in their trade with Turkey to ensure cheaper prices for silk brought by Indian merchants to Persia. The fictional territories of Forde's narrative thus feature the zones of an intensive and often contentious mercantile politics, areas in which England had already invested much of its diplomatic power and skill in an effort to clear the flow of trade in both directions.

Explored against the background of growing commercial knowledge elaborated in the expanding literature and translations about travel, resources, and conditions of trade in the East, romances set in the East show that what appear to us now as narratives about chivalry and courtship may have been organized otherwise in the past. Randomly sequenced kingdoms of the East, from the Macedonia of *Montelyon* to the Persia of *The Seven Champions,* only appear arbitrary, even invented, if we regard them in isolation from the literature about the East in which those countries are destinations to be considered in preparing and mapping a mercantile trip within and beyond the Eastern Mediterranean. As a romance exclusively directed towards the East, within and beyond the Ottoman Mediterranean, *Montelyon* came out of the new knowledge of the East. It is one of those romances that seem to have had the discursive power to equip writers of non-imaginative literature with stories about the East and narrative formulas with which to structure their treatises about that region.

Lewes Roberts offers an example of this crossover of narratives and discourses. When English commercial travels in the East developed in the Caroline period, Roberts produced a detailed merchant's guide to the East, suggesting that a "gentleman's" motives for travel are "*curiosity* of mind and search of *novelty*."[22] Here he privileges the adventurous aspect of travel over commercial intelligence, the avowed subject of his book. The merchant's travels in the East are thus imagined as no different from any young man's at the beginning of a romance, who leaves the paternal home for adventure and the maturity required in order to establish his own household, often in parts foreign. What moves the romance narrative forward – novelty, adventure, and curiosity – is thus what also moves Roberts's account about trade in the kingdoms of the East forward. And when Roberts justifies the writing of his treatise, saying "How then shall this *land-travelling Merchant* know whose kingdome he is in? What *Prince* commands, or who is *lord* of that ground he treads upon; but by a speculation *herein*?,"[23] we do not need to know whether Roberts was familiar with any of the Elizabethan and Jacobean romances to recognize the romance potential in this preamble about the whereabouts and identity of the ruler or master of an unknown land. We encounter this narrative formula in many romances as the knight travels through, and the narrator speculates about, the unknown lands. By 1637, when Roberts's treatise was entered in the Stationers' Register, romances had already flooded the print market and had become familiar reading for anyone even remotely interested in eastern travels. Literary texts have the potential to imagine how the emerging historical interest in the East could unfold or even be challenged by an unexpected turn of events – as when The Knight of the Oracle, Montelyon, is wrongly accused of trying to rape Praxenia and is therefore prevented from continuing his eastern travel. In the romances, such episodes are opportunities for the knight to prove his intentions and moral stance, so that the narrative of the East could continue.[24] But instances that are visibly about the violation of a woman's body invite us to think about the problem that frequent instances of rape in romances denigrate masculine agency, making the desire that moves it towards purchasing kingdoms also the desire that undermines the virtuous path of masculinity on its way to marriage.

In Forde's romance, then, empires of the East are both territories of pleasure and spaces for pragmatic effort. If *Montelyon* reverses the situation of *The Seven Champions,* insisting on the fact that the Arabian knight's success can be claimed for the West, it also prevents these victories from being claimed by England. The closing victories and celebrations at the end of *Montelyon,* including Montelyon and Philotheta's wedding ceremonies, which are enabled by the Macedonian king's release of Montelyon from imprisonment and overseen by the king of "Almaigne,"[25] are not only important because they symbolize the establishment of peace and the household, as in most romance endings but because they suggest the reverse of the claim to glory at the end of an arduous sojourn in the East. The sight of trading routes cleared of obstacles not by the efficacy of Christian knights but by the skill of England's eastern and western competitors, working in tandem, and with the aid of an English and a German ruler, suggests that Forde's romance is advancing a new meaning. Glorifying the success of an eastern knight within a form of narrative usually reserved for his western counterpart, *Montelyon* relativizes the anti-Islamic discourses that often characterize early modern writing about the Eastern Mediterranean.

Dynastic Marriage between the East and the West

In this section I will analyse *The famous Historie of Palladine of England* (1588) and *Oceander* (1600), two anonymous romances in which empires are imagined as a territorial merging of East and West, as products of a romantic union and the non-erotic connection between men through religious conversion. Both texts stylize the contact between East and West as imperial and emotional exchanges. While in *Palladine* the process of the imperial marriage of the kingdoms of East and West comes from the West, in *Oceander* this process is initiated from within the Eastern Mediterranean. These fictions also register a change that romance writing underwent after the 1580s. Early on in the intensified contacts between England and the Ottoman Empire, the Eastern Mediterranean was treated as a somewhat generic non-Christian space. (This is the case in *Palladine.*) After about 1600, however, following more extensive relations with Turkey, the Eastern Mediterranean was redefined around Turkey, with an emphasis on Constantinople.

Unlike any other prose romance of the period, *The Famous Historie of Palladine of England* (1588) narrates the meeting point of male friendship across religious lines, and the national trading power symbolically extended from England to the Eastern Mediterranean. The translator of *Palladine,* Anthony Munday, says that the French published the work "in the honour of England."[26] His patriotic verve suggests the nationalistic framework of this romance. The narrative's see-saw structure, oscillating between London, the English court, and the Eastern Mediterranean, situates the discourse of power within the context of Anglo–Mediterranean mercantile politics. The story of male friendship, manhood, and cross-ethnic marriage is played out within this political framework. In the process, England's expanding power in the Eastern Mediterranean is symbolically narrated through a negotiation of friendship and marriage between the eastern prince Zorian and the English knight Palladine, culminating in their marriages across religious and ethnic lines. In both of these texts, the difference between East and West is initially marked when strange beasts enter the narrative just at the point when Palladine crosses the boundary symbolically separating West and East. In both *Palladine* and *Oceander* religious conversion is only a pretext for an extension of political rule over the territories of the Eastern Mediterranean.

The story of *Palladine* begins with an account of the travels of five young men. The group includes Zorian, the infidel prince of the Eastern

Mediterranean country of Aquilea, and his fellow-knights Broantine, Lyboran, Lycelio, and Palladine. The narrative then focuses on the friendship of Zorian and Palladine, and the brokered, cross-religious, and cross-ethnic marriages of these two friends that are meant to seal that friendship and bring the two kingdoms, England and Aquilea, closer together. Zorian, about to convert to Christianity, first requests of Palladine that the conversion be enabled by his father, the King of England, and that it take place in London. In exchange for his conversion to Christianity, Zorian then offers to arrange, through his Aunt Orbiconte, the enchantress of Aquilea, for his sister, Nonparelia, to marry Palladine, rather than the "great Turke,"[27] whom she is expected to wed. Once this marriage takes place, Zorian asks to marry the Flemish princess Gratiana,[28] a union that Palladine will procure. *Palladine* ends with Zorian's marriage to Gratiana and Palladine's union with Nonparelia. When the fleet of English and Ottoman ships carrying Zorian's sister to England is just about to leave the Mediterranean Sea at Gibraltar, Orbiconte conjures a big storm, separates the ships, and attempts to take Nonparelia and deliver her to the "great Turke." Saved by a passing English ship just as her own vessel is being attacked by pirates, Orbiconte is delivered to England by the English admiral. There she realizes that the marriages between Palladine and Nonparelia and Zorian and Gratiana are about to take place. Faced with this turn of events, Orbiconte miraculously flies back to Aquilea on a red griffon.[29] Before her dramatic departure, she advises Zorian to care for his young son, Floriano, and prophesies that "this prince Floriano be married to Pamphilia, Daughter of the Emperour of *Greece*, yet unborn."[30] The oracle delivered, Orbiconte flies to Aquilea "to confirm your [the King of England's] pieace with my Brother ... and lay down order for his revolt to Christianity."[31] At first a conjurer, Orbiconte has now become a peacemaker in the Mediterranean.

The story of this marriage is not that different from the fiction of the dynastic marriage between the King of Tunis's daughter and a Neapolitan prince in *The Tempest*. Like this union, the marriages in *Palladine* imagine the extension of power from West to East. But unlike *The Tempest*, where the profit of the dynastic marriage goes in one direction only, to Italy (Sebastian: "'Twas a sweet marriage, and we prosper well in our return" [2.1.70]), in *Palladine* the double dynastic marriage, uniting a western man with an eastern woman, and vice versa, implies a mutuality and parity of power. That a Flemish princess is involved in the marriage scenario here suggests that it is not just English but

Anglo-Dutch trading interests in the Eastern Mediterranean that are protected in any contacts. Acknowledging the symbolic English control of the triangle connecting the Flemish lands, England, and the Eastern Mediterranean, the two marriages, Zorian to Gratiana and Palladine to Nonparelia, enable England to seal control over the trading waters of the Eastern Mediterranean. In *Palladine* the symbolism of marriage is extended even further, to the yet unborn heiress, thus ensuring that the significance of the union of the two worlds continues in the future. Yet this condition, made late in the romance with the intention of securing a long-lasting claim over land and power in the Eastern Mediterranean, does not minimize another issue that looms large in this romance and that enables this political ending: the non-sexual desire that brought two friends, Palladine and Zorian, together. In an age of contractual marriage, a model of marriage promoted, moreover, by romances, with their tales of young men and women leaving home in quest of a partner – *Palladine* privileges another story. The quest and desire here is for the rival, another heroic male; it is a quest for a social equal of a different race, with the goal of making marriage the political and legal contract between enemy lands. But the emphasis in *Palladine* is not so much on marriage, but on enduring male friendship. It is friendship, not marriage, that will provide the cultural assurance of a stable trading route between West and East, whereas the meaning of marriage remains largely symbolic. The emotional closeness between the two men proves a socially viable union in bringing Eastern Mediterranean bounty closer to England, even part of England. The close relationship of two men of a similar social rank in *Palladine* reflects the emerging practice in the late sixteenth century of the model of friendships as marriage for "household service gains."[32] The passion, however, that such a private union between two men of equal status might enable, remains safely removed from the eye of society, and from the readers of *Palladine*. The story of this intimacy, which appears less disturbing than the dramatic scenarios of lineal family in Jacobean drama, is modelled on the same social scenario that *Palladine* exploits so boldly. The question of who controls the marriage, a wife or a friend, complicates the very nature of fictionalized marriage in this romance. It also reminds us that marriage in England "does not seem to have been primarily aimed at maximizing procreation," which linked it intimately "to a number of other equally unusual features."[33] One of those "unusual" features, as *Palladine* shows, is the importance of a male friend in redirecting marriage into a new realm of social and erotic imagination.

The dynastic marriage in *Oceander*, between this romance's eponymous hero and Phianora, daughter of England's invincible King Argamont, forms part of a narrative similar to *Palladine's*, wherein personal power is solidified through dynastic marriage and affective friendships between men. The narrative suggests an extension of the national corporate power of royal London over a kingdom in the Eastern Mediterranean. But, like *Palladine*, the storytelling in *Oceander* emphasizes masculine agency over matrimonial politics as an example of the best strategy for achieving advantage in matters of state. In this regard, *Oceander* extends the humanist idea of virtue as a central effective instrument in exemplary history and matters of state politics. Born out of the clandestine union between Olbiocles, Prince of Greece, and Princess Almidiana, daughter of Rubaldo, the Hungarian king, Oceander, a man of the ocean, as his Greek name suggests,[34] was orphaned and cast into the sea, "wrapped in warme swaddling clothes put in the ruines of an olde chest, which by the help of an honest mariner … was with pitch so cun[*n*]ingly fastned from taking any violence from the waves."[35] Oceander experiences the same fate as his character-antecedent Amadis de Gaule, who was "found in the sea" and "so thence forward … called … the Gentleman of the Sea."[36] Found by a fisherman "about the shores of Asia,"[37] Oceander was taken to Carthage, where he was adopted by Kanira, Queen of Carthage. Unfamiliar with his origins, she converted him to Islam. From the beginning of this romance, Oceander straddles two worlds: the West, place of his birth, and "the shores of Sun-burnt Barbary"[38] in the East, where he grows up. This is a rare example of a romance in which the central hero, chosen by the Thebans as their hero and referred to as "our Africke Champion Oceander,"[39] fights both the Barbary challengers (Troglador, the Tyrant Marcimodes, the usurping King of Carthage; and the Knight of Leopard), and Christians, who come from all over Central Europe and England. (In this, Oceander is an obverse of Othello. Whereas Othello, born in Barbary but converted to Christianity, fights Muslims as a Venetian general on behalf of Venice, Oceander is a Christian converted to Islam who fights Christians in the name of his "Northern African" heritage.) This makes Oceander less of a "national" hero belonging to one side or the other, and more of an exemplar of the heroic virtue to which the narrative pays consideration:

> Although perhaps some man (whose insight might bee more deepe, and whose wisdome and iudgement bee sounder to conceive more sharply

> of this matter the[n] my selfe) might happily maintaine violence to bee the stranger, in regard it so often (and almost ever) overthroweth and overwhelmeth the vigour of Virtue: yet not him which continually giveth the foyle: but him which longest endureth."[40]

This virtue is displayed in the endurance of Oceander's actions and suggested in his continued success in defeating tyrants, giants, and usurpers. Thus the message the author of *Oceander* sends to the readers of this romance is that masculine agency free of national belonging is an idealized model of manhood.

The heroic plot of this romance thus focuses on an exemplary narrative of virtue that goes beyond both the political and religious conflicts in the Eastern Mediterranean and the imperial projections of the West. The Knight of the Sea, "the incomparable Oceander,"[41] is the most curious of all the knights-errant in romances: he fights for both religious camps, in the service of the King of Tunis "to maintaine the honour of their holy Prophet Mahomet"[42] against the advancing Christians, and alongside Argamonte, "King of fertile England,"[43] against the infidel, in the conquest of Constantinople, which "the magnanimous English"[44] are besieging with the help of a score of small armies from Europe's East, in the hope of restoring the government and Christian religion of the Greek emperor Claranex. Oceander's involvement on both sides appears as parity, but the stylistic ornament used to render his virtuous actions gestures towards nationalistic advantage. "Fertile" and "magnanimous" are adjectives reserved in this romance only for England and the English, who are not even major agents in the heroic actions in *Oceander*. Meanwhile, Oceander's dual allegiance is presented less as a sign of religious ambivalence, or even shared loyalty, and more as a heroic display of a virtue that surpasses religious belonging.

It is one of the peculiarities of this romance that it portrays the Knight of the Sea as belonging to both worlds while at the same time making him an agent of success for fertile England, a land also made up of magnanimous heroes. Thus a narrative of heroic adventures in both camps comes to focus on the use of religious ambivalence itself in the virtuous endeavours of those who are destined to win in Constantinople. The piling up of Oceander's heroic victories across the religious territories of the Eastern Mediterranean, between Tunis and Constantinople, is only a narrative colouring, as it were, used to exemplify virtue as it was developed in humanist rhetoric. In *Partitione Oratoria*, a rhetorical treatise used at the universities in early modern England, Cicero offers advice on virtue which seems to be manifested in the actions and arguments used by *Oceander*.[45] Cicero considers the epideictic, ethical and social functions of virtue, which

> has a twofold meaning, for it is established either in knowledge or in conduct. The virtue that is designed prudence and intelligence and the most impressive name of all, wisdom, exercises its influence by knowledge alone ... The virtue of prudence when displayed in a man's private affairs is usually termed personal sagacity and when in public affairs political wisdom.[46]

Cicero's word "actione" (from "actio") has a meaning broader than "conduct," which is how it is translated. Implying the notion of action, it gestures towards verbal display and effectiveness in speaking, and covers both epideictic virtue and virtue in agency. Attaching epideictic, social and political meaning to the notion of virtue, the *Partitione* casts a new light on *Oceander* and its protagonist's cleverness in oscillating between religious and political opposites, with the aim of ensuring both peace and profit in Constantinople, the nexus of trade in the Eastern Mediterranean.[47] The epideictic quality of virtue is revealed in Oceander's ability to concede to a heroic task that promises a yield or advantage. That it is this goal, not details of various battles or military successes, that is emphasized, is pointed out by the couplet on battles: "No Rhetoricians tongue in words can paint / The sorrows great, that did their souls attaint."[48] These lines illustrate a self-consciousness of stylistic expression, reminding us that a romance battle is after all only a rhetorical construct and convention.

While *Palladine* is presented as a patriotic romance, at whose centre the royal throne in London projects power both within and outside its kingdom through religious and politico-commercial manoeuvring, *Oceander* extends nationalism to the anxieties of dynastic prospects and victories in the Eastern Mediterranean. This narrative fictionalizes a merging of kingdoms and an extension of English power and rule in the Eastern Mediterranean. The didacticism of *Oceander*, displayed in the individual examples of Oceander's virtuous actions, in his triumphs over the threats to peace and stability, is presented not only through teaching by individual example of virtue but also by illustrating strategies for achieving advantage in the larger realm of imperial fictions, in which religion, territories, and individual ambition overlap. *Oceander*, like other romances, displays the blurring of the distinction between fiction and rhetorical instruction offered through illustrations and accompanying elucidations. The fact that from chapter 22 until the end the narrative is little more than a series of conversions of Barbary knights to Christianity, together with the revelation of Oceander's own Christian origins, only confirms that the advantage sought lies in the victory of Christianity.

In this interplay of imperial and religious discourses, romances arouse a love of virtue, and their story-telling strategies extend the humanist interest in promoting practical virtue. In the preface to his *Life of Pericles,* Plutarch says: "we ought to seek virtue not merely in order to contemplate it, but that we may ourselves derive some benefit from so doing."[49] That Plutarch associates the acts of a Roman warrior with examples of virtue that a classically trained humanist man should follow sheds an important, double, light on the heroic stories of prose romances. It reminds us that romance writers invested the knight-errant's action not simply with virtue but with an exemplary virtue, which, as both acts and ethics, was intended to offer models of conduct. We do not know anything about the author of *Oceander*, and very little, if anything, about most of the other minor romance writers, so we are not in a position to make persuasive arguments about these writers' grounding in humanist education. But we do know that the imaginary heroes of prose romances embody virtue as it is elucidated in Cicero's prose (available in the vernacular translation in the humanist school curriculum); and we know that romances present this form of virtue in their narratives in such a way as to render them models of agency.

The ending of *Oceander* brings into question the two main formulas of early modern romances, by which they are distinguished from their medieval antecedents: the unstable dynastic future and mercantile interests as a promise of the future. Against the anxiety over "a safe and peaceful transition to any future true heir,"[50] the last pages of *Oceander* temper such anxieties by fictionalizing the kind of scenario that befell England after Henry VIII: the wished-for princess who Orbiconte imagines will be born to Floriano and Pamphilia looks back at the success that Elizabeth had brought to England during her reign. Thus the prosperity of the Anglo-Mediterranean kingdom envisioned at the end of this romance is associated with the happy history that has already been rehearsed.

However, the resolution of this ultimately dynastic future through its displacement in the Eastern Mediterranean and the concomitant story of masculine virtue raises further problems about how that virtue is fictionalized in *Oceander*. The way in which the marriages came to be at the end of the romance does make the point that the crucial relationship in this romance is between two men, not between a husband and wife. The homosocial bond between the two young men is presented in this romance as the model for marriage. Yet it is precisely this coming together of a man from the West and a man from the East, as friends whose bond is based on parity and affection, that makes it possible for us to imagine that corporate and commercial power, not solely the felicity of romantic marriage, will guarantee hope for the future at the end of this romance. Thus conceived as secondary to inter-ethnic friendship between men, the marriage turns into the resolution of an impasse encountered by an imperial romance of the Eastern Mediterranean. In *Oceander*, both the friendship and the marriage lead towards a political goal – the extension of England's mercantile power in the Eastern Mediterranean – but not without attentiveness to a distinction between how emotions are gendered within these political relationships. *Oceander* surprises us not only because it is yet another anti-parental romance, but because it is an instance of yet another romance featuring companionate marriage presented in opposition to paternal control. Thus the writer of *Oceander* reserves affect and agency for male bonds but allegorizes the mingling of kingdoms through an instrumental dynastic marriage.

The end of *Palladine* fulfills what Lori Humphrey Newcomb, speaking of Shakespeare's late plays in relation to prose romances, has astutely called "a masculine line of narrative authority" of romances.[51] The powerful patriarchal men of *Palladine* have not only found their heroic predicament in romance fulfilled by becoming rulers of a land, they have also found solace and felicity in the new certainty that that rule is solidified through their marriages, which span both East and West. As in the case of Palladine's offspring, the romance has also confirmed that the next-generation assurance is achieved, that linear succession is not compromised, and that female autonomy, embodied in Orbiconte, is overcome. This overthrow of autonomy in the form of female authority and agency is both a masculinist defeat of femininity, and also a subjection of the Eastern Mediterranean, gendered feminine, through Orbiconte's origins there. The defeat of Orbiconte is not simply a triumph of masculine strength over female power; it also points to the fact that the writer's primary interest lies in the purchasing of kingdoms in the Levant. Tension between the narrative of heroic quest and the fiction of inter-ethnic, international, marriage reflects the gendered tension in the romance narrative, in which the masculinist charge of the romance runs, at different times, both counter to and alongside of the feminine stream of the romance invested in marriage.

An episode at the end of *Oceander* is another reminder of how the remoteness of the Eastern Mediterranean from England affects the ways in which gender is presented in this romance. Sailing in the south Adriatic Sea on the way to the West, Oceander and his knights dispose of the enchantress Mardegua's body: "they presently conueid her where what became of her body or mantle afterwards, was neuer since, either knowne or hearde of."[52] The peace at the end of this romance is made possible by evacuating the fictional world of feminine magic. Serving as a burial ground for the magic and evil that taints the chivalric mission of a heroic knight, the Adriatic becomes a signifier of the purpose indicated by many merchant-travellers in their travel accounts of the period.

Because the eastern coast of the Adriatic was known for piracy and was associated with Turkish rule in its immediate hinterland, and because it was generally considered to be "a sea tempestuous and unfaithful,"[53] as George Sandys reports, the Adriatic was a sea full of danger. William Lithgow even associates it with monstrosity, as if suggesting the backwardness of the region bred distortion of humankind.[54] It is true that necromancers and enchantresses are associated with the regions further to the East in this romance. But it is difficult to shake the impression that while the waters of the Mediterranean are reserved for trade with luxuries and exchange of wealth and goods, the Adriatic is thought suitable only for a swift passage. One of the features of romance writing is that of a body found or dropped in the sea, and so the writer of *Oceander* remains within the formal boundaries of romance narrative when he adapts this meme to his story. Yet given the reputation of the Adriatic for danger and tempests, one might wonder whether this conception of the Adriatic as a mysterious zone separating the two worlds, of the Christian West and the Islamic East, helps to explain why the knights in *Oceander* inter the body of the dangerous enchantress there.[55] The rest of the Eastern Mediterranean often appears to be "a pretty Paradice of eternall pleasure."[56] Dragging the body of the enchantress here – in a territory claimed for England and in a region that is the source of commercial marvels and profit – would mean polluting it with the evil of which it has just been purged. But getting rid of it in the Adriatic, a sea under constant threat from the Ottomans and political pressure coming from Venice, returns the necromantic body to where it symbolically originated.

Rapists and Tyrants in the Commonwealth of Trade

Eastern kingdoms cast a long shadow over the stories of masculinity in romances, where narratives of rape overlap with the fictions of mercantile travels. Yet if we read rape strictly as the ravishment of the female body, and thus symbolically as the ravishment of land, in other words as just one of the forms of "the association between femininity and tyranny in Renaissance culture,"[57] we are leaving out a significant dimension of the meaning of rape as a form of erotic violence, a characteristic of romance with which this genre contributed to the history of sexual violence, as an act that is beyond law, consent, and coercion.[58] Since the heroines in romances rarely suffer the fate of Shakespeare's Lucrece, from his narrative poem *The Rape of Lucrece* (1594), who is raped and commits suicide out of guilt and humiliation, rape narratives take a specific meaning in relation to the discourses of eastern trade, a meaning that cannot be offset against the danger of violence that forced trade posits to the body of woman as a prize for men's passage in the East. One of the recurrent critical views of romances has been that "the narrative sequence eschews logic" and that "[c]onnectives are suppressed, leaving the plot full of temporal and geographical gaps," but that "these lapses are challenging and exhilarating."[59] While this cannot be denied, the challenge in reading romances is to consider how examples of characters' actions shape meaning in sequencing episodes. Rape narratives form part of that system of sequencing exemplarity that is aimed at providing the knight with an opportunity not just to prove his manly virtue in instances in which he defeats the raping and often infidel tyrant on the battlegrounds of the East, but also to remove the threat to the commonwealth of trade, embodied as a raped maiden or a woman threatened with rape.

Here is an example from *The Famous, pleasant, and variable Historie, of Palladine of England* (1588), given here in an adapted translation by Anthony Munday from Claude Colet's French original. In chapter 16, Palladine comes to the kingdom of Dace, somewhere in the Aegean archipelago, on a mission to rescue from imprisonment a knight "of high and especiall desert" who is being held in a castle by four other knights, the sons of Dace's king.[60] The knight was imprisoned because he killed one of the king's sons, who had threatened to rape the daughter of a poor tenant, and then, in a rage, killed her. In the knight's recounting of the causes and history of his imprisonment, he tells Palladine that he first "beheld the poore virgin before him [the king's son] on her knees, he hauing his Sword drawne in his hand, threatening therewith to cut her throate, if she would not accomplish his unlawfull desire" while the "poor mayden was out of breath, with struggling and striuing to defend her chastitie."[61] The virtuous knight tries to persuade the wicked son not to kill the maiden, but just when it looks like his persuasion has been successful the wicked son turns and kills the maiden, at which point the virtuous knight kills him – only to be caught by the king's other sons who, as befits romance, suddenly and mysteriously appear on the scene. This short episode, characteristic of the romance's discourse about the violence of intemperate men against the chastity of women, is rich with meaning produced both by the sequencing of episodes and the intertextual layering of allusions. A female character that is completely silent in this narrative, as is the case with the one in *Palladine*, is also symbolically erased from the narrative about the shaping of subjectivity. The violence of man against "the poore virgin" (I1ᵛ) represents aggression against the social order of women, and by extension against the formation of the domestic household. The episode also makes romances anatomies of masculinity and male agency, pitting the most aggressive extremes against the temperance inherited from the tradition of romance writing.

Both Palladine's and the imprisoned knight's actions are meant to be understood as virtuous, in Cicero's sense of virtue displayed in conduct.[62] Their masculine agency is contrasted to that of the son of the King of Dace, who threatens to violate the maiden's chastity. The two kinds of action represent the two sides of the narrative coin in which masculine agency is represented in romances: temperate and intemperate. The account of the maiden's rape, with references to ravishment and murder if the culprit's desire is not satisfied, compresses the story of Terseus and Procne from Ovid's *Metamorphoses* (6.3719–81), turning Procne's suicide into the murder of the maiden. The motif of rape frames the episode of the murder of the maiden, which is reported in matter-of-fact fashion ("he stabd her to the heart with his dagger").[63] Appearing in a masculinist text, this motif connects two parallel narratives of chivalric virtue, Palladine's and that of the imprisoned knight. The reader is encouraged not to dwell on the episode of the death of the maiden, but instead on Palladine's next adventure: driven by his desire for Aquilea, he is "determined to trauaile thither,"[64] deeper into the East. I have dwelt on this episode to illustrate the point that if we read the narrative of rape and violence against women in isolation from the larger narrative context in which these episodes occur we can (mis)read them as misogyny only, and thus miss their function in structuring the narrative about the crossover between mercantile and heroic travel and masculine agency.

The example from *Palladine* demonstrates that rape enables the meanings of the body and violence to acquire other signification in the narratives of heroic adventures. In romances, rape is often perpetrated by an intemperate knight or by a Muslim man. That rape is framed ironically, as in the following example, suggests that the signification of rape lies beyond, not only within, the rape narrative itself. Yet what are we to make of the following example from Johnson's *The Seven Champions*, in which the Earl of Coventry's attempt to rape Sabra goes awry when Sabra snatches his sword and drives it through his chest (part I, chapter XV)? The narrative oscillates between Coventry's thoughts of suicide stirred by thwarted desire (Sabra rejected his advances) and a threat to rape and then cut out her tongue:

> First will I wrappe this dagger in thy lockes of haire, and naule it fast into the ground: then wil I rauish thee by force and violence, and triumph in the conquest of thy chastetie: which being done, Ile cut thy tong out of thy mouth, because thou shalt not reueale not discrie thy bloody rauisher.[65]

By saving Sabra from Coventry's aggression, the narrative preserves her as a prize in the mercantile possession of the Eastern Mediterranean, claimed by St George. The author juxtaposes the rape episode with the triumphant wandering of St George, directing the reader to one of the most common literary signifiers and discourses of rape in early modern literature: Ovid's story of Procne. The self-conscious irony of this remarkable chapter about the danger to women posed by the rejected lover derives not only from the sudden reversal of roles between the perpetrator and the victim, when a threatened woman suddenly turns into the murderer of the culprit, but also from the image of blood sprinkled over the grass and the violets, dropping not out of the violated female body (a stylistic and rhetorical cliché in rape narratives), but from the dying culprit's chest. But this does not mark the end of irony's role in the rape narrative: the narrator tells the reader that he has accelerated the narrative, "passing over the speedy prouision made by the Christian Champions in *Egypt* for the inuasion of *Persia*,"[66] in order to finish this story and tell more about what befalls the knights-errant "in the Confines of *Persia*."[67] The emphasis is not on the fate of the woman (who, after all, saved herself) but on the eastern kingdoms in which libidinal and commercial temptations abound. The irony of the chapter, self-consciously playing with literary clichés, directs readers' attention away from the gendered narrative – cautioning them to read it as a rhetorically exemplary narrative about the effect of the lack of masculine virtue and the effectiveness of rhetoric in saving female virtue – and towards the narrative of acquisition of mercantile kingdoms. Like Persia, which resists the invasion of St George and his knights, Sabra resists the Earl of Coventry's attempts to violate her body. Thwarted rape, like failed invasion, preserves the prosperity of trade, with which the country is linked. By making the rapist a character from the homeland, from England, the narrative throws the moral weight of violence back onto domestic culture. The narrative becomes a negative example of chivalric masculinity out of control and thus a critique of placing ethical value in bygone ideals of heroic masculinity.

The narratives of rape and murder run counter discourses of marriage in prose romances; they shift the attention, not to marriage with the woman at the core of it, but to the unruliness of masculinity that threatens the stability of state that rests on the household. Particular representations of rape narrated in prose romances are part of a much larger body of early modern writing that focused on rape and the connection between rape and state politics, but in a way that rape is often cut out of the historical circumstances that frame those representations of it, a process which Stephanie Jed calls "chaste thinking."[68] In this sense, it is impossible to think chastely when writing about rape in romances, because, among other reasons, as an act of violence, rape in romances is denuded of the often complex rhetorical milieu that surrounds it in other literature, in which the victim speaks (or writes out, as Lavinia does in Shakespeare's early tragedy *Titus Andronicus*) her defence and in which moral and legal arguments against rape can be presented. Romance writers present rape as an act of masculine aggression as such, as an act of intemperance that romances are meant to condemn at the same time they display it as an aspect of Eastern masculinity that cannot be governed by the moral or legal rules of the Christian West.

The symbolic resonance of rape and its avoidance, however, runs even deeper in *The Seven Champions* and is connected with the question of imperial boundaries around and within which mercantile discourses are presented. It might have not escaped the attention of early modern readers of Johnson's fiction that St George's union with Sabra takes place somewhere on the borders between the Holy Land and Syria.

It takes place, in other words, against the background of many of the discourses about the soul, the body, sexual renunciation, and Mary's conception of Christ in the writings of early Christian writers and monks, for whom woman's body was a "sacred boundary, unbreached by intrusion from the outside world."[69] The boundary is between the permissible and the forbidden, between the sacred and carnal.[70]

Yet in the context of a romance in which the knight-errant's travel is through lands whose borders are fluid, it would perhaps be a critical provocation to think of Sabra's body not standing for a land but demarcating a frontier that would be violated if it were not for the knight's ability to stop this intrusion. This frontier now marks the new mercantile territory of the early modern world as it extends its commercial activities in the East. Johnson's narrative thus stops short of the violence of acquiring land that would physically augment England's territory, the process later to be identified with colonization, and resorts instead to a cross-ethnic dynastic marriage as an alternative way to solidify power and interest in an eastern land. But such marriages, we should remember, were only subjects of literature, and did not occur in early modern England. It is therefore hard to equate them with an attempt at colonization, or the romance's imperial ambitions, even if at the level of speculation and imagination they resemble colonial enterprises. In the end, the narrative of Johnson's romance emphasizes the knight's virtue and England's symbolic claim to trading routes in and beyond the Eastern Mediterranean, not on the fact of the knight's acquisition of land.

Recalling Gerard de Malynes's allegorizing of the threat and obstacle to trade in the figure of a giant, the episode involving the giant king of Sicily and his brother (part 2, chapter 14) seems to belong to the same complex of fictions in which rape, a threat to trade, and a challenge to heroic masculinity are combined in writings about the Mediterranean. It would not have escaped the contemporary reader that Sicily, as George Sandys reminds his readers, was often referred to as "the Queene of the Mediterranean Ilands"[71] because of the wealth of its land but also because it is where Proserpina was raped by Pluto.[72] Similarly, readers would not have missed the allusion to Sicily as an island of bounty, a prosperous mid-point for trade between the Western and Eastern Mediterranean. Killing the giant of Sicily is not just about saving a maiden's chastity but also about erasing the obstacle on the path of mercantile exchange on an island through which goods travelled to both the East and the West. When romance writers fashion men from the

East as rapists, as does the author of *Palmerin d'Oliua* (1597), who imagines "the Turkes, Moores, Arabes and Medes" as satyrs and "horned" fauns assaulting women's chastity (they are "giving new invasions of the Nymphes of Diana"), they adhere to the Renaissance cliché of representing the infidel as sexually insatiable and threatening.[73] The lascivious Turkish emperor who attempts to rape Princess Agriola in *Palmerin D'Oliva* (1597) is not merely dissuaded from ravishing her but entirely eliminates the element of sexual desire for her by pledging that "I shall therefore account you [Agriola] as my Sister, and death shall not make me doe contrarie to your appointment."[74] The language of filial relationship is then strengthened by action, when Agriola leaves the sultan's court bearing "many rich presents,"[75] which she and her maidens take back to their Christian countries. This gift giving is symbolic of a culture in which productive relations between the West and the Ottomans were constantly being forged. In this episode the infidel–rapist is reformed through the rhetoric of women's defence of chastity. The narrative invites the reader to consider this rehabilitation both as an effect of women's rhetoric in defence of chastity and as redemption of Muslims through the new alliance.

If what starts as an attempt to violate the Christian land, symbolically embodied in the female body, has turned into an episode in which the relationship is changed by gifts and the rhetoric of filial affection, then the Muslim who can be swayed from his violent act by effective rhetoric has become a partner in rhetorical communication within a culture of increasing contacts and exchanges with the Ottoman Empire. In contrast, Brunoro, the intemperate giant-knight and ravisher of a young virgin in the third part of *Palmerin of England* (1602), is incapable of hearing the virgin's plea to save her chastity and will soon be fought by Palmerin of England.[76] The difference in the statuses of the rapists, a Muslim and a giant, hints at the change that the image of the Muslim was beginning to undergo in late Elizabethan romances. He is no longer seen as violent – the giant has taken over that place – but as someone whose intemperance can be tamed with rhetoric, a listener susceptible to persuasion, and a partner in exchange with the West. When the idea of mercantile empires had first begun to take shape in the writings about the East, the infidel inhabiting the lands along the trade routes was an ambiguous figure associated with threat and pacification.

In romances, the tyrant suggests civilizational decline, posing a threat to virtue and female honour. This association of cultural fall with existential threat is one of the motifs of the literature in which the western narrative eye observes the East of the Mediterranean for the first time. Reporting on his travels in the Eastern Mediterranean in *A Relation of a Journey begun An.Dom: 1610*, George Sandys writes:

> countries once so glorious, and famous for their happie estate, are now through vice and ingratitude, become the most deplored spectacles of extreme miserie: the wild beasts of mankind hauing broken in vpon them, and rooted out all ciuilitie; and the pride of a sterne and barbarous Tyrant possessing the thrones of ancient and iust dominion. Who aiming onely at the height of greatnesse and sensualitie, hath in tract of time reduced so greatnesse and goodly a part of the world, to that lamentable distresse and seruitude ... vnder which it now faints and groaneth.[77]

Sandys's account of the Levant is written in accordance with the stylistic cliché, dominant in travel accounts and romances, about the civilizational and religious, and therefore moral, decline of the ancient Christian lands now ruled by the Ottomans. In the hands of the tyrant, "those rich lands at this present remaine waste ... goodly Cities made desolate; sumptuous buildings become ruines; glorious Temples either subuerted, or prostituted to impietie; true Religion discountenanced and oppressed."[78] When Sandys personifies the Ottoman invaders of Natolia as the "barbarous Tyrant," whose indulgent "sensualitie" renders him a creature of lower nature, indulging in senses and physical satisfaction,[79] Sandys turns the lustful Muslim into a low-natured tyrant, and the land he rules into a cultural and natural wasteland, both tyrant and ruined land instantly becoming a challenge to the virtuous and entrepreneurial knight. It is within this land of former glory and present danger that the chivalric knight battles the Tyrant, who, remembering Sandys, we should read as a concretized Islamic threat to Christian honour and to women. It is this danger that the knight has to eradicate in order to remove the threat to virtue and chastity (the tyrant's "violence and rapine [is] insulting ouer all"),[80] but also to claim, to free, the land under the barbarous tyrant–Muslim threat to "the rest of the world,"[81] to other commonwealths. The fight against the tyrant, then, is prompted by both moral and economic urges.

Yet when the Muslim became England's partner in trade and diplomacy, and when Turkey began to be seen ambivalently as both political enemy and commercial ally, something also changed in fictional representations of Muslims. The Muslim switched from being pictured as an intemperate rapist threatening the chaste body of the western maid (or the West as maid) to a collaborator warning about the threat of the giant infidel. Henry Robarts gives us one example of this change in *Honovrs Conquest.* A Muslim, who has joined a party of knights "to attende to their horses" as they travel, warns the knights that they are being approached by "a verie faire and beautifull woman, attired in a petticoate of crimson damaske, which was pursued by two Negroes slaues, which would violence haue abused her bodie."[82] Reflecting the changes in economic circumstances that were transfiguring the relations between West and East, the "Negroe" would-be rapists play the role of Muslim rapists from the earlier fictions, when the Ottomans were regarded as the arch enemy. Displaced by skin colour and social rank (not only black, the rapists also figure as slaves), the rapist of the maiden (dressed in damask, a commodity imported from the Levant) is imagined to come from beyond the boundaries of Mediterranean Greece, in which Robarts's romance is set. When this cultural–historical shift occurred, the Muslim's position changed, becoming multilayered in the English cultural imagination: on the stage and in the propaganda pamphlets that continued to be infused with the old rhetoric of religious conflict, Muslims were still seen as a threat; but in the neo-chivalric prose romances they were regarded more favourably, as facilitators of exchanges with the West that benefited England but did not seem to harm the Ottoman Empire.[83]

From the narrative signposting of the East, which throughout Johnson's fiction naturalizes the East – from his descriptions of the pyramids of Egypt to an account of a pilgrimage to Christ's tomb in the Holy Land to an evocation of "the sweete Orenges and ripe Pomegranades"[84] growing on an island off the coast of Armenia – a more complex, historically determined picture of the East emerges. The knight-errant's search for a woman intersects in this Mediterranean romance with the quest for eastern trade routes. On this trading path, Constantinople becomes a terminus for the knight's Mediterranean adventures, so the second part of Johnson's romance ends with the knight settling there. Yet Constantinople is not only the end point of the knight-errant's heroic travels but also the centre of the new household organized around a model different from marriage based on conjugal love. With the reunions of the two fathers long separated from their sons – St George with his sons and the Islamic emperor with his missing son, the Prince of Constantinople – the narrative of confirmed patriarchy figures not as the imagined household, involving a wife (who is absent from the end of the romance) but as more of a corporate household bringing together western and eastern men. This is precisely the kind of union that was the centre of the diplomatic and mercantile Eastern Mediterranean, and at the centre of western trade with the Levant; it is a union upon which England would have depended to secure its place in the theatre of mercantile exchange and contacts in the East.

The end of Johnson's romance reminds us of the importance of these popular and cheaply produced prose fictions for the development of mercantile discourses of the East in early modern literature. Richard Helgerson has argued that in the 1590s verse romances of Tasso and Ariosto, "the ruler is a marginal figure and his imperial project of negligible importance."[85] If the ruler is removed from the "imperial project," the knight re-imagines that project into a different version of superiority and advantage. Prose romances, which are close in narrative structure to travel and historical writing, are more directly engaged both with emphasizing the importance of rule and succession and with the varied meaning of the ideas of empire. The triumphal establishment of England's rule, displaced to the East, in *The Seven Champions* emphasizes the importance of both the ruler and the imperial vision in prose romances.The 1590s romances were more a product of the English (and European) mercantile urban culture than of the feudal romance tradition of tilt and chivalry. And so, in Johnson, both the ruler and the "imperial project" occupy the central, yet different, role in a story in which nationalism and power are connected with the trading success and creation of conditions for England's future endeavours. If we only read romances as texts invested in fantasy and fictional geography, or if we treat them simply as narratives promoting royal ideologies, peaceful rule, and prosperous households on which the power of the early modern kingdom depends, we miss a crucial aspect of those romances' historical framing as fictions stylizing mercantile contacts, conflicts, and exchanges.

I want to revisit the question with which I began this chapter, about what empire stands for in these romances of the Mediterranean's East. Against the criticism that has interpreted romances as texts anticipating the colonization of the New World and the rise of a western imperialism that apprehended the idea of "the East" as a subaltern "other," I have argued that the kingdoms and empires that romances stylize are not consistent with the modern-day idea of either colonization or imperialism, partially because romances were texts that served various purposes and were addressed to a varied readership. Rather than being simply texts about colonial expansion, romances imagine the epideictic and pragmatic strategies of an effective virtuous agency that is in tune with the humanist vernacular writings on the efficacy of history, here illustrated in the varied ways in which it began to imagine its power on the seas and in the trading markets, what I would call romance maritime imperialism. Romances present not the shaping of the maritime empire (as opposed to the land-locked empires of some European states) that England was later to become, but a form of literary fiction of imperialism that as yet lacked the inspiration of concrete empires. Their acts are not about governance, but about claiming (temporary) power, demonstrated by the repeated success in defeating enemies and seizing land and frontiers for commercial passage and mercantile profit.

Here at the end of this chapter, I turn to Richard Willes, who prepared for print the second, 1577, edition of Richard Eden's translation of Pietro d'Anghiera's treatise *De orbe novo* (*The history of trauayle in the West Indies*) originally published in the early sixteenth century. In the Epistle to Lady Brigit, Countess of Bedford, Richard Willes pauses to caution his ambitious and entrepreneurial travellers of the moral consequences of their colonial undertakings. Dated in print 4 July 1577, this Epistle represents what is perhaps the most extraordinary critique of colonialism in early modern English literature,

> What is the matter, you Christian men, that you so greatly esteeme so lytle portion of golde more then your owne quietnesse, which neuerthelesse you entende to deface from these fayre ouches,[86] and to melt the same into a rude masse. If your hunger of golde be so insatiable, that onlye for the desire you haue thereunto, you disquiete so manye nations, and you yourselues also susteyne so many calamities and incommodities, lyuyng lyke banished men out of your owne countrey, I wyll shewe you a region flowing with golde, where you may satisfie your rauenyng appetites: But you must attempt the thing with a greater power, for standeth in your hand by force of armes to ouercome kings of great puissaunce, and rigorous defendours of theyr dominions ... Albeit that the greedie hunger of golde hath not yet vexed us naked men, yet do we destroy one another by reason of ambition and desire to rule. Hereof sprynegeth mortal hatred among us, and hereof commeth our destruction.[87]

Rarely have free trade and exploitation of resources received such harsh critique in early modern writing as in Willes's sharp language which curiously anticipates some of the social and ecological devastation to come later in history. Invoking the destructive effects of ambition and the desire to rule, two of the human vices that made the Renaissance troubled, Willes is warning against precisely the kinds of energies that are fully animated in the prose romances at the turn of the century: colonialism with all its negative consequences, the colonizer's hunger for wealth, and the overestimation of the value of gold. What Willes unfolds here is not just a critique of resorting to power to conquer regions rich in gold, but a forceful warning that the hunger for gold will fuel hatred and conflict between Christian nations, between those that defend gold in their land and those that ruthlessly seek to possess it.

Willes's warning against greed's destructive consequences for the stability of nations is articulated alongside his call to overcome the mighty kings ("kings of great puissaunce") in their exploitative quests. A pronounced moral undertone resonates throughout Willes's impassioned warning, as he views the insatiable hunger for gold as the seed of hatred and the destruction of (Christian) humankind. Considered in the context of Willes's response to the exploitation of resources, the purchasing of kingdoms in romances of the East seems a milder rendition of the emerging politics of England's engagement with the East. What appears in romances is not a self-destructive politics of exploitation of a foreign land, but a different emerging polity, an early political relationship between England and the East. In this relationship England is emerging as an early mercantile nation imagining its prospects in the Eastern Mediterranean.

Knights-errant comfortably ensconced in Constantinople, having furnished London with silk, pearls, and other commodities from the East, are the product of a literature that is the obverse of Eden's caution. They have not conquered the East, or integrated it into England, but have been absorbed by it. Their thirst for heroic victory and desire to rule have been displaced from England to the Eastern Mediterranean in a vision that portrays the knights-errant, led by St George, as the champions of England's commercial interest in Constantinople, the nexus of Eastern Mediterranean trade – and this in 1582, only a year after the appointment of William Harborne as Elizabeth I's first ambassador to the Ottoman Empire. Harborne's embassy was entrusted with the task of providing intelligence for the expansion of trade with the Ottomans. The number of fictions imagining the benefits of trade in the kingdoms of the East, anticipated in romances and related fictions of the 1580s and elaborated in those at the turn of the century, demonstrates the extent to which those fictions used the power of persuasion to instill in their readers the idea that the Eastern Mediterranean was the territory in which the conquest of routes, resources, and commodities could bring power and glory to the West. They tell us that in an age of bustling Mediterranean traffic with the Ottomans, the terms of heroic valour and victory had long lost their chivalric meaning and had acquired a new import measured by prudent estimation of success in the competing arena of trade with the East.

PART II

Intimacy, Sexuality, and the Queer Levant

4 Desire and Knightly Masculinity

The eight romances that I discuss in this part provide compelling examples of how the fiction of the Mediterranean shaped literary versions of masculinity, male sexuality, and homosocial intimacy. In the following pages I will explore Emanuel Forde's *Ornatus and Artesia* (?1595), Lady Mary Wroth's *The Countess of Montgomery's Urania*,[1] Lawrence Twyne's rendering of *The patterne of paineful aduentures* (1594), Margaret Tyler's translations of Diego Ortúñez de Calahorra's *The myrrour of knighthood* (I, 1580; II, 1585), Anthony Munday's translations of the anynymous *Palmerin of England* (1596) and *Palmerin D'Oliva* (1588), Henry Robarts's *The Historie of Pheander the Mayden Knight* (1595), Robert Greene's *Arbasto, the Anatomie of Fortune* (1594) and *Gwydonius or the Card of Fancy* (1584), and Robert Parry's *Moderatus* (1595). Page after page in these romances, the reader is drawn into the world of masculine agency dependent upon male characters' involvement with the ideological, racial, commercial, and culturally alien but attractive contingences of the Eastern Mediterranean. There is a sense that the Eastern Mediterranean is a magnet that draws male characters into its fold; that those characters embrace the alien and mystical allure of the Eastern Mediterranean, a process that opens up hitherto unknown layers of their interiority and western identity to new possibilities for sexual pleasures and masculine identification.

Prose romances and men inevitably encounter the instability of sexuality, desire, friendship, and economics, producing at times intense stories of male attachment and erotic bonds. Although prose romances do not provide sufficient narrative and discursive space for an exploration of men's inwardness – they are more fictions of action than of introspection – they are nevertheless an important and still under-examined literary resource for the study of male subjectivity. And so prose romances take us back, from a discussion of a pre-modern male subjectivity and sexuality as they are situated within sexual subjects, not within sexual categories, and thus occasion a discussion of different ways in which those male subjects could occupy different erotic positions, indeed, different roles, within the neo-chivalric world of romances. As a literary type whose sexual and erotic agency changes flexibly and freely in prose romances that were flourishing at the time when middle-class culture had just started to emerge in the agrarian England of the late sixteenth century, the romantic knight of sixteenth- and early seventeenth-century romances stands at the threshold of history of sexuality as a modern phenomenon.[2] He occupies an important place in the still growing discussion of the "historical emergence of sexuality itself."[3] The knight also helps us understand how that sexuality started to be understood, and how sexual acts were imagined, before the next major phase in the development of the history of sexuality as a bourgeois phenomenon in the eighteenth and nineteenth century.

Literature that, like prose romances, focuses on masculine agency offers ample opportunities to examine that agency in the different scenarios in which it occurs and within the genre of fiction, where most of sixteenth-century subjectivity was negotiated outside the spheres of religious, legal, and political writing. Male subjectivity as it is fictionalized in romances thus offers a corrective, a different perspective, on the idea of the male subject as it was, often prescriptively, narrated in other forms of literature that, unlike prose romances, targeted only select classes. Courtiers and students, apprentices and merchant travellers, were not the only readers of romances. Men of socially diverse classes read romances, and those fictions sometimes perform the role of conduct books for maturing young men, providing narrative scenarios for prudent actions in the future. When prose romances became more interested in civic and middle-class concerns and militant chivalry became less important than courtship and love, romance writers started to be more interested in emotions, desire, and eroticism in detail, as if deliberately testing the limits of the social and religious boundaries of erotic expression.

The display of heterosexual and heteronormative acts, which occasionally occurs in romances and which is intended to bolster the knight's masculinity, in fact subordinates a woman to yet another instance of aggressive male sexuality and raises questions about the historical forms that erotic masculinity and subjectivity take in romance.

In Emanuel Forde's *Ornatus and Artesia*, a prose romance set in Phrygia and infamous for an uncontrolled display of sexual acts and sexual scurrility, Artesia's loss of virginity after "shee permitted" Ornatus to enter her bedroom raises the question of reading romances in the period and of how we assess the transformation of masculinity from heroic to romantic and the role (and fate) of women in that transformation. "Sometimes blushing, sometimes shrieking," writes Forde, "and yet yielding, denying, and yet graunting, willing and unwilling; yet at last, she gaue that she could not recall, and let him possesse her spotlesse virginitie."[4] Passages like this may have been understood as a market ploy, intended to boost the sales of cheap print fiction, intended for buyers among the young men of London looking to satisfy their voyeuristic desires with light reading. Women who bought romances could equally identify with male virtues or be cautioned by the male acts depicted in these texts. In a way, then, romances are a literary barometer of the ways in which early modern England fantasized about sexual agency and its moral and social consequences for both women and men. In a culture in which pornography did not mean what it means today and in which censorship was designed only to catch heresy, episodes like the one quoted from *Ornatus and Artesia* open a window into the possibilities of a broad range of erotic acts.

At the same time, the misogyny of such lengthy episodes – the one quoted spills over two pages of black-letter print – shows that when sixteenth- and seventeenth-century romances started to be interested more in different civic, middle-class concerns and when therefore the ethical boundaries of their narratives loosened – and when the readership of romances tilted more towards the middling sort – the narratives of courtship turned into openly erotic discourses, and masculine aggression towards women became pronounced, subjugating women into sexual experience. Even though marriage still ends the knight's adventure in the East (as in *Ornatus and Artesia*, set in Asia Minor), the knight's path towards it became filled with more incidents of either misogynistic aggression or homosocial distraction, which puts into question the idea that marriage remained the primary concern of these fictions. Moreover, the question may be raised, too, whether woman is always the goal of man's quest for a mate in these romances in which we can follow the shift from a heroic or chivalric knight to an erotic knight, from a knight seeking love to a knight looking for carnal pleasure.

Under the surface of the stories of heroic adventures and heterosexual courtship, another story is told, that of affective and erotic bonds between men, a story that is sometimes expressed in "the sparest of signs and gestures,"[5] as, after all, all stories of intimacy are told. In the Eastern Mediterranean, the chivalric knight also becomes the erotic knight. Writers like Philip Sidney, Robert Greene, Lady Mary Wroth, Lawrence Twyne, the writers of *Palmerin of England* and *Palmerin D'Oliva*, the author of the *Booke of the myrrour of knighthood*, Robert Parry, and Henry Robarts use erotic romance not only to demonstrate "how all sense of political and social responsibility can be eroded by passion"[6] but how desire and sexuality facilitate political contacts between men, how they give energy to the social and political commitment to purchase kingdoms.

Among the "sexual types" as "recognizable figures of literary imagination and social fantasy," the erotic knight does not quite stand out as a figure culturally identified by his sexual practices, distinguished by his mannerisms, and attributed with character deformation, like the sodomite, the masculine "tribade," or the effeminate and narcissistic courtier.[7] The erotic knight is not characterized by "the definitive traits of a particular sexual type,"[8] being only a literary figure, not an actual person. However, the erotic knight, with other sexual types, shares manifestations of ideological constructions that "extend beyond sexuality,"[9] and that expand both the erotic space within which the culture imagined sexuality and that push the boundaries of literary criticism and "disciplinary authority"[10] within which sexuality is debated in historical and theoretical terms. As a literary figure of erotic historiography, the erotic knight is not a fixed type in the sense that his fictionalized erotic life takes a number of forms and casts the knight in a number of different roles. The erotic knight shares some of the characteristics of the sexual figures that appear in other literary genres, such as poetry and drama, but because the knight's fictionalized life is not bound with anxiety or presented as subversive or socially threatening, his sexuality and the desires that drive him to other knights and men make him one of the most flexible erotic types in early modern fiction, absorbing valences of sexual agency and erotic desire. As a literary erotic type that does not fit a specific sexual type as defined in historicist interpretations of eroticism, the erotic knight poses a challenge to both the historical field and the sexual domain. He interrupts "the universalizing scope of historicism" that often "moot[s] different makers of sexuality for the sake of categories claimed to be more general,"[11] helping to open up the field of sexuality, not by a difference that is historically determined, but by the difference of a literary genre, itself produced through an interaction with other texts, with which romance shares both the stylizing strategies and cultural investment in the ways of knowing and articulating the East. The scope of sexual and erotic possibilities characteristic of the erotic knight will show that the literary past of sexuality cannot be reduced "to one of mere difference or development."[12] Displaced in places geographically remote from England, wrapped in an anachronistic literary milieu, and belonging to a genre generally associated with a high level of fantasy, the erotic knight has more freedom than other types to negotiate his erotic fantasies and his sexual body to unexpected invitations that the unknown, curious, and strange world of the Eastern Mediterranean provides. Yet by precisely displacing the erotic body of the knight in the exotic milieu of romance writing, romances actually exercise their own narrative versions of control of the male body thus eroticized. By keeping the erotic body of the knight confined mostly to the East, the narratives of prose romances indicate that erotic discourses in popular literature are subject to a strict control of erotic discourses on the part of a culture that acknowledges unhindered sexuality as something that does not belong to national space, but that befits the foreign and the faraway, where wonders and mysteries freely occur. As a literary figure of sexuality, therefore, the erotic knight is a site of frequent demystifications of critical assertions hitherto made about the crossover between national politics and male sexuality.

In the early modern period, masculinity was "an inter-related and variable mix of three main factors: genital signs, somatic deeds ... and behavioral indicators."[13] Scholars writing on masculinity across several disciplines, including literary and social history, are still mapping the historical and conceptual territory of what it meant to be a man in the early modern period. The historical and philological story of masculinity that is emerging from romances offers a specific perspective on the subject because this gendered story is the product of different yet closely intertwined discourses that had defined masculinity for a long time – travel, chivalry, combat, friendship, and mercantilism. These discourses and ideological projections work together within the locus of one figure, the knight, to produce a range of ideas about masculinity, male sexuality, and affection between men at the crossroads of the narratives of romantic quest and the commercial and mental "discovery" of the East. While the ideas about masculinity in romances could not be classified as experiential evidence of male behaviour, they are not "foolish beliefs"[14] either, because they reflect the ways in which a specific genre imagined for its male and female readers alternative debates, new ways of imagining the sex and gender of men, and of male roles in society, outside the religious, political, and medical discourses about sexuality that shaped the knowledge about the body and sexuality in the early modern period. The other side of chivalric masculinity, the one that reveals itself when the knight diverts himself from courtship and combat, is a provocation to political homosociality that leads to commercial ends, a challenge to romantic chivalry driven by the ideology of conjugal marriage and procreation and the pressure put on men to embody social ideals and fulfill the goals set out for them by the political and social culture at home.

Erotic Ethnography

Translations of the classical romances by Longus, Achilles Tatius, and Heliodorus exerted a major influence on erotic writing in early modern England, especially in prose fiction. English translations of these classical writers were readily available by the second half of the sixteenth century, and they seemed to have become hugely popular among writers of fiction. The structural and thematic elements of fictions written by these classical authors have deeply informed the narrative and stories of the vernacular romances in the sixteenth and seventeenth centuries.[15] These three classical writers also influenced non-fictional writing as well. Contemporary texts about the Eastern Mediterranean, in which the body and desire become the filters through which the East is described, understood, mystified, and misunderstood imbued romances with the material for fiction. One of the striking features of mercantile romances is their power to fictionalize close male–male relationships both within and across ethnic lines in the East. In this chapter I demonstrate how both fictional and non-fictional accounts of erotic practices in the Eastern Mediterranean create a discourse of erotic ethnography and, particularly in relation to male sexuality, as a source of strategic (and pleasurable) alliances with men from the East. Masculinity and male sexuality are therefore not only imagined in the fictions of the Eastern Mediterranean, but through them the Eastern Mediterranean also becomes a cultural text about sexual difference, uncontrolled desires, and sexual violence, of intimacies between men, and of a libidinal history different from that of the Christian West. Yet criticism about male sexuality in early modern England has not explored the subject of masculinity and male sexuality in prose romances at any greater length.[16]

Yet in fictions about the Eastern Mediterranean the narratives of undoing the gender of a man lie at the heart of the European perception and interpretation of that space. We have been accustomed to read in criticism about the sexual liberties and transgressions that the western traveller purportedly observed in the East. Thus, in early modern writing sodomy was frequently troped as a Catholic and Muslim sin. Notoriously, for example, Robert Greene writes in *The Spanish Masquerado* (1589) that the Roman cardinals' pride, shown in their dress, reflects the lechery and sodomy in their lives:

> their Sodomie, as they kepe not very secrete, for they in their Palaces, imitating the heathen God IVPITER, gette them Ganimedes, which ... serue for Pages: yet theey as much as they can obscure, but their Lechery they feare not to make manifest, as being fathers of many Bastardes, and Paramours of sundrye Courtizans.[17]

This is an example of the kind of rhetoric and mythical iconography associated with the sodomitical figure of Ganymede; it was a frequent feature of Protestant propaganda against Catholicism. While the period's fear of Muslims became a trope in anti-Islamic writing, the actual threat of the Islamic invasion of Europe was often relativized and, in writing, it was played off against the religious tyranny of Catholicism. Thus John Foxe writes in his 1580 treatise, *The Pope Confuted*: "I became not a little doubtfull in mine imagination, whether the tyrannie of the Turke haue more grieuously wounded the Christian common weale, or the doctrine of the Pope hath beene more preiudiciall too the Gospel of Christ."[18] In the Newberry Library copy of Foxe's book, an anonymous reader underlined this passage, suggesting that the passage is important to him or her, as well as to the cultural moment in which the reading occurred. This kind of presentation was not surprising, given England's recent history with the Spanish Armada and the anxiety over Philip II's threat to invade Britain. It also reflects the changing relationship that England had developed with Turkey in the 1580s, a transition from hostility to commercial and diplomatic exchange, whose purpose was partly to counter Spain's economic and military power in the Mediterranean.

Critics have documented the English travellers' sometimes obsessive attention to the somatic habits of Muslims. Among them, Bartholomeus Georgeuiz's treatise, *The offspring of the house of Ottomano* (1569) is no exception. Yet, unlike most writers on the subject who pay attention to male bodies, Georgeuiz is interested in details of male anatomy and in the practices that concern male bodies, as they appear to him within a foreign cultural milieu. In that respect Georgeuiz's homosocial eye follows the habit of many other traveller-ethnographers who write about the social and gendered practices of Muslims. Like Nicolas de Nicholay, for example, Georgeuiz describes in some detail the dervishes (different orders of Muslim friars "who have taken vows of poverty and austere life"),[19] paying some attention to their practice of inserting a ring ("of the weight of three pounds" [D4r]) in their penis to prevent intercourse. The weight of the ring is exaggerated and a product of Georgeuiz's own fantasy about the strangeness of the custom and the religious figure he is describing. But the strangeness of his description in this respect also draws attention to his curious, even queer, fascination with the dervish's member, fascination that makes his interest in the cultural and religious status and significance of the dervish almost secondary to his interest in the marker of his status by his genitals. Georgeuiz also describes circumcision, which English travellers never failed to observe, and the method by which it was performed,[20] conflating in his description ethnic and erotic difference from the westerner, whose site, again, is the Muslim man's penis. He also tells a story about the young male captives (known as janizary) from other parts of the Ottoman Empire, who were taken away from their families, converted to Islam, circumcised, and turned into soldiers or high state officials, either in the sultan's court in Constantinople or in governing distant provinces in the Ottoman Empire.[21] Muslims' marriage practices for women interest Georgeuiz only as a means of curbing men's lust and erotic violence,[22] a projection, perhaps, of the arguments in favour of marriage in early Christianity.[23] This kind of male-centred writing not only reflects the interest of one masculinist culture in the affairs of men in another such culture; it also creates the sort of textual environment within which the male-oriented stories of romances set in the Eastern Mediterranean originate. Such "microhistories,"[24] writing in which the author's focus is on recording the erotic habits or corporeal details of eastern subjects, create textual conditions for sexual and erotic differences to be explored and expanded in the figurative language of romances.

Contrary to some arguments about the effeminizing effect of the Eastern Mediterranean, travel writing imagines it as masculinist, if curious and strange in that regard. Travel accounts that registered the sexual practices of Muslims tend to oscillate between abhorrence and ambiguity, treating sodomy, at best, as an ethnic idiosyncrasy.

Almost routinely infusing any writing about Muslims, this kind of imbalance in anti-religious representations of Catholics and Muslims, redirected in discourses on sodomy, was the result, on the one hand, of a growing cultural awareness of the importance of the Ottomans in the expansion of English trading interests, and, on the other, to the activities of Catholic Spain in Mediterranean trade. This view of the Ottoman Empire puts the English perceptions of the sexual proclivities of Muslims in a different light. But, as I argue in this chapter, romances offer a different story of sexual desire in the Ottoman Mediterranean from that presented in travel and ethnographic writing.

By the time these cultural conditions had aligned themselves to such representations of Asia Minor in ethnographic writing about the Eastern Mediterranean, however, there already existed literature with romance elements that furnished plots about contacts between men from the East and West. These became literary intertext, if not direct sources, for the narratives in the 1590s romances. Early Italian novellas, in E.C. Pettet's words, reflected "something of a new bourgeois and urban society," and they "did to a certain extent transform the traditional background of romance." Pettet refers to a shift in setting, where "shepherds and shepherdesses" were substituted with "knights and their ladies."[25] But this is only part of the story.

In addition to furnishing plots for Renaissance city comedy, Italian novellas anticipated the plots of romances. One such novella sheds a particularly noteworthy light not only on the development of romances but, more specifically, on the shaping of discourses of affective friendship, central to romance, and the homoeroticism that sometimes accompanies it. It is the ninth story of the tenth day, about Torello and Saladine, from Giovanni Boccaccio's *Decameron*, retold as the twentieth "nouell," "Of Maister Thorello and Saladine," by William Painter in *The Palace of Pleasure* (1567).[26] The story of Sultan Saladin's act of grace to a knight originates in early medieval romances, but it is Boccaccio's version of it that is taken up by the writers of humanist fiction.[27] Lorna Hutson has demonstrated the influence of Painter's version of the story on Ben Jonson's city comedy, *Every Man in His Humour*.[28] The original story in Boccaccio involves the wealthy and hospitable merchant, Torello, from Pavia, and Saladin, the twelfth-century Sultan of Egypt and Syria, who, in Painter's story, travels from Alexandria "into Christendom disguised as a Cypriot merchant in order to gain intelligence of Christian preparations for another Crusade."[29] Painter's version of the story contains many romance formulas: sea travels, miraculous events, magicians, curious coincidences, disguises, and mistaken identities. At the end of the tangled narrative, the Pavian husband and wife are reunited just at the moment when things could have gone the other way.

As Hutson has shown in relation to Jonson's *Every Man in His Humour*, Painter's story acted as a conduit for the homoerotic desire that originated in Boccaccio and that defines the erotic charge between Thorello and Saladine. Thorello (Boccaccio's Messer Torello) turns from a merchant into a *miles christianus*,[30] a crusading knight, when he decides to join the Crusades, only to become the object of Saladine's affection when he discovers his erstwhile Pavian hosts imprisoned in Alexandria. He then decides to return the hospitality he received from Thorello when he lodged with him in Pavia. Earlier, when Saladine was about to leave Pavia, he was "mutch greeued" because "so farre in he was already in loue with him [Thorello]."[31] When Thorello is about to return to Pavia, Saladine says: "before I byd you farewell, I pray you for the loue and friendship that is betwene vs, that you do remember me if it be possible before our dayes do end, after you haue giuen order to your affayres in Lombardie, to come agayne to see me before I dye."[32] Tearful, Thorello leaves Saladine, promising that it "impossible that euer hee should forget ... his worthy friendship," and Saladine reciprocates, "louingly imbracing and kissing him."[33] Painter's version of the story of commercial intelligence turns into a narrative of affective contact between men. "Syr, it may come to passe, that we may let you see our merchaudise, the better to confirme your beleefe,"[34] says Saladine in reply to Messer Torello's inquiry about the nature of his wares. But Painter's fiction, the story in which Thorello participates (and of which Saladine seeks intelligence), does not develop into a narrative of mercantile exchange. Rather, it becomes a fiction about the symbolic exchange of friendship, and about the ambiguity (even incoherence) of emotions that accompany that exchange. This kind of story-telling strategy is characteristic of the conflict between friendship and love, and of the privileging of friendship over love, in romances.

In Boccaccio's version of the story the homoerotic charge emanating from Saladine is more apparent than in Painter's rendering of the story,[35] and it is balanced by Messer Torello's measured expressions of gratitude and amicability, rather than excessive emotional longing. The image of the "Ethnicke and vnbeleuyng man,"[36] that, appearing in the brief allegory of hospitality involving Ietro and Abraham (not in Boccaccio), anticipates Saladine at the beginning of Painter's fiction, turns into a story about the shrewd political calculation of a Muslim, oaths of friendship between a Muslim and a Christian, and the Italian's acquisition of riches through the generosity of the Muslim friend. The parity of friendship does not produce a correlative equity in the exchange of wealth. Yet the bond between the two men is further complicated. Thorello swiftly returns to Pavia (on a magic bed covered in gems, provided by Saladine's magicians ["Nycramancers"])[37] where he realizes that the period that his wife must wait for him to return before she is allowed to marry again is about to run out. The ring that Saladine gives Thorello as a gift for his wife, Adalietta, in addition to the ring that Adalietta had given Thorello as a token of her loyalty to him in his absence, is intended not only to bond the Pavian couple together but also to preserve the already established bond between Thorello and Saladine. The objects discarded in a symbolic exchange of wealth – Saladine's ring, the stones and jewellery on the magic bed, the other gifts given as proof of friendship and love – do not simply anticipate romance. As commodities signifying the East, they are features of an exchange that link giving to moral obligation, in the way Marcel Mauss describes the nature of the gift, as having the obligation to give, to receive, and to repay.[38] In the concrete scenarios of an exchange of gifts that carry intimate resonance with them, such as giving a ring, the process of receiving the gift, repaying it, and giving something in return translates into affective and by extension even erotic symbolism that, in this instance, frames the story of Thorello and Saladine. The sexual dimension of this gift exchange is not far from the economic and emotional exchanges that have already taken place. Along with the narrative of the exchange of hospitality, oaths of friendship, and Thorello's unsuccessful crusades, these acts of material exchange also point to a re-evaluation of the notion of honour in humanist fiction, a process that will continue in romances. For in Painter's fiction, honour is not measured by chivalric deeds enacted against the unbeliever, but by the oaths of friendship against the background of commercial traffic between West and East, which assures a profitable and, as both Thorello and Saladine would wish, a lifelong bond. Even the love narrative, characteristic of romance throughout its long tradition, privileges, in the story-telling space given to it, the emotional exchange between men, rather than that between a man and a woman. (It is, after all, Thorello's jealousy, not romantic love, that urges him to return to Pavia.) In this narrative scenario, marriage is a purely economic institution, assured through an exchange of affect between two men, affect that is also built into the gifts meant to confirm the permanence of the union between men.

Marriage is an event of secondary importance in both Boccaccio and Painter, as it is saved by chance and the magic of a Muslim man. Painter's novella furnishes us with an important discursive background for a discussion of homoeroticism in Mediterranean romances not only because of its romance elements, but also because it anticipates the kind of homosocial exchange characteristic of the commercial and emotional transactions between eastern and western men in romances of the Eastern Mediterranean.

In his book on male same-sex eroticism in early modern literature, Daniel Juan Gil argues for an "asocial sexuality," which brings male characters outside the social sphere into contact, representing a departure from critical arguments about sexuality bound to social life.[39] Both Painter's story and romances in general demonstrate that homoerotic charge and homosocial desire are not so much "inextricably intertwined with other registers of early modern social life,"[40] as Gil suggests, as they are integral to those "registers" that defined social life in early modern England. The closest register we have of the intimate lives of men is the humanist rhetoric of the oaths of friendship (and generally the writing about friendship) between socially equal men. Such oaths of friendship depended on the social situation between, for example, two aristocrats or two friends from university days.[41] Those oaths were the foundation of what Alan Bray has described as "an essentially private relationship that is necessarily set apart from the commerce and practice of the world."[42] However, as the example from Boccaccio and Painter show, private relationships in romance literature are negotiated through the language of commerce, and by extension politics, and they are sealed, in material terms, as gifts that are cultural signifiers of commercial and political discourses that have brought the men of these fictions together. The language available for articulating the intimacy between men was the language of commercial exchange and the contractual relationships that are part of that exchange, or the language of friendship, which has a particular relevance for neo-chivalric literature because of a long history of what I will call chivalric intimacy in the social and political culture of chivalry, and in romance literature. Men engaged in these processes of oaths of friendship and commercial transactions come to these states from within social life, and therefore the meaning of their exchanges with other men is culturally and socially produced. Prose romances (unlike *The Faerie Queene*, one of Gil's examples) are a good illustration of a genre that stands in contrast to Gil's notion of "asocial sexuality," because any meaning in them, including homoerotic interactions, emerges through a critical decoding of the story-telling and rhetorical technique of their social allegories and of the social agency of men that drives any kind of relationship between them.

In her analysis of several stories from Painter's collection, Hutson argues that Painter's stories "relocate the social agency of masculinity, and of male friendship, in the mastery of strategies for the evaluation and imitation of persuasive texts" and that, therefore, "any historicist criticism, especially a feminist criticism, needs to pay attention to them."[43] Queer early modern criticism could also pay attention to these kinds of contractual negotiations and exchanges between men, as the basis for analyses of early modern masculinity. There is no need to argue against the view that early modern queer criticism and explorations of masculinity have had very little to say about early modern fictions, especially romances.[44] To follow up on Hutson, though, one could ask what specific evaluative and imitative strategies these fictions invite, and what do they have to offer to a masculinist criticism, especially queer analyses? While I agree with Hutson that feminist criticism should be attentive to these fictions, I would push her argument even further and say that criticism and theories of masculinity should be even more aware of these fictions because at their centre are men who are conducting themselves as active agents in a variety of exchanges and in a production of persuasive arguments.[45] In this respect these stories are not-too-distant antecedents of the romantic fictions in which contacts between cross-ethnic men are "evaluated" in narratives describing oaths of friendship, cross-ethnic marriages, joint travel, and chivalric fraternity.

For students of the literary history of sexuality, especially homosexuality, romances offer an opportunity to explore strands of that history in which these forms of desire were not always bound up with suffering, denunciation, and violence. Here, analysis need not always lead to conclusions about difference, transgression, dissidence, and subversion of the social order. The long tradition of romance writing involving love and the idiosyncrasies of which love is made naturalized the ambiguities of love and desire as part of their romantic narratives, thus making love adaptable to the vicissitudes of romance plots. If it appears to us that romances are free of homoerotic scenarios, as we know them from Renaissance drama and poetry, it is because in romances love and desire are invested in other manifestations of men's social agency, like friendship, travel, and commerce, as well as being a separate discourse of intimacy and sex as an act. In that regard, romances are, again, a palimpsestic genre in which multiple desires accommodate larger political and cultural issues. Homoeroticism in romances is not denaturalized but naturalized through those discourses.[46]

Unlike feminist criticism, which has examined female sexuality in romances, scholarship on male sexuality has largely neglected the prose romances of the sixteenth and the seventeenth centuries, mostly, though not entirely, because drama and lyrical poetry have for a long time dominated the field of sexuality criticism in early modern studies. In the substantial, and still growing, body of critical writing about romances, politics, gender, and print history characterize this area of literary scholarship. Cross-dressing as an index of emasculation and, through that, of homoerotic masculinity, as some critics have interpreted the donning of women's clothes in Sidney's *Arcadia*, has for a long time been a topic that registered critics' interest in romances' investment in male sexuality.[47] But romances engage with male eroticism at a much deeper level than Protestant entrepreneurialism, ethical judgment, and political ambition, which are heavily promoted in the genre. For instance, in his *Arcadia*, Philip Sidney complicates the notion of the hero's masculinity through androgyny, which he stylizes in different ways and for different purposes.[48] In his female disguise as Zelmane, the knight Pyrocles becomes a figure that incarnates both masculinity and femininity. Zelmane's androgyny, asserted by Constance Jordan's "exemplary for both men and women,"[49] is employed by Sidney as a device that empowers, rather than weakens, both genders. For Jordan, androgyny thus fictionalized by Sidney runs counter to the views of "many modern feminists,"[50] who hold the view that "sexuality necessarily defines behavior," a view that does not allow for much latitude in gendered representations in the early modern period. Yet as Sidney's and other romances of the period, especially those that imitate *Arcadia* show, the loss of the attributes traditionally valorized as either masculine or feminine often represent the ways of positively expanding gender possibilities for both male and female characters. In *Arcadia*, and as, for instance, in Emanuel Forde's *Ornatus and Artesia* (?1595), written in imitation of Sidney's romance, cross-dressing is a device secondary to something more important that prose romances are engaged with on many levels of their narratives: power relations between male and female characters. As Laura Levine suggests, writing about early modern cross-dressing, in instances in literature where men don women's clothing, the issue is not whether it is not "worse for men to wear women's clothing than for women to wear men's,"[51] but with what sort of power a narrative device like cross-dressing imbues the gendered body of a male character. The masculinity of the knight-errant is made to appear anxious[52] in romances of the East, not because his romantic role supersedes his political purpose, but because the challenge of defeating Muslims and other allegorical obstacles that stand for Islam are often presented as too big to overcome, even if the knight succeeds in defeating them in the end. This degree of liberty in imagining the power and permissiveness of male sexual energy in romances of the East in these sixteenth- and seventeenth-century fictions was "Protestant erotic propaganda,"[53] whose readers came from all classes. This propaganda also had its vocal enemies among Puritans who attacked romances on moral grounds but who could not stop the endless flow of production and growing consumption of this cheaply printed and titillating literature in early modern England.

"Whoredome and sodometrie": Socio-erotic Anxiety and the Politics of Fiction

Returning to Painter, the "nonbeliever" Saladine in Painter's story is not the stock sodomite Muslim upon which Protestant England displaced its anxieties about sodomy.[54] What the story of Saladine and Thorello illustrates is how humanist fiction turns the historical Saladine, the leader of the Muslim struggle against Christians, into the central figure of a story in which reciprocal hospitality and an exchange of oaths of friendship became ways of imagining masculinity as an affective bond produced by mercantile exchange. This mercantile homosociality runs counter to the fading ideal of militant crusading Christianity, which, in any case, as a discourse, is lost in Painter's story, even though it is what initially brings men into contact with one another. It is this redefinition of masculinity, from chivalric and combative to reflective and hospitable, that apparently reduces the social gap between a Christian merchant and a Muslim sultan, a relationship that is offered to the reader as a proto-bourgeois, not chivalric, version of masculinity.

The new angle from which England viewed Asia Minor, and the earlier literary versions of the contacts between western and Muslim men, all contributed to the versions of the stories of men in which affective exchanges, not the horror of sodomy, were the subject of literature. What is new about romances is that, when Muslim masculinity comes into contact with its western counterpart, and especially when it becomes a conduit for the homoerotic pleasures for the West, sodomy is less often regarded as a stigma. Sodomy and Turkey have been frequent topics in queer early modern criticism, attempting to examine the cultural resonances of the word "sodomy" for the sexual politics within the early modern world, and not just accept that the word is only a term of deprecation, one frequently used to denigrate Muslims.[55] Alan Stewart has argued persuasively that accusations of sodomy followed a shift in social relations when the humanist system of values was replaced by another set of social relations.[56] The change from the earlier deprecation of Muslims, deriving from the history-long anti-religious stance, to a pragmatic relationship with the Ottomans that appeared both lucrative and threatening, gave rise to some of the sodomy-inflected writing against Muslims. But romances responded to this changing discursive practice by extending moments of male same-sex desire, both across and within racial and religious lines, by turning them into fictions of pleasure between early modern men. As literary fictions of these changed social relationships, they help me shift Stewart's argument about sodomy in a different direction. Romances show that the new contacts with Asia Minor gave rise to fictions in which an illicit sexual act is replaced with intense emotions shared among friends or trading equals. The Eastern Mediterranean described in travel and ethnographic writing was thus rewritten in romances from a place in which sodomy was recorded with disapproving curiosity to an arena for a display of affective exchanges between men.

William Parry's *A New and large discourse of the Trauels of Sir Anthony Sherley Knight, by Sea, and ouer Land, to the Persian Empire* (1601), an account of Sherley's travels in the East, not only summarizes some of the commonplaces in the representation of early modern homoerotic desire when it meets the Orient, frequently reiterated in queer early modern criticism, but, more important, shows how the rhetorical and genre conventions of ethnographic writing enable the circulation of homoerotic discourses in the imaginative prose of the period. After a banquet at the court of the Kurdish king, who was entertained "with boyes and Curtizans,"[57] Parry says, Anthony retired to his house, where a Catholic friar also found accommodation. But the first night at Sir Anthony's house the friar

> found the means to haue a Persian curtezan to lie with him, and so had night by night during his continuance there; which if he wanted, hee would hyre a boy sodomitically to vse. And that he was a sodomiticall wretch, it

> dooth appeare thereby: Sir Anthony at his first commiting, brought twoo Christian boies in the market, which afterwardes he bestowed on this Frier, whose name was Nicolao de Melo. He no sooner had them, but he was in hand with them concerning his sodomiticall villany. The boyes finding whereso hee was inclined (being incessantly importuned to his that solde them, hee likewise to the officer, the officer to the King), by meanes whereof the king espied his villany. Whereuppon the king send for the boyes from him, and send him worde, that were it not for sir Anthonies sake, he should loose his head.[58]

Parry appears to attribute this experience to Anthony Sherley, yet there is no evidence that Parry's version of the story is reliable. Rather, his narrative reaffirms the idea of reality that some of his contemporaries believed in. In the writing of traveller-ethnographers eyewitness experience often competes with cultural bias and prejudice.[59] Sherley expected to find sodomy in the East, and thus he apparently saw it. Yet the passage from Sherley's text is less a record of a scene he witnessed and more a self-consciously crafted fiction that engages a number of homoerotic scenarios, from the cliché of an infidel nobleman indulging in sordid luxuriousness to the more curious detail of procuring Christian boys for the sexual use of an older Catholic priest, an episode in which the culturally expected scenario of obtaining a slave on the eastern market becomes the obverse of the usual narrative concerning the discourse of homoeroticism in English narratives, where the disparity in age and status between a man of higher rank with a younger man of lower status, or, in this case, of no status, are the basis on which historicism discusses sexual difference. That this is also an occasion for Parry, writing about Sherley, who was Catholic, to invent an anti-Catholic narrative is also obvious from the choice of the figure of the old lecher. This account sets up Christian boys as bait, through a chain of informers that goes all the way to the king about to have the sodomitical friar killed. Parry's account of Sherley's story does not offer his readers evidence of the allegedly riotous homosexuality in the Eastern Mediterranean, but provides them with a familiar fiction involving a sodomitical Catholic friar, which makes homosexuality not a foreign but a familiar sin, and not heinous either. Anthony, after all, saves the Catholic priest from death at the hands of the infidel king, himself presented as a sodomite earlier in the text. Parry's narrative is self-consciously concerned with inventing a foreignness that enables sinful sexuality to circulate in fictions shared among his readers at home in England.

Anthony Sherley, however, never travelled to Asia Minor, although his brother Thomas was imprisoned there.

Because of its remove from Protestant England, the Eastern Mediterranean became a suitable location for displacing narratives of non-reproductive sexuality. There, the continent body of an English knight could exercise and display desires that were otherwise controlled by the strict prescriptions of Protestant morality and codes of somatic behaviour at home. While Parry's text links sodomy to Asia Minor, it also makes it a speculative possibility for his English readers, who would have read his travelogue not only as reportage but also as a text intended to inspire new travels. The narrative model within which Sherley's fiction imagines sexual encounters between men correlates with similar fantasies in romances, where homoerotic narratives often take the form of a digression intended to offer respite from the arduous travel of the wandering knight. As the remaining pages of this chapter show, these episodes are often presented as entertainment.

Occurring at the moment of England's entry into the arena of trade with the Turks, the presenting of the Ottoman Mediterranean as a home of sexual vices became a frequent ethnographic cliché and narrative formula in literary defamations of the Ottomans. At the turn of the century, during a series of Ottoman financial crises, when the empire was particularly vulnerable to western political interests, there was hardly a western traveller to the Levant who did not associate the Ottoman Mediterranean, especially its emperors, with sodomy. That association became a form of shorthand for the West's obsessive denunciation of the Ottomans. Robert Couverte, a traveller, observes that the Persians "are common Buggerers, as the Turks are."[60] Yet when Fynes Moryson reports that after the death of the Turkish sultan Amuranth, his son sent out of the court all of his father's "sodomieticall boyes," the common rhetorical jibe against the Ottomans receives an implicit rebuttal, as Moryson's observation implies that the Ottomans themselves dealt with sodomy harshly, and did not indulge in it freely, as many other English accounts suggest.[61] The emphasis on sodomy in English travel accounts says more about the English responses to sodomy in the period than about the sexual practices of the Ottomans. It is a matter of cultural rhetoric infused with prejudice, not an accurate ethnographic recounting of intimacy.

The English prejudice about the sordid nature of the Islamic Mediterranean, shared by the Christian West, is best demonstrated in the chapter called "The oriental Peregrination" in Nicholas de Nicolay's account of his travels in the Mediterranean. Nicolay says that "the Ilands and Coastes of the Sea Mediterane, [are] giuen all to whoredome, sodometrie, theft, and all other most detestable vices, lyuing onely of routings, spoyles, & pilings at the seas, and the Ilande, beyonde them."[62] Just as in Nicolay's narrative the poverty and desolation of the Eastern Mediterranean gives rise to sodomy and lewdness, so in romances the desolate Natolia becomes the breeding ground for illicit desire. In his account of travels to Jerusalem, Gaza, "Grand Cayro" and Alexandria, Henry Timberlake pauses to observe that the Ottomans living in the Holy Land "vse the sinne of Sodom and Gomorah very much in that country," so much so, in fact that,

> the poor Christians that inhabit therein, are glad to marry their daughters at twelve yeares of age vnto Christians, least the Turks should rauish them: and to co[n]clued, there is not that sine in the world, but it is vsed there amongst those Infidells that now inhabit therein, and yet it is called Terra Sanctra.[63]

In this account, sodomy is imagined to be a sin that only vaguely has anything to do with men. More pointedly, it is imagined as a sin that threatens Christian maidens. The intersection of religion and erotic violence fits the early modern discourse of the infidel invasion to the lands of old Christianity in the Eastern Mediterranean, by presenting the infidel, unlike the implied Christian assumed in the background of such narratives, as incapable of sexual renunciation. Yet this kind of emphatic denigration of the Infidel is emphasized by the specific Christian context, the Holy Land, which, because of its biblical significance, animated some of the most pronounced denunciations ofi in early modern literature. In Timberlake, the discourse of sodomitical sex becomes a way of denigrating Muslims, not a comment on the material practice of sexual habits observed at the centre of the Ottoman state. But the biblical land of the East has also become a hiding place for illicit sexuality presented as a pleasure of the East to English readers. What these early ethnographers record as evidence is very likely a projection of their own perception of sodomy in the Islamic Mediterranean, a view shaped by prejudicial discourse about it in the West. But looked at from the perspective of the Islamic Mediterranean, the picture of male–male intimacy appears to be different from the fantasies told in English romances.

Assessing discourses that presented male same-sex contacts in the Ottoman world of the Mediterranean in the early modern period,

Khaled El-Rouayheb has documented in detail the valences of affective contacts between men within the strongly homosocial world of the Ottoman East, arguing that these bonds are formed typically across a significant age difference between an adult male and a beardless boy and do not correlate to homosexual acts and behaviour. He has thus concluded, "The concept of male homosexuality did not exist in the Arab–Islamic Middle East in the early Ottoman period."[64] In this regard, at least, the early modern Ottoman Mediterranean was like early modern England, since in both worlds same-sex contacts and affects between men did not correlate with the notion of homosexuality. But unlike the English Renaissance where, as Alan Bray has demonstrated, male friendship seems to have been the only affective social bond between men that occupied both private and public spaces, the Ottoman Mediterranean recognized a variety of such bonds and responded to them in a range of discourses, especially involving adult men and boys. When English travel writers appear to be shocked at the "sin" of sodomy in Asia Minor it is more likely that they are strategically misreading local practices in order to warn their English readers of the social disapproval of the act of sodomy as such, superimposing the western horror of the act of sodomy over social practices whose meaning within a specific cultural context escaped them. Framing the male–male contacts presented in fictional discourses on "Turkish sodomy" from travel writing is thus not the most appropriate route for explaining what those contacts may symbolize in literature. Proto-ethnographic texts that dwell on the eroticism and sexual habits of eastern spaces use sex and sexual practices as one of the key ways of differentiating the East from the West, emasculating the East and presenting the West as more visceral and as a critical observer of the exoticism of eastern sexualities. But to read such accounts as always only about the subordination, denigration, and effeminization of the East is to offset any pleasure and any liberating effect they might have had for early modern readers to whom religious writing presented sodomy as the most heinous crime. In a sense, then, such reported or imagined sexual scenarios originating in the East, transmitted through travel writing, affect the reading and interpretation of sexual "sins" and alter the moral charge associated with illicit sexuality. In that sense, travel writing, like romances, participates in the production of literary fantasies about sex and sexuality at home by textualizing accounts from abroad.

Romances and travel writing make the unruliness of the infidel body one of the key ethnic traits of the Eastern Mediterranean. Once transgressive male desire is made into a foreign sin – Muslim, Spanish, Italian, Jewish, or Catholic – the implication is that the sin cannot be English. When Robert Burton refers to sodomy as "the Diana of the Romans," turning the goddess of the hunt into a sodomitical seducer who sets off from Rome but moves into other Italian cities, his rhetoric, like that of Reginald Foxe, is first a denigration of Catholics, and only afterwards includes "the Asiaticks" and the Turks.[65] Yet what is often missed in assessments of these accounts of sodomy in the Islamic world is that they were mostly used as additional arguments to prop up anti-Catholic propaganda, thus continuing a long history of prejudice as well as serving the specific purposes of religious rivalries. The sexuality and sexual proclivities of eastern men is one of the most resonant fantasies of travel writing in the Eastern Mediterranean. This fantasy permeates English writing about the space that stretches from the east coast of the Adriatic Sea to Constantinople and it has left a deep imprint in prose romances as well. Granted, the social history of sex in the region gave sufficient material for the fictions of sex to fire up the imagination of romance writers, and such history sometimes helps us see why in romances of the East this narrative became a fertile ground for fictions of homosexuality. This was the case not just with the parts of the Eastern Mediterranean inhabited by non-Christians but also in the areas inhabited by Christians.

In the Eastern Mediterranean, stories of sodomy among the Ottomans even prompted the enactment of anti-sodomitical laws and decrees, modelled on similar laws in Venice, Florence, and some other Italian cities in late fifteenth and early sixteenth century.[66] This occurred in Ragusa (Dubrovnik), where such laws were put into practice at the end of the fifteenth and in the early sixteenth century as part of a raft of measures against Ottoman rule in the hinterland of the Ragusan Republic in the southeast Adriatic.[67] Yet Ragusa's draconian anti-sodomitical law was less a reflection of a protective response against Ottoman sexual practices and more an expression of the authorities' wish to safeguard the city "at a time when an avalanche of novelties was threatening the old values" of this prosperous free city-state.[68] Unlike Venice, where only the passive partner was punished, in Ragusa both the passive and the active subjects in the sodomitical act were punished. The *Liber Croecus* (The Yellow Book), which the Ragusan authorities produced as a way of policing sodomy in this powerful and wealthy city state, lays down the anti-sodomitical law, saying that "whether active or passive, his head should be amputated and afterwards his whole body should be cremated and incinerated."[69] This legal practice represented the social situation on the social and cultural boundary between the Christian West and the Islamic East, in a place that in many ways was a protector of the West against further Muslim incursion. It kept the Turks at bay, in the hinterland, by paying a high price in yearly ransom for the freedom that ransom gave the citizens of Ragusa. Although "the Ottomans' menace" was one of the threats against which the Ragusan authorities wanted to protect their republic (a danger that seemed to grow after the Ottomans had consolidated their rule in the Balkan peninsula, which lay in the immediate hinterland of Ragusa), the anti-sodomitical decrees do not seem to suggest a specific cultural awareness of sodomy among Muslims. More likely, the decrees may have been a response to rampant sodomy in some Italian cities.[70] While it is likely that the Ragusan anti-sodomitical decrees betray domestic anxiety over sodomy, common in the period, they may also reflect the early modern paranoia over the spread of sodomy in the growing urban and mercantile centres in the world beyond this republic – places that profited from the flux of foreign traders and whose financial and commercial activities had started to compete with the interests of local merchants. As was often the case in this period, sodomy became a convenient and most effective discursive tool by which disapproval of public practices seen to threaten domestic interests could be voiced.

Scholars of early modern lesbianism have argued that one of the reasons that female same-sex eroticism does not incur anxiety or become connected with abomination is that in the patriarchal culture of the Renaissance, in which so much is at stake for men invested with public power, women's domesticated culture mattered less within the public sphere.[71] Apparently less socially disruptive and destabilizing than male homosexuality, lesbianism was less likely to be registered in literature than male sodomy. Indeed, a passage from *Amadis de Gaule* (1567) is one of the rare instances of explicit "lesbianism" in prose romances. The daughter of Mars, Alastraxeree, tells in detail how she was abducted by Arlanda. She says that Arlanda would carry her "into a house of pleasure, where she helde me fast and close, & daily solicited me to loue hir, using to mewards, gestures and amorous countenances, nother less [nonetheless] her more than if she had spoken to Florisell."[72] This kind of sexual enticement between women, which in its explicitness surpasses the more numerous erotic contacts between men (these are often shrouded in allegory or subsumed in disguise), confirm the literary evidence offered by feminist queer scholarship.[73] The construction of non-disruptive lesbianism in early modern literature is close to imagining male same-sex desire, even sodomy, in prose romances. The representation of male sodomy is hardly ever shown to be disruptive in romances. In fact, sodomy and other valences of male intimacy in romances are affirmed positively in the fictions that involve knights-errant who come from different but culturally related Christian backgrounds. What licenses fictions of male homoeroticism and dissociates them from anxiety is that romances are set in the mythical and exotic lands of the Eastern Mediterranean, far away from the rigorous proscriptions on male conduct at home. Where sodomy is implied in romances, it is almost always justified by the sense that it is a matter of wondrous digression. In such instances, verisimilitude is not an archaic feature of romance but a narrative ploy meant to inscribe a potentially disruptive sexual behaviour into the fabric of romance. In other instances, it is part of an imperial allegory in which political concerns overlay erotic actions. By virtue of these formalist aspects of romance, sodomy is naturalized by the fact that it represents a digression from the naturalized narrative.

Prose romances naturalize sodomy when they associate it with tyrants and giants (the extremes of allegorized masculine aggression and violence that the knight-errant is called to destroy) and when they invest the Turk and other men from the East with desire and affection within homosocial scenarios. They denaturalize it when it threatens a travelling knight. Thus, in the third part of *Palmerin of England* (1602), men's association with women is regarded as an insult that provokes violence, because the presence of a woman among infidel men incurs anxiety over effeminization and fear that those making such an implication are ravished homosexuals. Soboco, the Indian pagan, lashes out at Florendos, a knight, who had inquired about his abducted wife and niece among Soboco's knights-errant: "Thou shouldst be some pretty youthfull Ganimede, tha demaundest for women among Knightes in Armes."[74] The anxiety over sodomy, implicated in the figure of Ganymede, the pretty youth carried off by Zeus, here registers the anxiety over effeminacy, of threatening the knights' heroic prowess. At a moment in culture when chivalric masculinity is being displaced by its romantic counterpart, and when household masculine aggression is being projected onto the infidel, the heroic masculinity of Christian chivalry can be seen to have been displaced onto this figure of the infidel, thus showing that militant masculinity can no longer be traced to the post-Reformation culture of civic humanism, which promoted virtue textualized as readiness for prudent action. The scene brings together two kinds of knights: Florendos, the romantic knight of late sixteenth-century neo-chivalric romances, whose masculine agency is displayed in this effort to find his missing wife and cousin and reunite his household, and the militant knight-errant of medieval romances, whose otherness in this context suggests that he does not fit the new spirit of romantic masculinity focused on household management, which replaced the old chivalric model of masculinity in the late sixteenth and early early seventeenth centuries.

The splitting of sodomy and desire shows not only a more nuanced take on male sexuality but also calls into question criticism that accepts as a cliché the Turk as a sodomite in post-Reformation propaganda against the Ottomans.[75] When romances call attention to specific religious and ethnic markers associated with the Muslim world, they do so by invoking the same-sex affect, not sodomy. Sodomy remains reserved for the Infidel as a general category, a figure that is often hyperbolized as a tyrant or a giant. However, a critical equation should not be made between the sodomite and the Turk. The sodomite, rather, represents the much larger threat embodied by the East: the threat to power, trade, and religion that the English so often felt in relation to Turkey. The difference, then, is between the representation of sexual practice and desire, where anal sex was equated with the perceived risk that England would be overcome by the Ottomans, and the representation of affect, which brings men from East and West together, transcending, even erasing, the materiality of power relations.

However, accepting discursive constructions of the East as a space of aberrant and uncontrollable eroticism and anal sex as merely a way in which the West denigrated the East, leaves out other ways of interpreting the East eroticized in such a way. Displacing homosexuality and overt eroticism in the Eastern Mediterranean, romances create new possibilities for desire. As a space in which desire could be imagined as not circumscribed by domestic laws, or outside western law and morality, the Eastern Mediterranean became the future of desire. The West, then, is that which is old, that which the knight leaves behind, and the East becomes a new world of pleasure. The knight's movement and progress in the East is also the romance writer's quest for new ways of writing about sexuality. As the next chapter shows, romance's construction of the East's geographical subjects as affectively bound with western men shows that West and East have become inextricably linked with each other.

5 Cruising the Eastern Mediterranean: The Knight, the Friend, the Favourite, and Homoerotic Romance

Sodomites and Playfellows

By looking at the representation of homosocial exchanges in displays of erotic passions within the ethnic world of the Eastern Mediterranean we have been prepared to explore how these instances are fictionalized in prose romances. The fact that homosocial bonds serve as a metaphor for political anxiety and that those relations also shape economic transactions between men means that romances inevitably narrate the instability of masculinity and male sexuality, producing stories of friendship imagined as different structures of male relationship and levels of intimacy and imagining relationships between the knight and the men which whom he is in contact as spectacles of desire that sometimes oscillate between violent rivalry and affective commitment. In Philip Sidney's romance *The Countesse of Pembrokes Arcadia* (1598) the sodomite features as a tyrant. From the very first chapter, the sodomite represents extreme forms of power and abuse; he is a figure within which foreignness and homophobia interlock. Halfway through Book One, Pyrocles and Musidorus find themselves in the Eastern Mediterranean country of Pontus, where

> They were brought to the king of that countrey, a Tyrant also, not through suspition, greedinesse, or reuengefulness, as he of *Phrygia*, but ... of a wanton cruelty: inconstant in his choise of friends, or rather neuer hauing a friend but a playfellow; of whom when he was wearie, he could not otherwise rid himselfe then by killing them; giuing sometimes prodigally, not because he loued them to whom he gaue, but becaue he lusted to guie: punishing, not so much for hate or anger, as because he felt not the smart

> of punishment: delighted to be flattered, at first for those virtues which were not in him, at length making his vices virtues worthy the flattering: with like iudgement glorying, when he had happened to do a thing well, as when he had perfourmed some notable mischiefe.[1]

One might expect the tyrant to be deceptive, selfish, and vain, but his dependence on keeping a minion (whom the tyrant kills when he gets bored with him) instead of friends, which he does not have, embodies not just the extreme of masculine agency but also a sodomite, thus linking spiritual monstrosity with sodomy. The tyrant's behaviour illustrates the perversion of friendless man, the degradation manhood experiences when it exists outside friendship and outside secular and social laws that regulate men's roles within the culture of friendship. The linkage between tyranny and sodomy, or, of sodomy as a form of social tyranny, could be traced back to early Christian discourses of sexual renunciation and godly punishment for sodomy. Thomas Lodge says that "the very night Christ was born, sodomitical crue perished." He adds, "God should be thanked [because the] monsters are banished." In Lodge's version of the myth of Christianity, Christian faith is imagined as a miracle that purifies the earth of the sodomitical sin of paganism, and becomes the guardian of that newly gained purity. Yet Lodge also echoes St Augustine, finishing his tirade labelling the sodomite "as an enemie of virtue ... [who] consumeth wealth, & louing pleasure."[2] The singular tyrant-sodomite is thus threatening not only because of his inverted masculinity, but also because his selfishness and greed endanger the harmony of material abundance and love in the commonwealth. Because the stability of the commonwealth of the state offers a model for the micro commonwealth of the household, to which it also gives stability, protecting the state from the tyrant's poisonous effect on the state also means liberating masculinity for other forms of agency that do not only engage in battling such grotesque foes.

The Tyrant of Pontus also threatens because his destructive sexuality is further represented as deviant courtliness and abused favouritism. Sidney imagines the Tyrant as an infector of the state, as a unique form of plague, and as a kind of social and spiritual smallpox:

> He [Tyrant] chaunced at that time (for indeed long time none lasted with him) to haue next in vse about him, a man of the most enuious disposition, that (I thinke) euer infected the aire with his breath; whose eyes could not looke right vpon anie happie man, nor eares beare the burthen of any

> bodies praise: contrarie to the natures of all other plagues, plagued with other well being; making happinesse the ground of his vnhappinesse, & good newes the argument of his sorrow: in sum, a man whose fauour no man could winne, but by being miserable.[3]

The verb "use" suggests that the relationship between the tyrant and his favourite does not involve equals, but that the favourite is subordinated to the tyrant. In the figure of the tyrant, Sidney shows the obverse of heroic masculinity upheld and tried in his romance, making the tyrant's unnatural body the presence that can erode the commonwealth. This episode calls attention to the absence of equity which is required to exist between men in the humanist culture of friendship. It shows how without parity between men friendship threatens to become a parody of ideal relationships between men, turning the weaker in the pair into a potentially abused subject. In this scene in which everything is "contrarie" to nature, the abusive tyrant is the man who throws masculinity out of balance in a culture that promoted harmony across the commonwealth. The threat posed to masculinity in the commonwealth, where harmony is the ideal upheld and defended by the masculine subject of western humanist culture, comes from the foreign Mediterranean homosocial culture embodied in the tyrant and his favourite.

Homosocial bonds between unequal men, as between the Tyrant and his subordinate favourite, reveal the other side of masculine culture debated in Sidney's romance. Social inequality between men opens up male relationship to homosexuality. As Alan Bray has documented, social institutions that involved men of unequal rank, such as the household or the grammar school, became not only spaces that regulated the sexual lives of men who inhabited them, but spaces of homosexuality in early modern England.[4] The eastern tyrant who is "inconstant" in his choice of friends, by choosing not equals but subordinates, reveals the close connection between inconstant masculinity and homosexuality. The homosexuality of this episode is philologically inscribed in the notion of the "playfellow." The *OED* describes "playfellow" as "a playmate ... but in the early use often with sexual connotations." From the earliest occurrence in that erotic sense, in Thomas More's 1557 *History of Richard III* to the mid-seventeenth century, the word "playfellow" carried a sexual meaning, ambiguously covering both hetero- and homosexual erotic scenarios. The word occasionally crops up in poetry, but it mostly occurs in drama.[5] The term is childish, but the tyrant's "wanton cruelty" adds a rather macabre dimension, a kind of excessive sadism, to the childish sporting of the tyrant and his playfellow.[6] The core meanings of "play" between "mates" already suggests that the notion of a "playmate" does not simply involve equal relations, because a winner or a loser in the interaction between men can be declared.

In keeping with the dictionary definition, "playfellow" suggests friendship, love, and innocence. But the erotic ambiguity suggested by the term was not lost to early modern writers, including Sidney in this instance. For example, Shakespeare uses "playfellow" in *A Midsummer Night's Dream,* when Hermia calls Helena "sweet playfellow" ("farewell, sweet playfellow, pray thou for us," 1.1.220).[7] Shakespeare uses the term to dramatize the relationship between two women, but "playfellow" can also allude to veiled erotic affiliation between men. This is the case in More's *Richard III.* The young prince's mother sarcastically mocks Richard the Protector's attempt to get Edward V's younger brother out of her custody and back with his brother. She says:

> Troweth the protector (I pray god he may proue a protectour) troweth he that I perceiue not whereunto his painted processe draweth? It is not honorable that the duke bide here: it were comfortable for them both that he wer with his brother, because the king lacketh a playfelowye, be ye sure. I pray God send them both better playfelowes than hym, that maketh so high a matter vpon such a trifling pretext: as though they coulde none be founden to play with the kyng, but if his brother, that hath no lust to play for sickness, come out of sanctuary, out of hys sauegarde, to play with him.[8]

In this example, "playfellow" is a childish term that describes a relationship between men in which parity is not the only requirement, as in humanist friendship. Who would make a better playfellow to a young duke? Whereas friendship in humanist culture is formed between two men of equal social standing (in most cases they are two noble men), friendship fictionalized in this example replaces the humanist idea of parity with the parity of childhood play in order to neutralize and thus make acceptable desire that circulates between the playfellows. More, however, interrupts childhood play and wishes for Edward's younger brother a homosocial bond with another male aristocrat. More's use of "playfellow" helps to clarify the distinction between Shakespeare and Sidney's uses of that term as a relationship that complicates friendship. If Helena and Hermia are playfellows indeed, then their friendship should not be allowed to continue; they would have outgrown the phase in life when they were just mates in play. But since their friendship continues (despite their feud in Act 3), it seems that in Shakespeare "playfellow" only masks the amorous and erotic implications which go beyond the word's principle meaning of childishness and innocence.[9] If in Shakespeare "playfellow" represents a code word that enables the eroticism of female friendship to continue unchecked, in Sidney the term suggests failed friendship. Erotic friendship between Helena and Hermia makes these two dramatic characters both provocative and erotically autonomous figures in Shakespeare's play that constantly troubles heteroerotic relationships and patriarchal order. Thinking of them as early "lesbians" is "to lift the curtain on occluded practices within early modern culture."[10] But this scene, then, also lifts the curtain on the ambiguity of meaning with which the word "playfellow" is invested in early modern England, opening up a possibility to read similar scenes, but involving men, as examples of an exchange of desire between playmates. Sidney attempts to set failed friendship based on inequality off the culturally recognized friendship based on equality, by clearly marking his attempt in the narrative, since the tyrant episode follows immediately after the "enterchange" of the true friends, Musidorus and Pyrocles.

On the subject of friendship based on parity, Sidney says:

> And so vpon securitie of both sides, they [Pyrocles and Musidorus] were enterchanged. Where I may not omit the worke of friendship in *Pyrocles*, who both in speech [and] countena[n]ce to *Musidorus*, well shewed, that he thought himselfe iniured, and not relieued by him: asking him what he had euer seene in him, why he could bot beare the extremities of mortall accidents as well as any man? And why he should enuy him the glorie of suffering death for his friends cause, and (as it were) rob him of his owne possession?[11]

Contrasting true to failed friendship is an attempt to highlight *amicitia* as a positive form of male bonding.[12] These two episodes help us, not so much to uncover the queer meaning within terms that ambiguously straddle the space between erotic and non-erotic realms, as to reveal how certain terms were used to vocalize the period's own queer meanings for which there was no other vocabulary available.

Renaissance friendship is a political institution and, therefore, any sexual energy that may bind the friends together bears political significance. Sidney's romance is heavily infused with politics surrounding the anxieties over "the Anjou match" and other difficulties of Elizabeth's succession, and the question of kingship.[13] The distinction between the sodomitical Tyrant of Pontus and the two equal friends, Pyrocles and Musidorus, emphasizes the difference between destructive masculinity, which threatened to bring down the state, and constructive masculinity, which formed the scaffolding that constituted the state. Critical approaches to the homoeroticism of *Arcadia* have been broad, eliding the specific structures of desire that bind men in this romance. Thus it has been regarded as either a signal of male panic that resonates throughout this romance,[14] or as androgyny that is represented by cross-dressing.[15] These approaches to male eroticism in Sidney's romance are limited because they do not take into account that the *Arcadia* is primarily not about destabilizing but about solidifying male rule. Yet other critics, like Charles Casey, saw in Sidney's playfulness with male sexuality more obvious and consistent interest in male sexuality in this romance.[16] By referring to Pyrocles as "the erotic hero,"[17] Casey locates the literary identity of this remarkable character of early fiction in the realm of the sexual; he makes him one of the most prominent of sexually charged fictional characters of early romances. Yet more important, Casey views Pyrocles's cross-dressing, not as something that destabilizes masculinity, let alone a stratagem that unsettles femininity, but as a device that empowers masculinity, allowing Sidney to re-envisage heroic masculinity as a more fluid, freer, and ultimately a different kind of heroic subject. Thus, Casey argues, Pyrocles's "cross-dressing represents both his own willingness to challenge his masculine identity, and at the same time his surrender to a symbolic position of emasculation."[18] Even kingship in Sidney's romances is "not sacred" as a way of counteracting the anxieties over the aging Elizabeth's succession.[19] Sidney's emphasis on parity and friendship reflects the need to offset those anxieties with the stability of male rule, and against the threat of foreign instability to social order embodied in the sodomitical Tyrant of Pontus. Whereas Sidney represents true friendship based on equality in terms that make it a socially acceptable form of male alliance in a culture in which parity was the foundation of male friendship, he represents failed friendship in terms that make it the emotionless site of disorder. If in Sidney's *Arcadia* true friendship exists between equal friends and if Sidney does not make sexual desire part of such a socially sanctioned friendship, in other prose romances of Sidney's contemporaries true friendship and eroticism are privileged over heterosexual bonds and romantic love.

The two episodes from *Arcadia* illustrate how prose romances fictionalized sodomy and violent male sexuality by associating them with a more generic context of the infidel from an invented country of the East. Foreignness becomes a signifier for one who is outside sacred and secular law; it is unproductive, aggressive, violent, and one of the defining aspects of homoerotic relationships. When aggression and violence displace homoerotic desires they are associated with men with whom the knight, representing the elite and established rule, is not engaged in an exchange that assumes parity. But these stories invite us to reflect on whether we should read the homoerotics of romances as discourses that reveal problems that come with the idealization of romantic love, new protocols of courtship in which young men and women choose their own mates, and changes in the culture of marriage, especially a delayed age for marriage and a relatively large number of unmarried youths in England.[20] While the chivalric romances of Asia Minor celebrate marriage, promote courtship, and instruct in the acts and rhetoric of romantic love and virtue, they continue to fashion discourses of homoerotic desire as the narratives of female agency, and women's role as credit in exchanges between men, thus shaping the literary language of femininity. These early modern romances thus contribute to what Ruth Mazo Karras has identified as the tension between hetero- and homoeroticism in late medieval romances. Karras argues, "The importance of heterosexual desire to late medieval knighthood comes less from an attempt to overcome male anxieties about homosexuality or to promote marriage and reproduction, but rather because women were one of the currencies in which a knight's success was measured."[21] The tension between hetero- and homoeroticism is a product of the uneasiness and anxiety over heterosexual desire described by Karras. Karras draws our attention to the fact that in romances anxiety was not only about reproduction and heterosexuality, but also about the ways in which masculine virtue was measured in economic terms. Those terms related equally to courtship which was only about love but also, as Diana O'Hara has argued, about "property transfers."[22] Courtship presumed that the happy outcome will not only lead to marriage but to the doubling of property, and that was one of men's concerns in working towards establishing, and managing, a household. Any attempt to analyse masculinity in prose romances in terms of affective and erotic ability to attract the mate had to be offset with the larger project of romance to ensure economic advantage and profit whether or not women are involved. Returning to Karras, if the knight's deeds of prowess were only emphasized as his service to woman in order to "advertize [those deeds] more widely,"[23] then in Elizabethan and Jacobean romances in which homoerotic digressions interrupt the knight's heteroerotic acts of prowess we witness a further removal of those deeds of prowess from the original ideal of masculine honour gained and polished in battle. With more independence gained in choosing the mate (which George Whetstone advocates against "the reprehension of forcement in marriage"),[24] the knight was less dependent on the overstated protocols of chivalric courtship and, I would suggest, his body became the subject of erotic temptations.

Friends and Bedfellows

In Sidney's *Arcadia*, "playfellow" captures friendship as parity. But in some prose romances the friend becomes a bedfellow, a figure intended to solidify friendship as parity – through a potentially erotic contact with another male.[25] The term "bedfellow" changes meaning depending on the milieu in which it occurs, oscillating from the sexual partner in companionate marriage, to, as I argue, in romances, a more ambiguous state of closeness, which, capitalizing on the period's practice of men (and women) sharing a bed, exploits other meanings as well. William Gouge, in *Of domesticall duties* (1622), uses "bedfellow" as a term that describes husband and wife as sexual partners, but, we should notice: "Many husbands and wiues are much oppressed by their bedfellows vnsatiableness."[26] The term is already used in a discussion of spouses' unbridled lust, as an illustration of what is *not* "a right" behaviour in a section of part I of Gouge, entitled "A right conuinction of man and wife." Even if in this part of his text Gouge uses the term "bedfellow" to talk about the uncontrollable desire of a married couple, because of the implications it has invested at this point, the term is associated with situations that may lead to intemperate erotic actions. As the subtitle of his conduct book suggests, Gouge proscribes the rules of sexual conduct following the word of the Bible about sexual behaviour. Yet in romances, in which marriage occurs at the end, and which are not concerned with the marital life throughout (as Gouge's prescriptive conduct book is), bedfellows are very rarely a man and a woman, and hardly ever two women, but most often two young, travelling knights-errant. One could argue that these moments of bed sharing are a mere stylization in literature of the common domestic practice of sharing beds in early modern culture. While it is of course possible that as popular literature romances would borrow some of its features from domestic culture and turn them into fictional narratives, that still does not take away the discursive complications attached to such stylizations in romances themselves. The scriptural prohibitions of the body thus are loosened and often challenged in romances; knights as bedfellows are one way in which romances, in deferring, digressing from, and complicating marriage from the beginning, shape the all-male chivalric culture in romances.

Even when bedfellows involve a man and a woman, as in the second part of *Palmerin D'Oliva* (1597), they share it for the sole purpose of sexual pleasure: "The Fables withdrawn, and many pleasant speeches past between Palmerin and the Ladys Daughter, she conducted him to his Chamber, wishing (if her Honour might so avouch it) that Palmerin never might have any other Bedfellow."[27] The bedfellow clearly implies the sexual act. The act has taken place in another bed, in which the lady's daughter lost her virginity and is now concerned that Palmerin, taken to sleep in his own room, also takes with him her hope for the preservation of honour. Gendered contexts may change, but the "bedfellow" remains a notion associated with sexual pleasure, with a challenge to honour (and chastity), and as this example implies, with a rite of passage, which involves the loss of virginity: it is the Lady's daughter who is Palmerin's bedfellow; and it is because of what has happened while she was his bedfellow that she now wishes that he never find another one, and thus remain chaste. A similar, obverse situation, this time of an emperor's son becoming a bedfellow to a travelling knight, occurs in *The Honourable, pleasant and rare conceited Historie of Palmendos* (1589).

Involving a differently gendered but typologically similar situation – of a child paired off with a bedfellow who is a knight-errant – the scenario from *Palmerin D'Oliva* sheds a new critical light on the erotic nature of bedfellow occluded (because it involves two men) in the episode in *Palmendos*, where the Christian Prince Abenunco, arrives at the Emperor Palmerin's court at Constantinople. In an example of a religious conversion intended to solidify Christian power at the heart of the Ottoman Empire, a Christian knight-errant, Palmerin, has become an Ottoman emperor.[28] Happy to see Abenunco, Palmerin started "embracing him [Abenunco] very honourably in his armes, gaue him such entertainment as beseemed his estate, & for hee was not yet knighted, he willed he should be bedfellow to his Sonne Primaleon, which united a faithfull league of amitie between them, hoping one day to trauell as companions in Armes together."[29] Bedfellows, here, involve adolescent men – one already a prince, the other not yet referred to as such – and their future as two travelling knights-errant, two companions in arms, gestures towards one of the purposes of these romances – as fictional compendia or conduct books for young men.

But the father's projection for his son's emotionally based friendship or amity with another knight has a political dimension, too, for he is bringing "in arms together" not only two young knights-errant, but also two princes from the opposite sides of the religious line, one from the West, the other from the East. Romances exploit the possibility of such relations, in which the emotional and the somatic mingle, for political purposes, especially in shaping the empire in the Ottoman Mediterranean. The situation in *Palmendos* is evacuated of erotic meaning, though the shaping of amity as proposed contains a certain amount of emotional ambiguity involved, as we have seen, in becoming a bedfellow to another male youth. But since this situation imitates the humanist culture's idea of friendship, and sharing a bed as an act commonly done by men in early modern England, importing this habit in Constantinople means also replacing sodomy as a threat, so often part of the imagination of the contacts between men in Asia Minor, with a more acceptable version of the same-gender, non-erotic, intimacy, such as amity and bed sharing.

The term "bedfellow" is used in such a way in *The second part of the first booke of the myrrour of knighthood* (1585), translated by the romance writer Robert Parry. The book is a sequel of a highly popular romance cycle by the Spanish writer, Diego Ortúñez de Calahorra, whose fictions were formative in the popularity of the English romances in the 1580s. In addition to the chivalric stories of the knights of temperance, Ortúñez de Calahorra's romances enriched the English revival of the genre with an excessive "orientalism": pushing them further towards the East. In the English-adapted translations of Ortúñez de Calahorra's romances the further geographical remove of the narrative in the East appears concomitant with the reformulations of the narrative of male friendship and masculine bonds. While, as Lorna Hutson has argued, the temperate knight of this Spanish-inspired romance becomes the prudent knight waiting for the best time and most appropriate occasion to undertake his own imperial enterprises on the revised model of those of the Spanish imperial precursors, friendship between temperate knights in those same translations opens up the conceptualization of friendship in early modern English discourses in ways that have yet to be recognized.[30] It may not be an accident that Robert Parry undertook to translate this book of de Calahorra's romance, for it may have inspired his own romance, *Moderatus, or the Adventures of the Black Knight*, published in 1595. This romance is unique among prose romances of the 1590s in that it makes friendship between the knights its central topic, re-envisioning the humanist concept of *amicitia* in the context of chivalric adventure in which competition, not parity, fashions the narrative of friendship.

Among critical debates about the status and structure of friendship, the sexual nature of that relationship has been hardest to resolve. Although in his earlier elucidations of this problem Alan Bray distinguishes the sodomite from the "masculine friend" due to the latter's separation from the sexual, he acknowledges that these categories "in some respects ... occupied a similar terrain."[31] Writing about the contested and murky terrain of humanist *amicitia*, Alan Stewart has expanded Bray's argument with examples in which friendship and sodomy or homoeroticism could intersect in private spaces shared by men.[32] One of those spaces, in which friendship and homoeroticism touched, was literary collaboration, which Jeffrey Masten coined "textual intercourse."[33] While Laurie Shannon argues for a very specific nature of corporeality and eroticism in Renaissance formulations of friendship, Tom MacFaul inscribes eroticism back into the social fabric of friendship, but only to argue that it has nothing to do with sexuality, as we understand it, but "with the public (and private) assertion of the existence of friendship," of which he cites the examples of King James I's minion-friends.[34] In one of his last essays (with Michel Rey) and in his book *The Friend*, Bray returns to the idea of friendship, offering it as an alternative to the study of male same-sex relations through discourses of sodomy. While insisting that certain social signs of male togetherness (sharing a bed, eating together, embracing) were deeply infused with intimacy, Bray and Rey argue that the multifarious ways in which love between men could be interpreted in the early modern period leaves the actual erotic and affective nature of male bonds unclear.[35] In *The Friend*, Bray removes friendship from the realm of the erotic altogether. In Valerie Traub's succinct formulations of Bray's argument: "Friendship ... was not an unreserved good; it could be compromised by expectations of material interest, influence, and advancement."[36] If criticism on the erotic charge of friendship has been undecided, it is because the earliest formulations of *amicitia* were ambiguous on the subject. Thus Cicero, whose formulations about friendship became the foundation of humanist thinking about friendship, already registers the ambiguity in the nature of the affect that constitutes male friendship. "I do not deny," says Cicero, "that affection is strengthened by the actual receipt of benefits, as well as by the perception of a wish to render service, combined with a closer intercourse."[37] If there is any critical consensus about the sexual nature of early modern friendship, it is that, given the specific social organization and complexity of humanist friendship, which cut across social, political, and affective lines, the sexual signs could be displaced in a number of ways and embodied in a variety of rhetorical codes. Those signs appeared to be of secondary importance to the superiority of the cultural significance of friendship as a form of socially important male alliance.

Imagining friendship between men as an affective union more perfect than that between a man and a woman, romances in that regard extend the classical theory of *amicitia*. In Henry Robarts's romance, *Pheander, the Mayden Knight* (1595), Guenela says to Phaender: "Prince Dionicus, made choice of you for his companion: then vnder *benedictie* let me craue (all lawe of friendship exempted) did he not acquaint you with his determinations for me thinkes it is scant credible, that such an vnity shall be amongst men, their loves being so perfect, but he should disclose each secret intent whatsoeuer."[38] Questioning why Dionicus did not disclose the secret of his oath to Guenela to his friend Phaender, who has made "choice" of him, Robarts puts idealized friendship in tension with idealized love, which is customary in romances. The knight-errant thus occupies the space between friendship and love, space that puts the knight in the position of shared loyalty, but that creates interior conflict and psychological tension for him. Prose romances also exploit the old precept about the blurred boundaries between the erotic and non-erotic nature of friendship for narrative purposes.

We find a vivid illustration of this tension between friendship and heteroerotic love in a rare copy of the book *Historie de Aurelio et Isabelle* (1556), by Juan de Flores, a book whose English translation, *A Paire of Tvrtle Doves, or, the Tragicall History of Bellora and Fidelio* (1606), has been "dubiously assigned" to Robert Greene.[39] The book reads like a mixture of romance and a tract on love and desire between men and women. There is a curious passage that captures the affective turmoil of interiority of two knights grappling to reconcile emotions that have kept them together for a long time, with love for the same woman which each of them has started to experience. Brimming with ideas about the privacy of man's erotic imagination, the passage is worth citing in full:

> two braue Knights, and true-deuoted louers, were so fast tied together, with the bands of hart-knitting amitie, that they had both voluntarily protested

> in words and long time duly obserued in deeds, the sacred laws of mutuall societie between them: yet were they so secret in their loues-secret, that although they were both taken in ye same Net, and like (Salamanders) liued together in loues consuming fire, yet they doth so closely smothered ye flame of their burning harts, that not a little sparkle, of the firie [fiery] passions of the one, could once breake out to the open sight and view of the other. Wherefore either of them priuily consulted with himself in the priuate closet of his secret thoughts, how hee might view her with his eies, whose presence they esteemed as the only palace of their pleasure. But not time, was more seasonable to produce the happie issue of heir luckie hap, and no weather more faire to bring them the Port of their desired hopes, then the still silence of the darke and sleepie night. For what, will true louers doe? Yea what will they not doe? If they doe but so much as espie [watch] a suddaine shaddowe of appearing hope, to reape the haruest of their longing desires: when others feast they fast, when others take their solace, they indure sorrowe, when others sleepe; they awake, yet they accompt [explain] their soarest paines, sweete pleasures, and their greatest labours, no toile, and all to gaine the loue of their best beloved ... When as these vnknowne Louers, one to the other, and long knowne friends, who had often so kindly met, were nowe so unwillingly met together, and had scarce halfe an eie sight one of the other (for loue can indure no corriuall: raging furie, so incensed both their harts, that unsheathing the sharpe-eadged Toledo blades, without any further pause, beganne to lay about them, with deadly blows.[40]

Heteroerotic desire is imagined as a force that tears apart long-standing friendship between two knights, turning devoted friends into bitter enemies caught in a duel over the damsel Bellora, whose love possessed them both of them. This is not an uncommon scenario in sixteenth-century fictions of masculinity.[41] It is also not uncommon for chivalric fiction to represent, as is the case in *A Paire of Tvrtle Doves*, a bond between knights grounded in love, yet a bond that is not nourished by homoerotic desire. These kinds of unions between knights are closer in nature to the tradition of chivalric brotherhood that dates back to the early medieval period than to *amicitia*, that is, male friendship based on social parity, characteristic of the courtly culture of the humanism of the Renaissance. Yet, that the intense affect that brings and keeps the friends together should be explained, as the author of *A Pair of Tvrtle Doves* does, in terms of secrecy, privacy, and intimacy, directs the reader of this book to think that the affect that is constituent of male friendship is an alternative to heteroerotic desire, and of a higher order too. This fiction exceeds what might be expected culturally, that is, a philologically acceptable convergence of male friendship and the literary language of love. As the passage suggests, heteroerotic love is imagined as a secret that has to be suppressed so that friendship can be preserved. Furthermore, heteroerotic love is presented as a disturbing force that turns the knights' temperance into violence; it transforms love between male friends into a tragedy, of falling in love with a woman. And so we might want to ask what the ensuing duel is actually about. Is it about the rivalry between men over the love of a woman? Or is it about preserving the emotionally charged male friendship? The passage brings out the struggle for intimacy with the preferred object of desire, and the difficulty of actually ascertaining what, or who, that object may be in a culture where the lines that separate heteroerotic love and male friendship remained blurred, at least in fictional writing. In this fiction and in other romances where male friendship and heteroeroticism are at odds, narratives of heteroerotic love do not merely trouble fictions of male friendship, they reveal the extent to which any story of a successful heteroerotic love depends in fact on a resolution, or a suppression, of the emotions that produce male friendship in the first place. In this chivalric fiction, however, the bond between Fidelio and Agamio, two knights-errant brought together by love, is fiction's answer to the question announced in the long title of this work, "whether man to woman, or woman to man offer the greater temptations and allurements vnto vnbridled lust." Desire that attracts men to women and women to men is here translated into an extended battle of arguments on the subject between Bellora and Fidelio. But that desire is also contrasted by the expressions of gentle affections between two male friends, affections which are expressed in rhetorically simpler and less ornate terms.

In *The second part of the first booke of the myrrour of knighthood*, Ortúñez de Calahorra provides a model for the narratives of knightly temperance in English romances, replacing the story of the knight's quest for marriage with the narratives of intimate friendship, told against the lavish eastern setting that invokes unbridled desire. Because of the intricate density of this romance's narrative, I offer not a brief summary of its plot, but a summary in service to the point about the displacement of heroic masculinity into the realm of the eroticized friendship. Rosicler, nicknamed the Knight of the Sun, sets out to defend the Natolian princess Claridiana from the giants Crudamante and Rocardo. On his way to Natolia, ambiguously located on the border of Macedonia and Greece,

Rosicler comes across a strange procession somewhere in Greece. He sees a one-hundred-foot-long chariot on twelve wheels of ivory pulled by giants and accompanied by a procession of twenty maidens (followed by more giants) dressed in sumptuous clothes and adorned with "verie faire and gallant bunch of feathers" and riding unicorns "betrapped with cloth of gold."[42] On top of the chariot is a tent divided into two chambers, one of which the author calls a "closet." In the chamber sits a beautiful damsel; in the closet, a melancholy knight "of a high stature and well made, his face was verie faire and of a good and gentle proportion."[43] His armour is covered with gold and precious stones, and the scales of Atlantic fish. The melancholy knight is dressed in silk robes covered with feathers, fish scales, and diamonds. Rosicler's sword is made of fine gold, his sceptre adorned with emeralds, and on his head he is wearing a green hat covered with rubies. But these are not the accoutrements of a heroic male; their ornamental excess undercuts chivalric comportment, and turns the heroic armour into a display of luxuries from the East (gold, silk, and gems) as signifiers of the indulgence in commodities in the urban proto-capitalist world from which the knights set off. Rosicler ignores the lady in the chamber, set up to lure him away from his chivalric pursuit, but fixes his gaze on the knight in the closet, feeling "within himself a great weakness."[44] The sight of the adorned knight renders him speechless and weakens both his heroic stance and his masculine comportment. The knight's closet features here as a "site of sexual anxiety," a space associated with the particular kind of private, even intimate, space, which, as Stewart demonstrates, was located within and beyond the household. In this romance the closet is further removed in the Eastern Mediterranean, and stylized, not as a private space for contemplative withdrawal, but as an outdoor temptation, an enticing site that lures the eroticized male body that it encloses and displays.[45]

Is it the male body or the ornamental excess encasing that body as a replacement of the chivalric armour allegorizing the luxuries of the East, that paralyses the knight-errant? What is the knight-errant attracted to: the man underneath the armour of gems, or the wonders themselves? Is his gaze that of a lover, directed at a friend of ambiguous emotions, or of a proto-merchant–colonizer bedazzled by Eastern luxuries? The sight in the tent raises these questions, but the romance does not offer a resolution of these doubts. The absence of character resolution is not a deficiency of this particular romance, but a feature of romance as a genre not concerned with developing characterization.

This motif, however, allegorizes a critique of the excessive indulgence in new luxuries from the East and its effect on the heroic masculinity whose over-accumulation of luxuries separated it, as the tent is separate from the closet, from enticing femininity. The glitter of gems is at once magnetically attractive and conspicuously emasculating for men attracted to the wonders yielded by eastern trade. If the closet is a site that helped the creation of a new subjectivity, then what sort of a subject is produced in the closet narratives in romances?[46] By distracting the travelling knight from his hetero-romantic path, the wonders of the closet have the effect of redirecting heteroerotic romantic masculinity into the masculinity of homoerotic and/or homoerotic attraction. Is Rosicler being warned against the homoerotic and economic allure of the exotic Eastern Mediterranean, which takes away his chivalric prowess and distracts him from romantic pursuit?[47]

But this moment in the narrative is only a prelude to a further instance of masculine displacement from chivalric and romantic to homoerotic; the narrative flashback shifts the story of Rosicler in an unpredictable direction. Like many young knights of romances who leave their paternal homes against their father's wishes, Rosicler leaves his father's court in order to discover which of the two maidens that he desires, Claridiana and Lyndabrides, he prefers. But he has also set out on a journey meant to resolve his emotional dilemma with two friends, Princes Brandizel and Claueryondo, just returned to Greece from journeying at sea after a long separation from Rosicler. And just when the author informs us of this happy reunion of friends, the narrative slips into a curious digression depicting the amicable reunion of separated friends:

> when he [Rosicler] came to the place [where he met Brandizel and Claueryondo], he went straight vnto them and lead them into a secret chamber within the Chariot, whereas they made themselues knowen to the one vnto the other, where they embraced the one the other with great delight, as those which loued together like vnto perfect friends. And with the grete desire they had to see one another, they remined a great while embracing before anie of them could speake, but after than they were somewhat quieted, the two Princes Brandizel and Claueryndo did giue the knight of the Sunne to understand of all that euer they had passed.[48]

After the reunion, Rosicler departs to meet Princess Lyndabrides. But fearing that his divided loyalty between her and the other princess,

Claridiana, "would have troubled him," he abandons romantic pursuits altogether and returns to his two male friends, now joined by another, Floriandus: "there lodged all four together in one chamber, in foure beds."[49] Just as men sharing a bed, as Bray and Rey have documented,[50] was a common domestic practice in the early modern period, a practice which, as Stewart shows, could also enable homoeroticism, so was the effect of love between friends often a turning away from the pursuit of courtship and marriage towards male bonding and intimacy.[51] Yet when the four friends in Ortúñez de Calahorra's romance sleep together in one room though in four beds; or when Parry, the author of *Moderatus* says of the friends, Moderatus and Priscius, that "one chamber was common unto them both,"[52] what does it mean, to echo Foucault, "for men ... to share their room?"[53] And why does Parry need to qualify his mention of the friends sharing a room "in foure beds"?

Alan Bray first posited that "homosexuality" in the early modern period was something that "was not – could not be – a relationship with a stranger," but with a familiar, a neighbour or friend.[54] Romances both extend and divert from this view, because, as this chapter shows, both strangers and friends offer homoerotic satisfaction. This proliferation of erotic alternatives is the effect of the displacement of romance fictions well beyond England onto the erotic shores of the Eastern Mediterranean, conveniently tempestuous to enable the encounter with the stranger and the travelling, or crusading, English. For Rosicler the chamber shared with Lyndabrides incurs anxiety, for which the only respite is his own bed in the room shared with his friends. The separate beds suggest how the narrative arrests the story of a potential exchange of homoerotic desire, by almost imposing the physical obstacle of the bed between the friends. The narrative draws our attention to the deflation of the masculine comportment and heroic stance, which Rosicler experienced before meeting his friends, when he encountered the resplendent (and campy) pageant in which the site of the knight in the closet weakened his senses, not emasculating him but pushing him further away from the quest for a woman towards an affect for men – which materializes a few pages later when he ends up sleeping with his friends. If the narrative of Rosicler mixes the intimacy of *amicitia* with a homosocial charge, the chamber shared by Moderatus and Priscius reduces that intimate space onto a more intimate place of shared pleasure.

Moderatus's absence from the bedroom one night further removes doubt about the meaning of the shared bed in Parry's romance. "The absence of his friend Moderatus," says Parry, "greatly troubled him

[Priscius], both for that he longed to understand his successe with Florida, and also much maruelled, why he came not to bed vnto him the night before, as his manner was."[55] If Priscius's yearning for Florida, his beloved, is not compromised by his missing of Moderatus, because his thoughts about Florida are "frivolous and vaine,"[56] then the narrative in this romance re-imagines the role of women in a fiction preoccupied with male bonding. The absence of a woman, this fiction implies, produces only superficial and fleeting emotions, alerting readers to the fact that the romantic and heteroerotic courtship is, contrary to a long history of criticism on romance, not the romance's narrative priority – even if it ends up being its usually rushed ending.[57] Rather, it is the complex and complicated emotional and social fabric of male bonds, including friendship, that romances dwell on. In romances friendship is fictionalized as the absoluteness of faithful devotion to the body of a friend, the knight.

Narratives of friendship thus draw our attention to one of the structural paradoxes of romances: by redirecting the narratives of courtship away from the predictable idealism of heteroerotic love, friendships, not romantic courtship, dominate these romances, even if they appear to be only occasional digressions. Romances share with their dramatic counterparts a curious, but firm, focus on friendship, which Pettet lucidly identified: "friendship, while passive from a dramatic point of view, is certainly very prominent in these early plays and as much as part of their spirit and atmosphere as it is in *Arcadia*."[58] Male same-sex bedfellows in romances are figures that trouble romantic love because they reroute its affect to each other, and away from women they set out to quest. These episodes from Parry and *The myrrour* romance emphasize the kind of homosocial exchanges between men in the East, and between friends, which in other romantic fictions are combined in a story in which economic exchanges between men from the West and from the East fictionalize both affective and homoerotic relations.

In these examples friendship constitutes a union solidified through an affective exchange between men, a union whose consequences are political and, as in *Palmendos*, of significance for international politics in the Mediterranean. In other romances the female threat to friendship is troped as the insatiable sexual aggression with which a woman disturbs male friendship. A significant chunk of the second part of the *Palmerin d'Oliva* romance narrates the adventures of Palmerin and Prince Olorico, the King of Arabia's son, two youths joined "in a league of amity."[59] Inseparable, these two friends allegorize the ideal of partnership that surpasses religious intolerance, idealizing *amicitia* as a bond that erases the difference between the infidel and the Christian man. But even in the example of the most erotically subversive act of a woman found in prose romances, male friendship is imagined both as a triumph of *amicitia* over the fatal and unbridled sexuality of woman, and as a cross-religious alliance of men that resists and surpasses the fantasy of a heteroerotic cross-religious union.

Having just offered an exemplary narrative of women from the classical tradition – "Hypermnestra, Myrrha, Dejanira, Scylla, Phedra, Thisbie, Oenone, Phyllis, Salmacis, Hero, and Dido" – "whose deaths were procured onely by lavish love,"[60] the narrator in *Palmerin d'Oliva* introduces the eastern Queen of Tharsus enamored with Parismus: "her heart was so inthralled, and with secret fire so washed and consumed, as doth the Waxe before the fire" (G2[v]). But seeing the bond between Parismus and Olorico as a barrier to her intentions, she had a sleeping potion that would "prouoke forgetfulness"[61] given to them. Once the friends were drunk beyond waking and separated as bedfellows, "the Queene went to the Bed of Palmerin, whom she abused at her owne pleasure ... The Queen having satisfied her unchaste desire, caused Olorico to be brought into his place again, and then returned to her own Chamber."[62] A number of signifying threads intertwine in this story of seduction: the proverbial unbridled female sexuality is turned into satisfying the male sexual urge without taking responsibility, only for the unconscious urge of sexual fulfillment to be turned into a conscious guilt over disloyalty to Palmerin's beloved, Palynarda, with Palmerin fleeing the bed of friendship and a scene of sexual and adulterous satisfaction. Since the Queen's sexual rapaciousness is already punished symbolically in the list of classical women whose uncontrolled love was the cause of their death, this romance disrupts friendship that was announced as ideal, but only once it has provoked guilt over female-inspired (and repeated) acts of fornication.

This extraordinary episode of the seduction of a sleeping, thus vulnerable, knight not only augments that stock feature of romance and of Renaissance literature more broadly – we find it in the allegories of slipped temperance in Edmund Spenser's romance epic *The Faerie Queene*, but also in the episodes of Tancred and Armida in Torquatto Tasso's *Jerusalem Delivered* – of a sexually rapacious woman assaulting a temperate knight's sexuality, separating the sexual act, reserved for women, from affection, projected onto male friendship. By emphasizing the queen's origin in the Eastern Tharsus, the unbridled sexuality of the East that threatens the temperate virtue and controlled honour of the West, embodied in the knight-errant, is highlighted. (One is reminded here of Shakespeare's Cleopatra, even if fornication in Shakespeare's play of the East is more the subject of style and rhetoric than of action, as in the case of the Queen of Tharsus, another eastern empress imagined as sexually overbearing.) Writers of romances disrupt romantic love narratives to develop fictions about affective male friendship and tangled story-telling techniques to keep friends connected in the narrative in order for the romantic love to somehow succeed. This reiterates the long tradition of the competition between romantic love and male friendship in romances. But it also shows that love is not always at the centre of all romances, and that romances are more about exploring affective scenarios that better serve the political and economic ambitions of their young knights, than fulfilling the traditional requirement for the satisfaction of romantic love and matrimonial felicity.

Slaves as Friends in the Levant

Madeleine de Scudéry's prose romance, *Ibrahim or the Illustrious Bassa*, first published in French in 1641 and translated into English in 1652, brings together a number of issues discussed so far in a way that no other romance has done.[63] The romance must have been very popular in its time because two more editions appeared before the end of the seventeenth century; a tragedy based on this prose romance was successfully performed in London and printed in 1694.[64] Written by a talented writer of rich imagination, of an admirable sensitivity to details of topographical descriptions, and attentive to moral psychology, *Ibrahim* is not only a readable romance but also a text that self-consciously troubles the romance genre. De Scudéry's work raises a number of questions, not only about the genre of romance itself, but about the transformation of knightly masculinity in romance writing in the seventeenth century, about the nature of homosocial relations between western and eastern men, about verisimilitude and the geography of romances, and about the ways that eastern trade and merchant empire condition the construction of masculinity in prose romances of the Eastern Mediterranean. In her attempt to correct various "defects"[65] in romance writing, de Scudéry shows reservations about some of the formulas used in the writing of a "Romanze"[66] that may skew the reading and understanding of romance. Subjecting those "defects" to critical scrutiny, she instead pens a version of romance in which the unconvincing issue of verisimilitude is offset by a fiction of contemporary history. Writing *Ibrahim* is an act of conscious revision, not merely of romance as a genre, but of romance as a kind of text that draws on contemporary history, specifically, in this instance, on the history of the Eastern Mediterranean. In doing so, she has produced a historical romance deeply steeped in Eastern Mediterranean politics and contacts between two worlds, East and West, symbolically exemplified in a loving friendship between a white slave from Genoa, Justinian, whose Muslim name is Ibrahim (also called the Bassa of the Sea), and the young sultan Soliman.

In her "Preface" to *Ibrahim*, de Scudéry questions the effect of verisimilitude against that of geographical knowledge: "how should I be touched with the misfortunes of the Queen of Gundaya, and of the King of Astrobacia, when as I know their very Kingdomes are not in the Universall Mappe, or, to say better, in the being of things."[67] Having a romance reader in mind, de Scudéry maintains that invented names divorced from the geographical knowledge that shaped ideas about distant places have little power to affect the reader's affective and cognitive response to the fantasies of romance writing. In proposing ways to strip romances of their high level of fantasy as much as possible to make them more enjoyable and of use to her readers, de Scudéry dismisses the miraculous aspect in romances, dismantling the structure of romance writing practised by her male counterparts. Having just critiqued the use of imaginary geography and choice of fictive rulers, de Scudéry continues her criticism:

> But this is not the only defect which may carry us from true resemblance, for we have at other times seek romances, which set before us monsters, in thinking to let us see Miracles; their Authors by adhering to much to wonders have made Grotesques, which have not a little of the visions of a burning Feaver.[68]

By implying that monsters and miracles of which there is an abundance in romances distort truth by obscuring it by false representations such as those exemplified by the grotesque, misshapen, and unbelievable creatures and monsters, de Scudéry questions some of the conventions of romance writing, especially the violation of decorum and of verisimilitude. Implicitly, therefore, de Scudéry also, with her pen, clashes with male authors of romances accused of letting fantasy prevail over true story-telling in instances where heroic deeds are the subject of their narratives. If male writers of romances indulge in fantasy and the violation of decorum, she will infuse her romance with a sufficient amount of realism to make her work a different kind of text. "It is not sufficient to say," de Scudéry continues:

> How many times they [heroes of romances] suffered shipwreck, and how [many] times they have incountered robbers, but their inclinations must be made to appear by their discourse: otherwise one may rightly apply to these dumb Heroes that excellent motto of Antiquity, Speake that I may see thee.[69]

In de Scudéry's critique of romance writing, the "defect" of verisimilitude also includes the linguistic mode of writing. De Scudéry privileges plain speaking intended to present heroism as speaking agency over heroic action presented as a set formula. One of the distinct features of de Scudéry's romance is that she turns the voice and interiority she gives to her heroes into copious prose. The hero of her romances does not talk in short clichés, as he often does in Richard Johnson's romance, but in long and often moving speeches that not only tell his story but also articulate his feelings and state of mind. The Italian knight turned white slave in Constantinople revels in conversation, communication, and introspection. So, in a romance that, instead of being set in a fictional land, is located both on the Bosphorus and in Genoa in Italy, and in a narrative that does not make his heroes roam through a vast geography of the East but contains their adventures between the extravagant houses and lush gardens of Genoa, and between the sultan's sumptuous Seraglio on the shores of the Caspian Sea and the marketplace of abundant luxuries in Constantinople's streets, a history of West–East contacts of the Eastern Mediterranean in the early modern period is reimagined within the narrative frame of romance. The orientalism of de Scudéry's narrative method and her revision of the mode of romance writing have a direct bearing on how we read the masculine agency within the fiction of friendship and conjugal love in this romance. De Scudéry's immersion in the East represents the pinnacle of the fiction of orientalism that increasingly sweeps the narratives of romance writing at the turn of the century, and progressively increases in seventeenth-century romance writing. Both Richard Johnson and Madeleine de Scudéry display a double vision of the East, one in which the East features as both a source of erotic pleasure and of economic interest.

Fictions of Pleasure for Men in the Levant

Among literary scholars, Lawrence Twyne's *The Patterne of Painefull Adventures* (1594) is primarily known as the source for the brothel scene in *Pericles*, a dramatic romance by Shakespeare, in which George Wilkins had a hand.[70] Twyne's text is a pastiche of romance, stories from the *Gesta Romanorum*, and travel literature. If Twyne's text gave rise to one of the most famous scenes of prostitution in Shakespeare, it also created one of the most humorous scenes of erotic bonding between men in prose fiction. Curiously, at the centre of both scenes, the brothel scene in drama and, what I will call the bathing scene in fiction, is either the governor or the king. In both scenes, that is, a figure of political authority becomes the body that violates the norms of sexuality and compromises procreativity. The episode that interests me here involves the event that befell Apollonius, a bridegroom on his way to marry Lucina. Shipwrecked in Turkey and stranded in an unfamiliar town, Apollonius contemplates how to "sustaine his life."[71] Bruce Smith has identified the shipwrecked youth as one of the stock figures associated with sodomy in Renaissance literature.[72] But the outcome of the story of Apollonius shipwrecked in an unfamiliar place, a typical romance locale identified as the setting for the homoerotically charged shipwrecked youth, differs from other motifs of shipwrecked youth where homoeroticism is veiled, as in Shakespeare's romantic comedy *Twelfth Night*.

Sunk in deep thoughts and contemplating his miserable state, all of a sudden Apollonius notices "a boy running naked through the street,"[73] with only a towel wrapped around his waist and his head shining with oil. The boy yells at the top of his voice, inviting everyone, citizens and strangers, masters and servants, to follow him if they wish to "exercise" and "wash."[74] Thinking that this might provide a way out of his misery, Apollonius obliges and follows the boy to a "Bania," where he takes off his clothes and lets the boy wash and anoint him with aromatic oils. Satisfied and anointed, but bored, Apollonius notices Alistrates, "king of the whole land,"[75] playing tennis with his men and joins them. Apollonius ends up being a good tennis player, which wins him the King's favour. After the game, which ended as soon as the King has developed a liking for Apollonius, he and the King jump together into one of the "banias," where Apollonius "washed the king very reuerently,"[76] so much so that the King says gleefully: "I sweare unto you of truth as I am a Prince, I was neuer exercised nor washed better than this day."[77]

After the stray Christian bridegroom has finished playing an "oriental" boy to the King, he and the King part company. The substitution of an Ottoman (boy) for a Christian (youth) in Twyne's homosocial fiction inscribes homoerotic intimacy in the narrative of men's play. It is in the playfulness and privacy of this narrative, implying homoeroticism, that Apollonius represents two of the most common types upon which homoeroticism was projected in early modern culture: the shipwrecked youth and the King's favourite. Twyne's fiction is thus both a warning to a wandering youth, who might be reading romances as conduct books for male youth, and young women reading the male versions of the matrimonial conduct books,[78] to beware the erotic allure of the Eastern Mediterranean and invitation to the same. In some of the earliest travel accounts, the westerner misreads the Muslim's sodomy for an aberrant sexual practice.

In the first decade of the sixteenth century, the Portuguese traveller Tomé Pires observes the sexual habits of the Persians, whom he considers the Moors, as he does with other non-Christians:

> The Moors in generall are all jealous men, and thus for all their good looks most of them are sodomites, including the Persians and the people of Ormuz. And they do not consider this to be unsuitable to their condition, nor are they punished for it, and there are even public places where they practise this for money. And those who suffer this are beardless and go about dressed like women, and the Moors laugh at us when we point out to them the turpitude of this sin.[79]

It is the westerner, not the Muslim from North Africa, who is disgraced in this account. Pires's text reverses the early modern "sodomania" (the propagandist discourse about homoeroticism in the Islamic context common in the early modern period) by turning an Islamic sodomite into a debased Christian.[80] Pires's account circulated only in Portuguese manuscript redactions in the sixteenth-century and therefore may not appear to be shedding direct light on English romances. Yet his text is a record of an alternative view of sodomitical proclivities of Muslims, augmented in the writing at a time when deprecating Muslims was in vogue in England. But as an account of sexual alterity in the Eastern Mediterranean, it runs counter to the pathological demonization of sodomy in western travel and ethnographic writing.

Read alongside Pires's story, Twyne's fiction shows that the accommodation, even normalization, of homoerotic sexualities was the other side of the history of its pathologization, which became prominent in the Protestant propaganda against sodomy. Both Twyne and Pires encourage us, then, to look for other, broader ways of looking at the representation of religious alterity and the sexual practices attributed to it from just denunciation alone. Romances offer another perspective on sodomy, which both intersects with, but mostly diverges from common practices, in presenting sodomy as a heinous and culturally destabilizing sin. It is the rhetorical game of representation that at the same time displaces that sin beyond the borders of the national and the familiar and gives that representation a form that makes the foreign sin potentially also a domestic one.

Interpreted through the lenses of travel writing, which linked Turkish baths with sexual filth, it would be easy to conclude that this scene does not carry homosexual symbolism. But this is an example of how Twyne's fiction is more accurate than travel writing about what went on in those baths. Seventeenth-century Egyptian scholar Abd al-Ra'uf al-Munawi "inveighed against men making use of beardless boys as masseurs when they visited the baths. He also urged the owner of a bath not to employ beardless boys, and not to allow them to strip in the bathhouse, since such practices lead to improprieties that are 'as clear as the sun.'"[81] The impropriety attributed to these beardless boys "who stood for the scrubbing and massaging" was likely to have been prostitution, to which such the secluded and private environment of the baths was particularly conducive.[82] The magnitude of the sin implied in the scene from Twyne is augmented by the fact that it is a king (albeit an infidel one) who lures the boy into the privacy of his baths and then brags about enjoying the service. Could it be then that under the guise of pleasure and enjoyment that appears to occlude the sexual act, Twyne's fiction emulates a very specific erotic scenario from the East more accurately than travel writing – that of the prostitution of boys as objects of sexual pleasure? Since it was also suggested that these bathhouse boy-attendants, who helped the bather undress and scrubbed oils into his body, be "of amiable character and handsome looks," pederastic enticement is further revealed here as more a matter of degree than kind, as was customary in Muslim countries, since those norms were defined by categories of "halal" and "haram." And Twyne's text offers it to his English readers as an equally pleasurable and reinvigorating experience.

What is more extraordinary about this tale is that it is penned by a Christian writer who fictionalizes a scene reminiscent of the motif of the beautiful boy seduced by, but also seducing, an elder Ottoman from the elite circles in Ottoman literature. The motif of the beautiful boy in early Ottoman poetry traces its origins in Persian literature, which flourished in the sixteenth century in elite cultural circles.[83] In that tradition, now adapted in the early modern Ottoman culture, boys could come from the upper class, they could be apprentices in any of the trades, or they could be city youths outside a specific trade, that is, "young, urban, nonslaves and nonelites," called "shehir owlanları."[84] Twyne's tale begins with a city boy, who, acting as a town crier, sets the stage and mood for the scene. But the story ends up featuring another boy, Apollonius, in a reversal of the scenario involving a youth and an elite Ottoman. This reversal reimagines within the fictionalized Ottoman context the corresponding cultural trope by which male homoeroticism was imagined in England, involving an aristocrat and a man of lower social rank. Yet Twyne makes the encounter pleasurable and socially tolerable by narrating a cultural reversal of male bonding within the space associated with homosocial bonding in another culture. By rendering pleasure shared between men free of anxiety, Twyne's fiction also idealizes the possibility of male intimacy for his western reader. The correlation between western and eastern treatment of homosocial pleasure in Twyne's narrative reveals the western writer's desire to erase the difference in the two cultures' attitudes towards pleasures shared between men in the realm of privacy. Does Twyne's fiction intend to incur what Roland Barthes termed "a *desiring* reading," a kind of clandestine state in which reading animates the "body's emotions"?[85] Just as the western visitors happened upon the baths but recorded them from a distance, Apollonius is shipwrecked into one: displaced by force to a foreign yet alluring place, he relinquishes the cultural constraints that in travel writing created obstacles for what one might call, via Barthes, a desiring writing.[86] Twyne's fiction could be said to imagine the intimate closeness of the homosocial bonding that might have occurred in Turkish baths, which never made it into the travel accounts. The motif of a male youth of lower rank lured into the private and intimate space of a royal adult immediately evokes homoeroticism, which in this scenario implicates an adult from the West. As we shall see, such episodes are cancelled from the travel writings, purporting to be authentic, but, as the account from Twyne illustrates, allowed to flourish in romance fiction, whose meaning readers understand is produced by the writer's lapses into fantasy.

Thus, in Twyne, homoerotic appeal is present even if there is a counter-appeal of an implicit homophobic discourse in these episodes.

In Twyne's fiction, a detour from the narrative of romantic, heteroerotic courtship to a digression of pleasurable play with a man from the East problematizes Apollonius's heteroerotic masculinity, by repressing romantic love and placing obstacles to marriage. In contrast to fictions that emphasize homoerotic acts practised among Muslims, Twyne's narrative of the Eastern Mediterranean excises sodomy from the narrative and, via a digression of homosocial erotic play, counter-balances an obsessive quest for a woman, an old cliché in romances. By privileging for a moment erotic dalliance between men over heteroerotic pursuits, Twyne's fiction reflects playfully upon a number of narrative and affective conventions of romances. The brief amiability shared between Apollonius and the king contrasts the violence, militancy, and rivalry that exist between knights and intemperate infidels in romances, but it also highlights the other kind of intimacy that is lacking in his fiction, that directed towards women by men. While the aggression and violence between men may be seen as affective and libidinal displacement, the homosocial dalliance between the Christian youth and an infidel king indicates the fictional attempt to recover some of the intimacy between men lost to militant chivalry, heteroerotic courtship, and pursuit of a woman and marriage. Courtship, heteroerotic love, and marriage – in other words, all heterosexual pursuits coexisted with the homosociality of chivalry at the time when the stories of romantic love, courtship, and seduction in romances increasingly started to take over the narrative space once devoted to displaying actions of heroic pursuit.

In Twyne's fiction, the illusion of events created in a narrative presented as a series of events that took place while travelling depends on the intertextual relationship between this and other typologically similar texts, but involving female–female sexuality. These texts create a network of orientalizing tales in which same-sex desire is represented as pleasurable if it concerns men, but disturbing if it involves women. Thus George Sandys, a seventeenth-century translator of Ovid's *Metamorphoses*, visited the public baths in Constantinople and observed that "Much unnatural and filthie lusts is said to be committed daily in the remote closets of these darksome *Bannias*: yea women with women, a thing incredible, if former times had no giuen thereunto both detection and punishment."[87] Sandys suggests that male homoeroticism is a matter of suggestion, which allows the reader to take pleasure in it; female homoeroticism is represented directly, and is therefore condemned in his masculinist perspective. Yet Sandys's account occludes the possibility that those who enjoy the "bannias" may exchange some kind of erotic pleasure, despite male readers' scandalized condemnation of those eastern women.[88] What is symptomatic about different versions of the account of women's baths lies precisely in what they are silent about: as Twyne's fiction suggests, only the men's baths are sites of pleasure. This occlusion of female pleasures in the baths locates women in the context of "filthie" desire, leaving men safely out of the realm of same-sex pleasures in Sandys's account. While Twyne's fiction relegates sexual pleasure between men outside the boundaries of Christianity, it makes the Eastern Mediterranean location the centre of pleasure, which it associates with an infidel's body as a seducer.

But in the same travel account, in which Sandys imagines "lesbianism" in the public baths and excises the possibility that the same "filthy" sin may occur between men too, he also excises sodomy from the sultan's court, thus occluding it in Constantinople. Sandys, apparently, visited the court of a young and ruthless sultan, aged twenty-three. There he witnessed the sultan "hauing caused eight of his Pages, at my being there, to be throwne into the Sea for Sodomy (an ordinary crime, if esteemed a crime, in that nation) in the night time."[89] The sultan murdering youth engaged in homoerotic acts is another instance of the fact that pederastic enticement, while it was certainly practised in Islamic cultures of the early modern era, was not theologically endorsed. Sandys's text is a record of the uncertain status the narratives of sodomy among Muslim men had even in English travel writing and among the travel writers keen to observe it.

In these fictions that cross over the boundaries of romance, travelogue, and ethnographic writing, we are also dealing with the fact that eroticism holds sway not only over the men and women imagined to enjoy the baths, it also keeps the writers of these fictional accounts captives to its mysterious and always elusive forces of empowerment and delusions. For these writers are the first to be overcome by the force of eroticism as literary inspiration, which colours other kinds of writing, from proto-ethnographic alterity to theology, so that their fictions about cross-gendered and same-gendered lives read like narratives bound by the "chains of Eros."[90] The issue in these proto-ethnographic fictions is not whether they are accurate, or even close to accurate, representations of the worlds they purport to reveal to their western readers. Rather, their thematic articulations of erotic vignettes are there to be shared in their own right with those readers; they are the subject of an exchange of ideas between the writer and the reader. It is the "textual unconscious"[91] of these proto-erotic fictions, which focus on erotic transgressions, that tell us more about those who write them and those to whom they write, than about the actual world of Asia Minor. It is fictions of erotic titillation clad in any number of thematic narratives that the readers of romances and of writing that draws on romance styles and structures, turned to for pleasure reading in the first instance. In that sense, then, prose romances and fictions inspired by them, by telling us about the Ottomans and their bodies, in fact tell us as much about early modern English readers' interests and appetites for erotic writing.

Sinning in Morea: The Homoerotics of Favouritism

Lady Mary Wroth's *The Countess of Montgomery's Urania*, published in 1621, was the most ambitious and voluminous romance written in the early modern period. It is also one of the very few romances written by a woman. In its complex interlaced narrative, the number of characters, and the breadth of the Mediterranean locations in which the narrative is set, it surpasses even Sidney's *Arcadia*. Written towards the end of King James I's reign, Wroth's romance resonates with the internal, international, and sexual politics that marked the court. The story of a wicked minion who betrays the unnamed duke and usurps his place has been said to allegorize the incident of Robert Carr's involvement, with his wife, the Countess of Essex, in the poisoning of Sir Thomas Overbury, one of King James's favourites. King James had the culprit and his wife imprisoned in the Tower of London, after first pardoning them.[92] Displacing this topical allegory to Morea, in the Eastern Mediterranean, enables Wroth to play out the homoerotic charge in the topical story of James's favouritism which puts kinship and sexuality into tension.[93] In Wroth, the intimacy of royal favouritism does not inhabit the physical and private "dark corners of the state"[94] but the larger plain of the Eastern Mediterranean.

Morea's status as part of the old Byzantium that has now declined to a place in the Ottoman Empire provides a convenient background for a story of a fall from dukedom to a melancholy hermitage. Of all the stories of his youth, the duke remembers the one that made him "issueless," that ruined him as a royal and denied him natural reproduction.[95] Mindful that romance is a genre of political teaching, one wonders, then, what the pedagogical and moral significance of this story is. Since its protagonists, including the unnamed King of Morea, disappear from the romance after this digression, the duke's story has the effect of a narrative emblem about the political consequences of sexual impropriety. The youth, "the son of wickedness," the duke says,

> though adopted to me, esteeming possession for better then reversion, gave place so much to covetousnesse, as much crept into credit to attaine the profit, wherefore he practiced to make me away: my friends and kindred had before left me, expecting nothing but my ruine, seeing me so bewitch'd with my undoing.[96]

The royal and sexual honour, or credit, in this exchange between the duke and the favourite, is undermined by the political profit the favourite intends to gain, by staging the duke's "ruine" by separating him from his friends and relations. But the duke's reputation is not only compromised by the favourite's exploitation of his sexual and royal honour, but also by his own failure of the profit the favourite is making: "I consented to the concealing, but never could be wonne, to think of harming him, whose ungratitude I beleev'd sufficiently would one day burden him."[97] Despite the duke's knowledge of the favourite's "devillish cunning," his affection "could not so much alter it selfe as to hate where once to earnestly I affected, or seeke revenge on him, whose good I ever wished."[98] The duke is only freed from the favourite's grip when the King of Morea intervenes in the favourite's treason and imprisons him. Social isolation becomes the duke's punishment for his neglect of duty, his version of the favourite's prison, and a form of private space from which he voices the story of his demise.[99] The duke's concealment of the favourite's misdeed puts the blame on the royal, not the favourite, and compromises one of the "princely deeds," which Margaret Tyler identified as "the aduancement of their line,"[100] causing the "issue-less," thus ruined, duke to lose his office. Lorna Hutson argues that in the fictions of women, female sexual honour is textualised as credit in the verbal transactions between men,[101] but in romances of men, as in the duke's story in *Urania*, male sexual honour is rendered as profit, therefore pleasure, which one, greedy, man usurps from another in an unequal exchange of sexual desire. Thinking about credit, profit, and greed, in interrogating the most prominent story of homoerotic contact, may seem a departure from the flow of Wroth's romance. This is only so if we treat the scene as yet another digressive incident, one of chance, characteristic of the literary form of romance. Yet thinking about this narrative in the light of political topicality involving King James can be more of an obstacle to critical assessment than explaining this story. Critics have used this scene to describe homoeroticism in Wroth's romance as "frank"[102] and "almost always an escape from the miseries of marriage and the inconstancy of love."[103] If homoeroticism is an escape from the misery of marriage, why are both sexual partners punished in the end? More is involved in this curious and miserable erotic transaction in Morea, and it involves the gendered economy of favouritism.

Within the complex sexual politics of *Urania*, and indeed of Wroth's writing in general, including her poetry, the homoeroticism of favouritism interacts with other forms of desire exchanged across gendered lines. Representations of "the public status" of female same-sex intimacy in Wroth's writing, as James M. Bromley has shown, coexist in Wroth's poetry with the poetic articulation of heteroerotic bonds.[104] While this kind of division is evident in Wroth's sonnet sequence *Pamphilia and Amphilantus*, whose subject is the love of (and for) women, it is also one of the main concerns of Wroth's fiction of the world of heroic male characters in the prose romance, *Urania*. In *Urania*, we can see how easily the boundary between the public and private, and between public role and social standing, can be disturbed under the pressure of homoerotic desire. And how at once dangerous and appealing that transgression can be. Wroth's interest in exploring same-sex male desire at the crossover between public and private realms, which correlates with her exploration of same-sex female bonds in the sonnets indicates a depth of social and literary concern with the queerness of relationships that cross over the limits of public status and therefore also gendered relationships.

Moving beyond the topicality of the scene, we can view the punishment as a move to consolidate the story within the conventional ideology that promotes marriage and procreation. Wroth applies the terms of credit and profit in imagining the structure of homoerotic relationships by echoing terms, credit and profit, that are used in humanist literature about household management, which underpinned the thinking about marriage in early modern England, to recommend equality between husband and wife. Thus, profitability, as Xenophon describes it in his influential *Treatise of Householde*, requires parity: "this couple is so much the more profitable, the one to the other, because that [the] one lacketh the other hath."[105] However, the rhetorical economy of Wroth's episode replaces the wife with the favourite. Read alongside Xenophon's views on profit, Wroth's romance shows that an imbalance in emotional "profitableness," therefore greed, leads to the demise of the relationship.

In resorting to the dynamics of credit and profit in textualising the sexual economy between the duke and the favourite, Wroth looks back at theories of matrimony and at discourses that undermine what secures woman's position in the household, that is, a profitable and equitable marriage, not, say, to other discourses of credit and profit and profit and loss, which circulated in the economic sphere dominated by trading men. The duke's erotic and love credit, his virtue and autonomy, is exploited by the favourite, for whom profit is the benefit gained (at least prior to imprisonment) from usurping the value of the duke's virtue in the "covetous" exchange with him. The damaging potential of such profit, and of favouritism, in this episode is manifested in the duke's fall from power, in much the same way it is constructed in Christopher Marlowe's historical tragedy *Edward II*, which pushes the fall even further in staging the deaths of both King Edward II and his favourite, Gaveston. In Wroth's version of men's exchanges in Morea, homoeroticism is seen in the conventional, not liberating, sense as a threat to marriage and procreation.

If Wroth's adaptation of chivalric romances is an "act of 're-vision' from a female perspective – not merely of one text, but of an entire tradition," intended to reimagine the "often bitter" divide between the idealized status of woman in fiction and the "restrictive realities"[106] of Jacobean woman, then the episode of the duke, the kind of story that does not feature in romances written by men, represents a curious example of that revision. In her adaptation of the literature of favouritism typically written by men, Wroth reimagines a conventional message within an unconventional story: the violation of the profitable relationship with a wife within the household for an unprofitable sexual attachment to an undeserving man comes as a punishment for abandoning the main goal of the romance: marriage that brings stability not only to the commonwealth, but also to a woman striving, in the romance tradition, to attain social status and economic prosperity through marriage. In a story in which the woman is left out, Wroth's romance reflects a conventional view of the homosexual as a social outcast, and in that, her fiction differs from romances written by men that envisage male desire in ways that are unconventional and run counter to discourses of difference in travel literature.

The stereotype of the Levantine man (like the stereotype of a Catholic, Jew, or Italian) as a sodomite continues the stock representations of religious and ethnic groups as sodomites in Reformation and post-Reformation propaganda literature.[107] But romances show that sodomy was rarely associated with Muslims in imaginative literature and that erotic and affective contacts between men in romances are more nuanced and varied, and, most important, that they do not close down but open up possibilities for men to experience both their masculinity and their intimacy. The man from the Levant thus turns out to be not a figure of sexual abhorrence, but a companion in shared emotions, and a facilitator of desire that cannot be exchanged among the knights. Romances thus run counter to the post-Reformation denigration of the Turk as the stock figure of the sodomite, and by reserving sodomy for tyrants and giants, but desire and non-somatic contacts and affection between knights or between a western traveller and an eastern man, they rethink Christian masculinity and subjectivity.

Afterword: Mediterranean Masculinities

Knights in arms at the time of social transition from feudalism to protocapitalism, from Philip Sidney to Madeleine de Scudéry, challenge masculine identification with chivalric militancy and with battles in which other knights are regarded as rivals. Transformed by the changes in masculinity from heroic to romantic at the end of the sixteenth century and reflecting the shift from chivalric militancy towards circumspection, required as a result of the strategies of England's political and commercial involvement in the Eastern Mediterranean, romances now abound with scenes in which masculine agency is tested as a private and public force away from the battlefield. In all the romances that I have examined throughout this book, knights in arms remind us that masculinity in romances was changed in an encounter with the new, both strange and increasingly familiar, world of the Eastern Mediterranean. Within that world, the knight of romances moves through the often treacherous territories of the East and through the seductive private spaces of the Levant with the same force that once drove his passage through the lands of dragons and supernatural mysteries. In places where giants once challenged the masculine virtue of the knight-errant, trading routes now stretch towards the lucrative markets of the East, navigated with vigour by the knight. His eastern counterparts, men from the East, are no longer the infidels, that is, the non-Christian believers who have to be defeated in the romance of chivalry because they pose a threat to Christianity. Rather, the new framework for romances means that every aspect of the knight's agency, be it pragmatic or erotic, in his engagement with the East, is put in the service of circumspection which is required for his negotiation of power and profit in his contacts with Levantine men. In the narratives in which the knight's desire redefines the idea of a moral story that romances were generally associated with, that desire also changes the notion of the Eastern Mediterranean. The Eastern Mediterranean is no longer a place of danger; it has become a space that produces and absorbs pleasure.

The erotic masculinity that emerges from the pages of prose romances reveals the instability of heterosexuality, whose chivalric manifestations assume dominance in romances. If romances are predicated on heterosexual masculinity, given that they are driven by the ideology and rhetoric of courtship and marriage, then the erotically ambiguous male contacts represent a departure from the heteronormativity of romances. That departure suggests that romances are interested almost equally in new models of male desire based on sexual difference as in promoting heterosexual desire. The tendency of prose romances to move away from, and in some instances reject, heteroerotic love and marriage as a norm in romance writing is not altogether new. For example, in Achilles Tatius's Hellenic romance *Clitophon and Leucippe,* boys are openly promoted as more desirable objects of male love than women. This makes us aware of the fact that sexuality in romance literature was a category that was always under scrutiny in the history of romance writing, that it has driven romance narrative. The study of the literary discourses of male sexuality in prose romances of the early modern period has for a long time been an almost blank page in written histories of the discourses of masculinity in western literature. Translated into English by William Burton and published in 1597,[1] Achilles Tatius's work deeply influenced erotic romance writing at the turn of the century, as Victor Skretkowicz's detailed analysis of the erotic romance in the Renaissance amply demonstrates.[2] While the privileged erotic ideal in Hellenic homoerotic romances is pederasty, and while Burton's translation could be said to add an important prose romance to the body of homoerotic writing in early modern England, it is the prose romance of late Elizabethan and of Jacobean periods that offers a new perspective on male eroticism to this body of work. Erotic masculinity is both a matter of intimacy and sexuality as much as of politics, and it reveals how the formation of subjectivity in romances is concomitant with the creation of a new political order that often assumes the inscription of western power in the East. As fictions of masculinity show, when we speak of exchanges and contacts with the Eastern Mediterranean we should not always assume a two-way flow of interests and desires. Rather, what romances show is that those exchanges are often imagined to work to the West's advantage and that surrendering to the sexual allure of the

East mixes erotic with political energies that imbue romance narratives through and through.

The paths of travelling merchants and heroic knights-errant often meet in the Eastern Mediterranean, but this does not mean eliding literature with the social and political context against which it is written. Western knights-errant following in the steps of the Crusaders may not have been seduced by handsome Arab boys offering to rub aromatic oils in their bodies; and real merchants most certainly did not share a bed with the sultan in Constantinople. But when writers of romances imagine these scenarios they make not only the East and the West, but also eastern and western masculinity, legible in ways that challenge the ideologies that defined masculinity as solely within the religious boundaries of the West. The East becomes as much as a defining principle of western masculinity as Protestant Christianity is. The conflict of power that permeates the geographical writing of the Eastern Mediterranean is as much the subject of erotic writing as it is of political writing and texts on mercantilism. The struggle that took place over the trading routes and territories in the Eastern Mediterranean, and between eastern self-identity and western claims on that identity through trade in the Mediterranean, also represents the struggle that is fictionalized in romances, depicted in geography (in maps and atlases), and narrated in travel and ethnographic writing.[3] It is a struggle channelled through masculinity as agency that is driving the early cultural history of the Eastern Mediterranean.

Nowhere is that struggle between knightly masculinity and the new demand placed on it at the time of the opening of mercantile routes in the Eastern Mediterranean played out in more exploratory ways than in Richard Johnson's romance *The Seven Champions of Christendom.* This romance marks the high point of romance writing in sixteenth-century England. The merchant empire that emerges from the pages of this romance is not just a space of probable profit in the East, it is also a zone where western masculine self-identification with royal service acquires a different meaning in the knight's contact with the East. None of the seven Christian champions who reach the Eastern Mediterranean are images of heroic male prowess that can be recognized from earlier chivalric romances. The romantic agency of these knights in pursuit of marriage is concurrent with their forceful political agency as heralds of new trading territories that are taking shape, that are not-too-distant versions of a mercantile empire whose contours emerge in a different kind of writing about the East.

In some of the most fascinating ways in which prose romances engage with the East, Johnson's Eastern Mediterranean stretches from the shores of Asia Minor alongside the Silk Road to the mouth of the Persian Gulf and the nexus of eastern trade, Hormuz. The geographical sweep of lands that created this route is a reminder of an area of criticism still waiting to be fully examined: the stories, fables, and travel writing about the Silk Road route, and of eastern trades, as resources in the transformation of prose romances in the early modern period. The caravans that trundled down the busy Silk Road to and from the Mediterranean, which connected the East with the West through commerce, moved along the same geography that Johnson's champions are securing for western trade with the East. In a romance in which silk and eastern luxuries create a cluster of related images connected with the commodities originating in the East and arriving to the Mediterranean via the Silk Road, eastern trade is written in the stories of the heroic achievements of the knight whose masculine agency is an instrument of the West's mercantile politics in the East.

The cultural story that material objects and matters of the East tell within the romance history of the heroic knight-errant transform those objects and matter into what Jonathan Gil Harris perceptively calls "an oriental–occidental palimpsest," emerging at the point where the East and western literature are joined in one text.[4] Such a palimpsest of history and knowledge of the East becomes legible as the West–East narrative in which the knight's agency creates material conditions for profit in trade to be gained in the future. The orientalism of romances, therefore, is never too far removed from the romance of the East in Johnson's fiction. The Orient as an intertext in romance writing is imagined in fascinating detail in Madeleine de Scudéry's romance of the Levant. Alongside Wroth's *Urania*, and together with Johnson's romance, Scudéry's *Ibrahim* represents a major achievement in turning the Levant into the defining story of emotions, gender, and sexuality in western romances, produced through contacts with the East as both a material entity and an eroticized space.

The merchant knight of these eastern kingdoms, and the erotic knight, who crosses the border between the West and the East via the homosocial route, represent two sides of the same coin of writing masculinity in romances of the East. But they are not antithetical types. Rather, knights in arms in romances trouble the incongruity between the hero and the lover and between reason and passion, that criticism has sometimes assigned to the knight's role in prose fiction, arguing that such duality "represents the locus of desire" in texts like Sidney's *New Arcadia*.[5] When the knight ceased to be the model of aristocratic and heroic masculinity that he was in feudal aristocratic romances, this model became open to other kinds of cultural inscriptions that romance attached to it as part of negotiating its main concerns of love and eroticism. And when with the decline of chivalric culture the militant knight ceased to be the model for masculine identification, the merchant emerged as the ideal of civic masculine agency of the nascent middle class. This is why the heroic paths of knights-errant often intersect with the routes travelled by ambitious merchants sailing from the West to eastern ports. Prose romances collapse the knight and the merchant into one type, the merchant–knight. In the body of the merchant knight, both intimate and public acts of masculinity offer a basis for a new exemplary story of actions based on circumspection and for new fictions of intimacy.

Explored against a variety of records of the Eastern Mediterranean across a diverse body of writing, prose romances reveal a different, competing picture of the Eastern Mediterranean, precisely fictionalizing that region through the prism of eroticism. In that sense, any critical account of how early modern England viewed the Eastern Mediterranean, or how the East shaped the aesthetics and text of early modern England, will continue to be incomplete if the Mediterranean prose romances of the East are not added to the rich archive of early modern orientalism. In the eyes of English travellers in the Eastern Mediterranean, every inch of this region was regarded as a poetical site of sexual vice. But in the pages of English writers of romances, the same sites are reimagined as spaces of emotional fulfilment, sexual pleasure, homosexual companionship, or amorous friendship. For instance, in his travel account of the Holy Land, *A True and strange discourse of the trauailes of two English Pilgrimes* (1608), Henry Timberlake chooses not to dwell on the sacred and ritualistic significance of Jerusalem, but records the apparent epidemic of sodomy among the non-Christian citizens of the Holy Land. Those citizens "vse the sinne of Sodom and Gomorah very much in that country, whereby the poor Christians that inhabit therein, are glad to marry their daughters at twelve yeares of age vnto Christians, least the Turks should rauish them." Timberlake finishes his tirade against sodomy by saying that sodomy "is vsed there amongst those Infidells that now inhabit therein, and yet it is called Terra Sanctra, and the Arabian Tongue Cutelha, which is the Holy Land, bearing the name only and no more: for all holyn[e]s is clea[rli]e banished from thence, by those Theeues filthy Turkes and Infydells that inhabit the same."[6] Here, we read the requisite Christian rant against Muslims articulated through language of sexual denunciation. The catastrophe that befell the biblical cities of Sodom and Gomorrah as the result of God's ire is here read as a catastrophe that befell Christianity when it fell to the Ottomans. As Alan Bray has reminded us, the reference to these two biblical cities was one of the many images that conjured up the horror of homosexuality in Renaissance England, but that these images "came most readily to hand when a round-about description was needed of the vice not to be named among Christians."[7] Once Sodom and Gomorrah had unleashed their signifying sodomitical energies in early modern English writing, the observers keen to infuse their writing with the stories of wonders and marvels of the East did not miss any opportunity to add sodomy to the list of strange things in their histories of eastern curiosities.

One of those attentive observers of the East was William Lithgow, who, like many of his contemporaries who travelled in the East, was ready to infuse his travelogue with a fair dose of fiction. In one of his travelogues from Turkey he reports that the Turks wash after "they commit any copulation with Christians, or their own sex" before sunrise "thinking thereby to was their sinnes."[8] In examples like this, it is important to note that it is Lithgow who projects the Christian model of "sin," which pertained only to Christians, onto the Islamic context of his writing. In the course of this projection Lithgow implicitly censors homoeroticism at home, where it is regarded as sin. Against such constructions of the East as a space of uncensored sexual acts, episodes of sexual aberration and violence in romances are almost routinely reserved only for fictionalized accounts of male violence against women. The moral of an account of the young woman, Rosella, seduced by "a man of comlie personage, debonaire, well qualified, and rich"[9] in Constantinople, told in *The third and last part of Palmerin of England* (1602), is an instance of the misogynistic tendencies of some romances. But this episode is an exemplary narrative in which the author mounts a critique of hypermasculinity as the type of masculinity that romances, in fact, abhor. Once the man in *Palmerin* has dragged the woman into the woods and "seduced" her with "kisses" and "flatteries" in a small tent, the man "like a monster and no man, glutted his libidinous and insatiable desire,"[10] and ordered the tent and the bed in which the raped young woman lay be taken away, leaving her, "unmanlike," to wake up naked in the woods.

At once a story of tyrannical sexual aggression and a fiction that critiques such masculine agency through the vivid language of violence, this episode provides a sharp contrast to a very different model of masculinity in which homosociality is the only source of sensuousness between men. The narrator in *The second part of the first booke of the myrrour of knighthood* (1585), tells the readers that a reunion of three friends, Florinaldus, Blandizel, and Claueryondo, also in a wood in the Levant, was a scene involving "those which loued together like vnto perfect friends" (P5^{r}).[11] The three men from the *Myrrour of knighthood* are joined temporarily as friends in the privacy of a closet-tent, separating them from the world of heroic masculinity outside the tent. In Anthony Munday's romance, *Zelauto* (1580), friends are joined for life. "Betweene these twayne," Munday says, "were ioyned such a league of Amytie: that neyther bitter blastes should procure the breach thereof, nor any accident whatsoueuer, moue them to mislike one of the other, but euen brotherlyke were vnited, fyll terme of lyfe were vtterly expired."[12] Permanent and tight bonds of friendship between men, based on emotions whose depth and permanence resembles devotion to a female partner in marriage, does not merely reflect a shift of romance from heroic to romantic concerns. Rather, this literary movement relieves masculinity of its obligation to serve only the requirement of heterosexual romance and to be always on the course of courting women. These two antithetical examples of masculinity and desire – the aggressive masculinity of heterosexual desire and the romantic masculinity of friendship and homosocial eroticism – also display instances of unnatural and natural masculinity in romances. Moral degradation and denigration of a rapist removes the most extreme version of hypermasculinity from the narrative space of romance. In his place, the romance discloses homosexuality and brings into full view loving and lasting friendships between men. Prose romances rank very high on the hierarchy of literary genres that naturalize same-sex eroticism and male erotics, not as effeminizing, but as a productive alternative to heterosexuality that eliminates the boundary of threat and rivalry between the West and the East.

Prose romances have been termed inescapable, erotic, and exceptional.[13] Each of these adjectives has attempted to capture the fact that romances overreach the limits of their own genres and imbue other literary genres. These qualifiers also indicated that romances assimilate some of the most provocative aspects of literary writing across historical periods, that they themselves become the wells of new knowledge about the time that produced them. Romances of the Levant, or the Eastern

Mediterranean, have not only been mediators of knowledge about the Eastern Mediterranean at a time when that knowledge was being created, contested, and rewritten in different forms. They also shaped the idea of masculinity as produced by the Eastern Mediterranean and imagined the Levant as a space of the economic and erotic interests of enterprising and curious adventurers from northwest Europe.

Early modern studies of subjectivity, sexuality, and queer desires have not drawn on the wealth of romance narratives of the body and interiority to compose arguments about the erotic subject and homoerotic masculinity in the early modern period. But in the pages of the texts explored in this book – *The Seven Champions of Christendom, The Countess of Pembrokes Arcadia, Moderatus, Pheander, Ornatus and Artesia, Montelyon, Oceander, Palmerin d'Oliva, Palmerin of England, Amadis de Gaule, Montelyon, Ornatus and Artesia, Palmendos, The myrrour of knighthood, Gwydonius, The Patterne of Painefull Adventures, Ibrahim,* and *Urania* – the Levant is made into a political and affective force that engenders fictions about different manifestations of masculinity and male erotics as something that is negotiated between the two divides of the Mediterranean, the East and the West. At first glance, almost all of these texts, with (perhaps) the exception of Sidney's *Arcadia,* strike us as non-canonical literature. Yet the originality and freshness with which they present masculinity make these texts central to the still developing canon of gender and erotic writing in the Renaissance. If in this book I did not deliberately place romances, even for the sake of a short comparison, side by side with other texts that are most revealing of the early modern presentations of sexuality, it is because I wanted these romances to speak with their own voice, with their own language of men's diverse sexuality. The orientalism of western masculinity and male sexuality that emerges from the pages of these romances reflects the internationalizing tendencies of late sixteenth- and early seventeenth-century fiction, and of the role the East plays in the erotic imagination of early modern English writing. The 1580s and the 1590s in particular were the decades when romance writers' interest in the East peaked. The transcultural and multi-confessional global Mediterranean that takes literary form in the romance writing of this period reveals little about the culture and society that constituted it, but says a lot about the rich literary imagination that brought, and translated, that distant world for and to English readers. If we want to know, as we increasingly do, more about the origins and nature of western interests in, and representations of, the Islamic world of the Eastern Mediterranean, both in literature and early modern culture, we have to take prose romances seriously as imaginary versions of the early, and changing, western attitudes towards the East. Without paying attention to prose romance, the historiography of early English ideas and fantasies about the East will remain incomplete. Prose romance shows that the East became increasingly familiar to the West; that it became a space of limitless projections of western political and mercantile ambitions; and that it ended up being a generator of stories, a great resource for literary imagination translated into new fictions that enriched the early modern literary canon. In many ways, prose romance prepared the terrain for the abundance of fiction about the "fabulous Orients"[14] that flooded the literary scene and market from the Restoration well into the eighteenth century.

The orientalism of the Eastern Mediterranean and of the erotic subjects and their activities that are associated with this region is not the only ideological feature that we can use to describe the dynamic engagement of the West with the Ottoman Empire. In an attempt to expand historical approaches to the study of the Mediterranean, historians of this sea have proposed the term "Mediterraneanism," offering it as a "comparable ideology"[15] to orientalism. Mediterraneanism refers to the construction of the Mediterranean alongside the North–South economic divide and a more broadly conceived understanding of the terms covering various ways in which the Mediterranean gives meaning to a variety of writings about it as a sea, history, and imagination. This book has argued that Mediterraneanism was the powerful ideological charge that was responsible for the transformation of prose romances as a literary genre that took place at the end of the sixteenth and in the early seventeenth century.

The Eastern Mediterranean that prose romances fictionalize was an imperial space, absorbed and governed by the Ottomans. It was not a coherent political entity either. Within this imperial Eastern Mediterranean dominated by the Ottomans, prose romances developed their versions of the lines of trade and of the subjectivities that are formed under the strangeness of that sea as much as romance features, in an attempt to imagine the same space as a dominion of western imperial ambitions. "The end of the Mediterranean,"[16] as two historians have suggested, may have arrived with Fernand Braudel's history of the sea and its shores, a history whose romantic view of the Mediterranean in all its abstractions marked an era of Mediterranean historiography. Braudel looked into just about every corner of the Mediterranean and the archives that preserve its history. But his monumental history of the sea is heavily preoccupied with the western presence in the Mediterranean. In David Abulafia's comprehensive history of the Mediterranean, which covers the period from the early centuries BCE to the twenty-first century, the early modern period occupies the central place in his study. His focus on the early modern world is of interest to my study of romance writing because of the particular argument Abulafia makes shedding light on the burgeoning of Mediterranean romances particularly invested in fictions of the Levant. Namely, Abulafia reminds us that in the period between the 1570s and the 1650s, political tensions in the Mediterranean "calmed" as the result of "the tacit settlement between the Ottomans and the Spaniards,"[17] which in turn made the sea crossing less dangerous than before this fragile truce. He goes on to argue that "once Spanish patrols limited themselves to protecting the coastal waters of southern Italy, Sicily, and Spain,"[18] the Ottoman menace on the sea became confined to the Eastern Mediterranean. Thus, with the Catholic opponent defeated, the attention of the English could now be directed towards the other big rival in southern Europe: the Ottomans. In a way, then, the interest in Islamic figures and an ambivalent relationship towards the Muslim world, a relationship that mixes attraction with prejudice and pleasure with horror, could be said to have replaced the preoccupation with Catholicism with which Protestant and Puritan critics of the sixteenth and seventeenth centuries often associated prose romance. And it is precisely within this space of uncertainty and danger in the Eastern Mediterranean that romance writers fictionalize both heroism and the mercantile opportunities awaiting western merchant-knights. What became a socially and politically – and commercially – treacherous zone of West–East contacts thus became a space imagined in various ways in the pages of early modern prose romances. In those pages, an alternative history of the Eastern Mediterranean is written. The fictional history of the Eastern Mediterranean is a history of these once highly popular books of light reading, in whose narratives the knight-errant's ability to reclaim the East with his prudence is the source of unending stories of desire. As fictions of desire in which fulfillment is imagined both as an affective and a material, or pragmatic, accomplishment, romances about the Eastern Mediterranean are also romances of ambition. In these fictions of the East, in these tales that honour and uphold both the romantic and economic aspirations of men, we can also see the slow emergence of the novel in the time to come, and the importance of the East in that process, for stimulating stories of ambition and profit, mixed with bravery and desire.

Notes

Preface

1 I have borrowed the phrase from the title of Sedgwick's book *Between Men*.
2 Werth, *The Fabulous Dark Cloister*, 3.
3 Hutson, *The Usurer's Daughter*, 112–13.
4 The link between the Mediterranean, romance, and the novel has been explored by Doody in *The True Story of the Novel*.
5 Cooper, "Introduction." *Christianity and Romance in Medieval England*, xiii.
6 Parker, *Inescapable Romance*, 5.
7 Fuchs, *Romance*, 4–5.
8 Moretti, *Graphs, Maps, Trees*; "The Slaughterhouse of Literature, 207–27.
9 Murrin, *Trade and Romance*.
10 I have borrowed the phrase from the title of *Sex Before Sex*.

Introduction

1 *The famous History of PALMENDOS SON of the most Renowned Palmerin D'Oliva*, sig. A4^{r}. The first edition of the same romance by Francisco de Moraes does not include the same epistle. It is entitled *The honourable, pleasant and rare conceited histories of Palmendos*. This romance was translated by Anthony Munday.
2 Lincoln Cathedral Library, MS 91 (A.5.2). This collection of romances is called "Thornton," after the Yorkshire scribe Robert Thornton.
3 Charbonneau and Cromwell, "Gender and Identity in the Popular Romance," in *A Companion to Medieval Romance*, 96.
4 Carey, "Structure and Rhetoric in Sidney's Arcadia," 245.
5 Cave, "Locating the Early Modern," 19. Emphasis included in the original.

6 Ascham, *The Scholemaster* (1570), 81.
7 Meres, in "Sketch of English Literature, painting, and music, up to September 1598," 22. There is also an entry in the Register of the Stationers' Company stating that on 13 February 1581 a certain John Charlewood "Lycenced vnto him by master watkins a booke intituled the historie of PALMERIN of Englande, vppon Condicion that if there be anie thinge founde in the Booke when it is extante worthie of Reprehension that then all the Bookes shal be put to waste and Burnte." Cited from Arber, *A Transcript of the Registers of the Company of Stationers of London*, 74.
8 Fuchs, *Romance*, 98.
9 Mentz, *Romance for Sale in Early Modern England: The Rise of Prose Fiction*, 32.
10 Fellows, "Printed Romance in the Sixteenth Century," 67–78.
11 Jewkes, "The Literature of Travel and the Mode of Romance in the Renaissance," 222.
12 Cavanagh, *Cherished Torment*.
13 Everett, "A Characterization of the English Medieval Romances," 3.
14 Burlin, "Middle English Romance: The Structure of Genre," 1.
15 Particularly important in that regard are the following studies: Jackson, "The Nature of Romance," *Yale French Studies*, 12–25; Clare, *Sovereign Fantasies*.
16 Frye, *The Secular Scripture: A Study of the Structure of Romance*, 177.
17 Finlayson, "Definitions of Middle English Romance," 168–81.
18 Dolven, *Scenes of Instructions in Renaissance Romance*.
19 Cavanagh, *Cherished Torment*.
20 Moretti, *Graphs, Maps, Trees*.
21 Warkentin, review of Franco Moretti's *Graphs, Maps, Trees*, 343.
22 Moretti, *Graphs, Maps, Trees*, 35–6.
23 Ibid., 29.
24 Ibid., 1.
25 Ibid.
26 Moretti, "Conjectures on World Literature," 57.
27 Davis, *Renaissance Historical Fiction* 7.
28 Ibid., 8.
29 Greene, *Gwydonius, or The Card of Fancy*, 82.
30 Ibid., 11.
31 Ortelius, *An Epitome of Ortelius*, sig. M8^{v}.
32 A town on the island of Lesbos in modern Greece.
33 Ortelius, sig. M4^{v}.
34 Ibid., sig. M5^{r}.
35 Said, *Orientalism*, 44

36 Ibid., 44.
37 Ibid.
38 Burke, "Did Europe Exist Before 1700?," 21.
39 Latin text accompanying the symbol reads: Hic Saladine turcar, rex babilonic, et damasci Soldanus uicit xpianor. The translation is mine.
40 Brotton, *A History of the World in Twelve Maps*, 6–7.
41 Marchitello, *Narrative and Meaning in Early Modern England*, 73.
42 Schwoebel, *The Shadow and the Crescent*, 93.
43 Moryson, *An Itinerary Written By Fynes Moryson Gent*, sig. X3v.
44 Gallagher and Greenblatt, *Practicing New Historicism*, 47.
45 In that sense, Morea is mentioned in Madeleine de Scudéry's romance *Ibrahim*, sig. Iii3v.
46 McCoy, *Sir Philip Sidney*, ix.
47 Imber, "The Crusade of Varna, 46.
48 Hadfield, "Travel," 137.
49 Hurd, *Moral and Political Dialogues*, 226.
50 Ibid., 295. The passage in *Paradise Regained*, to which Hurd refers, reads: "Such forces met not, nor so wide a camp,/When Agrican with all his northern powers/Besieged Albracca, as romances tell;/To city of Gallaphrone, from thence to win/The fairest of her sex Angelica/His daughter, sought by many prowest knights,/Both paynim, and the Peers of Charlemagne." (III, lines 337–43). Quoted from John Milton, *The Major Works*.
51 Bolgar, "Hero and Anti-Hero," 127.
52 Ibid., 141.
53 Ferguson, *The Indian Summer of English Chivalry*, 111.
54 Women and prose romances are the subject of Newcomb, "The Romance of Service," 117–39; Hackett, *Women and Romance Fiction in the English Renaissance*.
55 Hutson, "Fortunate Travelers, 88.
56 I explore this issue in more detail in my essay "English Renaissance Romances as Conduct Books for Young Men," 60–78.
57 *The Second Booke of Amadis de Gale*. Another example of a man owning a prose romance is found in the Bodleian Library copy of Palmerin D'Oliva, in which an owner wrote "Robertj My buk" on the title page.
58 Lucas, *Writing for Women*, 49.
59 Schwarz, "The Probable Impossible: Inventing Lesbians in Arcadia," in *Tough Love*, 178.
60 Foyster, *Manhood in Early Modern England*, 3.
61 Skretkowicz, *European Erotic Romance*.
62 Wells, *Shakespeare and Masculinity*, 34.

63 Traub, *The Renaissance of Lesbianism in Early Modern England*, 13.
64 Sanchez, *Erotic Subjects*, 3.
65 Shepard, *Meaning of Manhood in Early Modern England.*
66 Forde, *The Most Pleasant History of Ornatus and Artesia*; Johnson, *Seven Champions of Christendom*, 132.
67 Breitenberg, *Anxious Masculinity in Early Modern England*, 3.
68 I adapt the idea from Matchinske, *Writing, Gender and State in Early Modern England*, 6.
69 Abulafia, "What is the Mediterranean?," 11.
70 Ibid., 11.
71 Boemus, *The Manners, Lawes, and Customes of All Nations*, sig. A2r.
72 Ortelius, *An Epitome of Ortelius His Theatre of the World*, sig. M6r; Anon., *Oceander*, sig. Y2r; Also, John [Giovanni] Botero devotes many pages to a detailed description of the Mediterranean and the origins of the sea and its name. Botero, *The Cause of the Greatnesse of Cities*, 232–5.
73 Cooper, *Thesaurus linguae Romanae & Britannicae*, sig. Gggg3r.
74 Goody, *Renaissances: The One or the Many*, 39.
75 Braudel, *The Mediterranean and the Mediterranean World in the Age of Philip II.*
76 Chambers, *Mediterranean Crossings: The Politics of an Interrupted Modernity*, 1.
77 Heng makes a similar argument with respect to medieval romances. *Empire of Magic*, 5.
78 Worden, *The Sound of Virtue*, xxi.
79 Ibid., xxi.
80 Kahn, *Wayward Contracts*, 177.
81 Schwarz, *Tough Love*, 176–201.
82 Zurcher, *Seventeenth-Century English Romance.*
83 Fumerton, *Cultural Aesthetics*, esp. ch. 2, 29–66.
84 Britton, *Becoming Christian*, 5.
85 Ibid., 16.
86 Fredric Jameson, "Magical Narratives: Romance as Genre," 143.
87 Montrose, *The Purpose of Playing*, 5.
88 Jameson, "Magical Narratives, 142.
89 Bolgar, "Hero and Anti-Hero, 141.
90 Ibid., 127.
91 Ibid., 141.
92 Ferguson, *The Indian Summer of English Chivalry* 111.
93 Hamilton, *Historicism*, 17.
94 Cooper, "Introduction," xi.

95 McKeon, *The Origins of the English Novel*, 55–6.
96 Das, *Renaissance Romance*, 3.
97 Shuger, *The Renaissance Bible*, 120.
98 Robbins, "Commodity Histories," 456.
99 Newcomb, *Reading Popular Romance in Early Modern England*, 39.
100 Ibid.
101 MacFaul, *Male Friendship in Shakespeare and his Contemporaries*, 17. This line of argument was anticipated by Bray, "Homosexuality and the Signs of Male Friendship in Elizabethan England," 1–19 and in *The Friend*. It is also explored by Bray and Rey, "The Body of the Friend, 65–84; Shannon, *Sovereign Amity*; and Stewart, *Close Readers*.
102 Armitage, "Literature and Empire,"102.
103 Heng, *Empire of Magic*, 5.
104 Hutson, "Chivalry for Merchants," 34.
105 Andrea, "Early Modern Queens and Anglo-Ottoman Trade," 12–29.
106 Bearden. *The Emblematics of the Self*, 12.
107 Linton, *The Romance of the New World*, 8.
108 Robinson, *Islam and Early Modern English Literature*, 3.
109 Ibid., 3.
110 Fuchs explores identity in relation to early modern Spanish empire in *Mimesis and Empire*.
111 Davis, "England and the Mediterranean," 125.
112 Harris, *Sick Economies*, 3.
113 Edward Misselden, one of the first writers to write about free trade in early modern England, employed the rhetoric and narrative techniques of romance storytelling in his writings on mercantile exchange. His most notable treatises are: *The Center of the Circle of Commerce; The maintenance of free trade according to the three essentiall parts of traffique; The circle of commerce*.
114 Kahn, *Wayward Contracts*, 178.
115 Kamps and Singh, *Travel Knowledge*.
116 Dimmock, *Mythologies of the Prophet Muhammad in Early Modern English Culture*.; *New Turks*. Arguments about England's engagement with the Ottomans are extended in the essays in the collection *The Religions of the Book: Christian Perceptions*.
117 Vitkus, *Turning Turk*, 31.
118 Ibid.
119 MacLean and Dalrymple, *Re-Orienting the Renaissance*.
120 MacLean, *The Rise of Oriental Travel*.
121 MacLean and Matar, *Britain and the Islamic World*, 7.

122 Matar, *Britain and Barbary*, esp. ch. 2, "'Imperialism,' Captivity and the Civil Wars," 38–75.
123 I borrow Barbara Fuchs's useful term which captures the fictionalizing of empire in early modern literature, from the title of her book, *Mimesis*.
124 Brotton, *The Renaissance Bazaar*; Jardine and Brotton, *Global Interests*.

1 Purchasing Kingdoms in the Eastern Mediterranean

1 Johnson, *History of the Seven Champions of Christendom*, Case Y 1565.J.623.
2 This evidence is based on the editions in the Folger, Newberry, Huntington, and British libraries, and the library of The Harry Ransom Humanities Research Centre at the University of Texas at Austin.
3 Kirkman, *The Seven Champions of Christendom*, 1638.
4 Murrin, *Trade and Romance*, 216.
5 Cooper, *The English Romance in Time*, 389.
6 "Richard Johnson," *Oxford Dictionary of National Biography*, http://www.oxforddnb.com/public/index.html, 1, accessed 18 August 2013.
7 Johnson, *The Seven Champions of Christendom*, I, 6.
8 Ibid., 83.
9 Ibid., 52.
10 Ibid., II, 246.
11 Heylyn. *The historie of that most famous saint and souldier of Christ Iesus*, sig. A1ʳ.
12 de Malynes, *Saint George for England*, sig. A2ʳ–A3ʳ.
13 Heylyn. *The historie*, sig. C1ʳ.
14 Johnson, *The Seven Champions of Christendom*, I, 83.
15 Ibid.
16 Ibid., 86.
17 Ibid., 17.
18 *The Three Kings' Sons*, BL Harley MS 326.ff.8–123b. A similar romance is *The King of Tars and the Soudan of Damas* [the Sultan of Damascus]. This work narrates the heroic and amorous adventures of "mayden man," a young knight in Syria. It appears in BL Add. MS 22,283, ff. 126–8b.
19 Johnson, *The Seven Champions of Christendom*, I, 141.
20 McLeod, *The Geography of Empire*.
21 Munday, "Epistle" to his *The Admirable Deliverance*, sig. A2ʳ.
22 Ibid., sig. B2ᵛ.
23 Johnson, *The Seven Champions of Christendom*, I, 142.
24 Kerrigan, *Archipelagic English*, 54ff.
25 Kahn, *Wayward Contracts*, 174.
26 d'Anghiera, *The decades of the newe worlde of west India*, sig. A2ʳ.

27 Cormack, *A Power to Do Justice*, 228.
28 "empire, II, 5.a." OED Online. 18 September 2013. Oxford University Press. http://www.oxforddnb.com/public/index.html.
29 I expand the OED Online definition of "emporium" as "a place in which merchandize is collected and traded in. Often applied to towns or countries" (1a).
30 Ramsay, *English Overseas Trade During the Centuries of Emergence*, 34.
31 In the "Appendix: Medieval Romance in English After 1500," Helen Cooper provides details of a long afterlife of medieval romances in later centuries. See Cooper, *The English Romance*, 408–29. See also Cooper, "Shakespeare and the Middle Ages."
32 Heng, *Empire of Magic*, 5.
33 Vitkus, "Early Modern Orientalism, 208.
34 Johnson, I, 118.
35 Ibid.
36 de Grazia, "Anachronism," *Cultural Reformations*, 32.
37 Ibid., 21.
38 d'Anghiera (Peter Martyr of Angleria). *The decades of the newe worlde or west India.*, sig. H1^{v}. Also quoted in Maslen, "Sidneian Geographies," 46. The obsolete word "indocible" is glossed as "incapable of being taught or instructed; unteachable" (1a). OED Online. 13 June 2014. Oxford University Press.
39 Ibid., sig. H1^{r}.
40 Hakluyt, "Discourse of Western Planting," (1584) *The Original Writings & Correspondence of the Two Richard Hakluyts*, Vol. II.
41 Ibid., 325.
42 Brummett, *Ottoman Seapower and Levantine Diplomacy in the Age of Discovery*, 12–13.
43 Karras, *From Boys to Men*, 24.
44 I have borrowed the term from Karras, *From Boys to Men*, 51.
45 Simpson, *Reform and Cultural Revolution*, 287.
46 I have adapted this term from the phrase "to purchase kingdoms" which appears in the first part of Johnson's romance, *The Seven Champions* (41), where the narrator questions the purpose of the knights' advance into Asia.
47 Fuchs, *Romance*, 83.
48 Shepard, *Meanings of Manhood in Early Modern England*, 187.
49 Ibid.
50 The case of Elizabethan plantations in Ireland and the status of Ireland as at once a colony and a kingdom – Queen Elizabeth I was nominally the Queen of Ireland as well as of England and Wales – is a separate and complicated

instance of Elizabethan colonization, different in structure and organization from the fictional scenarios of merchant empire in prose romances.

51 Neal, *The Masculine Self in Late Medieval England*, 198.
52 Knolles, *The general historie of the Turkes*, sig. A4r.
53 Djurić, *Sumrak Vizantije*.
54 *Newes from Rome, Venice, and Vienna*, sig. C2r.
55 *Syr Bevis of Hampton*, sig. B3r.
56 Crane, *Gender and Romance in Chaucer's Canterbury Tales*, 27.
57 Smith, *Shakespeare and Masculinity*, 45.
58 Headlam Wells, *Shakespeare on Masculinity*, 47.
59 Cormack, *Charting an Empire*, 50.
60 Ortelius, *Theatrum Orbis Terrarum*, fol. 112.
61 Brummett, *Ottoman Seapower and Levantine Diplomacy in the Age of Discovery*, 146.
62 Foster, *England's Quest of Eastern Trade*, 94.
63 Skinner, *The Foundations of Modern Political Thought*, 53–4.
64 Ortúñez de Calahorra, *The mirrour of princeely deedes and knighthood*, sig. Ar.
65 Botero, *Relations of the most famous kingdoms and Common-wealths thorowout the world*, 23.
66 Botero, *The Mirrour of Policie*, sig. Hiijr. This work, influenced by Cicero's *Laws* and Book 6 of Aristotle's *Ethics*, is an anonymous translation from French of Guillaume de La Perriére's *La miroir politique*.
67 Kahn, *Rhetoric, Prudence, and Skepticism in the Renaissance*, 47.
68 Armitage, *The Ideological Origins of the British Empire*.
69 Drant, *Horace his arte of poetrie, pistles, and satyrs*, sig. Ciiijr.
70 Horace, *Satires, Epistles and Ars Poetica*, 321.
71 Kabbani, *Imperial Fictions*, 17.
72 Horace, *Satires*, I.x.34.
73 Guicciardini, *The Historie of Guicciardin*, sig. Iiiir. In The Harry Ransom Center's copy of this book a contemporary hand left a marginal note, which reads "From 1494 to 1533," on the title page. This may be the reference to the cut-off dates of the events covered by Guicciardini.
74 Johnson I, 91.
75 On Dubrovnik (Ragusa) and Mediterranean trade, see Kostić, *Dubrovnik i Engleska*.
76 Abulafia, *The Great Sea*, 550.
77 Johnson I, 36.
78 Gainsford, *The glory of England*, sig. C6r.
79 The "great Sophy" refers to the shah of the Safavid dynasty in Persia, which is how the Venetians and the Portuguese refered to the Safavid shah

in the first decade of the sixteenth century, as Sanjay Subrahmanyam suggests. According to Subrahmanyam, the epithet "great" stuck with the westerners and "was then carried over to his descendants." Subrahmanyam, *Three Ways to be Alien*, 81.

80 Grogan, "'Headless Rome' and Hungry Goths," 33.

81 Ibid., 32.

82 *Calendar State Papers Venice* (1913), 587.

83 Quoted from a transcription of Hakluyt's notes in Hackel and Mancell, "Richard Hakluyt the Younger's Notes for the East India Company in 1601, 432.

84 Ibid.

85 Ibid., 429.

86 Ibid.

87 Robarts, *Honovrs conquest*, sig. B4^{v}.

88 Hsy, *Trading Tongues*, 23–9.

89 Eden, *The History of Trauayle in the West and East Indies*, sig. iii^{r}–^{v}. "Calecut" is modern Kolkata, whose historical name in English is Calcutta.

90 Eden, *The History*, sig. iiii^{r}.

91 A 1595 account of English trade with the Levant lists as "principal" imports to England "oranges and lemons, timber, pitch and rosin, wines, flax and hemp, furs, cordage, linen, silk, currants, sugars, saltpeter, dates, molasses, sweet oils, spices, large onions, wood, wax, pitch, cross-bows and sword blades, prunes, tar, gold, silver, pearls, hides, salt beef, &c." *Calendar of State Papers, Domestic Series, of the Reign of Elizabeth*, 152.

92 Rothstein "Silk in the Early Modern Period," 536.

93 Hutson, "Chivalry for Merchants," 30–1.

94 Kahn, *Rhetoric, Prudence, and Skepticism in the Renaissance*, 30.

95 Ibid., 39.

96 Murrin, *Trade and Romance*, 2.

97 Ibid., 9.

2 The Knight on the Silk Road

1 Johnson, *The Seven Champions of Christendom*, II, 5.

2 Ibid., 1.

3 Hakluyt, *The Principal Navigations*, vol. 1, 50–1.

4 Hadfield, *Literature, Travel, and Colonial Writing in the English Renaissance*, 70.

5 Ibid.

6 Johnson, I, 151.

7 Greene, *The Spanish Masquerado*, sig. C3^{v}.

8 *State Papers Venice* (1905), 124.
9 Robinson, *Islam and Early Modern English Literature*, 30 and 33.
10 Johnson, *The Seven Champions of Christendom*, I, 161.
11 Shepard, *Meanings of Manhood in Early Modern England*, 70.
12 de Malynes, *Saint George for England*, sig. A2[r].
13 Ibid., sig. A6[v].
14 Ibid., sig. A7[r].
15 I follow Jonathan Gil Harris's astute interpretation of "Malynes's infected dragon," elaborated in his essay "Usurers of Color," 130.
16 de Malynes, *Saint*, sig. A6[v].
17 *The Honorable, pleasant and rare conceited Historie of Palmendos.*
18 Ferguson, *The Indian Summer of English Chivalry*, 111.
19 Murrin. *Trade and Romance*, 187–95.
20 Foster, *England's Quest of Eastern Trade*, 297.
21 Davis, "England and the Mediterranean, 125.
22 *State Papers Venice* (1913), 503.
23 Gritti, the Italian Consul at Aleppo, reports to the Venetian Senate, on 6 September 1623: "The King of Persia perceiving the great harm done him by allowing the English and Dutch to trade in Ormus and Bandel, their ships only bringing him [in] London, tin and spices to be disposed of in Persia and taking thence such a quantity of silk, has decided to make peace with the Portuguese." *State Papers Venice* (1921), 3.
24 Fumerton, *Cultural Aesthetics*, 189.
25 Wood, *The Silk Road*, 10–14.
26 Braudel, *Capitalism and Material Life*, 237.
27 Blunt, *The Golden Road to Samarkand*, 10–12.
28 Letts, *Sir John Mandeville;* and *Sir John Mandeville;* Bennett, *The Rediscovery of Sir John Mandeville.*
29 Morgan and Coote, eds. *Early Voyages and Travels in Russia and Persia by Anthony Jenkins and Other Englishmen*, 87–9.
30 Lach, *Asia in the Making of Europe*, Vol. 1, 81.
31 Epstein, *The English Levant Company*, 3.
32 Ibid., 304.
33 Arikan, "The Ban on the Export of Certain Articles from the Levant to the Mediterranean Ports during the Fifteenth and Sixteenth Centuries," 203.
34 İnalcik, "The Heyday and Decline of the Ottoman Empire," 324–53, 339.
35 Barbour, *Before Orientalism*, 13ff.
36 Brummett, *Ottoman Seapower and Levantine Diplomacy in the Age of Discovery*, 149.

37 Sandys, *A Relation of a Iourney begun An.Dom: 1610*, sig. L1[r].
38 Johnson, *The Seven Champions of Christendom*, II, 126.
39 The English silk production that began about 1560 soon became one of those enterprises that Joan Thirsk calls "new economic projects"; fast expanding industries producing lightweight consumer goods that expanded fast. Thirsk, *Alternative Agriculture*, 21. In the 1590s, silk trade in London had blossomed into a lucrative industry and silk had become a fashionable, if expensive, commodity sold on London's markets, especially Spitalfields, and in nearby market towns.
40 For example, when in Henry Robarts's romance, *Honours Conquest*, Edward of Lancaster, the Knight of the Cross, who protects the merchants from Tartarian pirates and robbers, observes "Portuguese merchants with 100 camels laden with spice and silk for Constantinople," the reader is reminded that the paths of the chivalric knights intersect with the routes of Iberian merchants trading with the Ottomans in commodities, spices and silk, which the English are only just beginning to contemplate. Through the imagined battles between Spain and Turkey Robarts's narrative figures disruptions of the established mercantile routes and, under the narrative guise of the knight's defense of Christianity, makes that knight also a defendant of something more pressing for English nationalism at the time: the sea and overland routes leading to the markets in the East. Those are the same markets from which, as Hakluyt advised, the English travelers should bring "Worme-seede" – the cocoon of the silkworm. Robarts, *Honours conquest*, sig. G3[r].
41 Johnson, *The Seven Champions of Christendom*, II, 13.
42 Ibid., 45.
43 Ibid.
44 Keene, "Material London in Time and Space," 67.
45 de Malynes, *Saint George for England*, sig. A6[v].
46 Stallybrass, "Marginal England, 33.
47 Johnson, *The Seven Champions of Christendom*, II, 36.
48 Liebler, "Bully St. George," 115–29.
49 Johnson, *The Seven Champions of Christendom*, II, 135.
50 Ibid., 157.
51 Ibid., 151.
52 Hutson, *The Usurer's Daughter*.
53 Johnson, *The Seven Champions of Christendom*, II, 153.
54 Potter, *Secret Rites and Secret Writing*, 75.
55 Johnson, *The Seven Champions of Christendom*, II, 123.

3 The Marriage of Merchant Kingdoms in Romances about Men

1 Jardine, "Companionate Marriage Versus Male Friendship," 234.
2 Wrightson, *English Society*, 92.
3 Houlbrooke, *The English Family*, 106.
4 Ibid.
5 Jardine, "Companionate Marriage Vesus Male Friendship," 234.
6 Ibid.
7 Ibid., 234–5.
8 Bray, *The Friend*, 110.
9 O'Hara, *Courtship and Constraint*.
10 I thank Tim Stretton for help with this part of my argument.
11 Forde, *Montelyon*, ed. Falke, v. Falke conjectures that the romance "was first published around 1600" (v). The 1599 date is proposed by Scanlon, "A Checklist of Prose Romances in English," 152.
12 Baker, *The History of the English Novel*, 124.
13 Forde, *The famous historie of Montelyon*.
14 Forde, *Montelyon*, ed. Falke, 191.
15 Ibid., 179.
16 Alfred C. Wood, *A History of the Levant Company*, 3.
17 Ibid., 6.
18 Forde, *Montelyon*, ed. Falke, 44, n.1.
19 Ibid., 171–85.
20 "These cruel wars [between Armenians and Persians] continued many years, the king of Armenia defending himself and keeping possession of the crown notwithstanding the Persian forces." Forde, *Montelyon*, ed. Falke, 89.
21 Wood, *The Silk Road*, 115.
22 Roberts, *The Merchants Mappe of Commerce*, sig. B1^{r} (emphasis in the original).
23 Ibid., sig. B2^{r} (emphasis in the original).
24 Forde, *Montelyon*, ed. Falke, ch. 35, 245–50.
25 Ibid., 291.
26 *The famous, pleasant and variable historie, of Palladine of England*, sig. Aa6^{v}.
27 Ibid., sig. U2^{v}.
28 Ibid.
29 Ibid., sig. Aa4^{v}–5^{r}.
30 Ibid., sig. Aa6^{r}.
31 Ibid.
32 Jardine, "Companionate Marriage Versus Male Friendship," 235.

33 Macfarlane, *Marriage and Love in England*, 119.
34 *The heroicall advuentures of the knight of the sea comprised in the most famous and renowned historie of the illustrious & excellently accomplished Prince Oceander*, sig. D3r.
35 Ibid.
36 *Amadis de Gaule*, ed. Moore, sig. G1v.
37 *Oceander*, sig. D3v.
38 Ibid., sig. F1r.
39 Ibid., sig. L2r.
40 Ibid., sig. J4v.
41 Ibid., sig. Gg2r.
42 Ibid., sig. Aa4r.
43 Ibid., sig. X4r.
44 Ibid., sig. Y2r.
45 Bodleian MS Lat misc. e.114 contains Randolph Cholmondeley's annotations on *Partitiones*, which Peter Mack identifies as possibly being "a record of a course of lectures" on rhetoric. Mack, *Elizabethan Rhetoric*, 53.
46 Cicero, *De Partitione Oratoria*, xxii, 76–7.
47 See Vickers, *In Defence of Rhetoric*, 57.
48 *Oceander*, sig. Dd1v.
49 Vickers, *In Defence of Rhetoric*, 51.
50 Cooper, *The English Romance in Time*, 370.
51 Newcomb, "The Sources of Romance, the Generation of Story, and the Patterns of the Pericles Tales," 21–46.
52 *Oceander*, sig. X2v.
53 Sandys, *A Relation of a Journey begun An.Dom: 1610*, sig. B1v.
54 Here I refer to a detailed description of the monster Child of Lessina (Lastovo in Croatia) in the Adriatic Sea, which was allegedly brought out to him as an after-dinner entertainment on the occasion of his voyage in the Adriatic. See Lithgow, *A most delectable, and true discourse, of an admired and painefull peregrination from Scotland, to the most Kingdomes in Europe, Asia and Affricke*, sig. D2r.
55 This motif from romances also appears in Shakespeare's *Pericles*.
56 *Oceander*, sig. Q3r.
57 Bushnell, "Tyranny and Effeminacy in Early Modern Culture," 344.
58 Dolan, "Re-reading Rape in *The Changeling*," 4–29.
59 McDonald, *Shakespeare's Late Style*, 90.
60 *The Famous, pleasant and variable Historie of Palladine of England*, sig. H4r.
61 Ibid., sig. I1r.
62 Cicero, *De Partitione*, xxii, 76.

63 *Palladine*, sig. I1r.
64 Ibid., sig. I1v.
65 Johnson, *The Seven Champions of Christendom*, I, 109.
66 Ibid., 111.
67 Ibid.,115.
68 Jed, *Chaste Thinking*, 12.
69 Brown, *The Body and Society*, 407.
70 Critics who have written about the abundance of rape scenes in early modern literature relate the violated female body to a violated national land. See Little, *Shakespeare Jungle Fever*; Jocelyn, *Writing Rape, Writing Women in Early Modern England; Women, Violence and English Renaissance Literature: Essays Honoring Paul Jorgensen*, ed. Woodbridge; Swarth, *Rape and Religion in English Renaissance Literature*; Saunders, *Rape and Ravishment in the Literature of Medieval England*; Solga, "Rape's Metatheatrical Return: Rehearsing Sexual Violence Among the Early Moderns," 53–72.
71 Sandys, *A Relation of a Journey begun An. Dom: 1610*, sig. X4r.
72 Ibid., sig. X3v.
73 *The first (second) part of the Honourable Historie of Palmerin D'Oliua*, sig. A8v.
74 Ibid., sig. A1r.
75 Ibid., sig. B1r.
76 *The third and last part of Palmerin of England*, sig. Ppp4v–Qqq1r.
77 Sandys, *A Relation*, A2r.
78 Ibid.
79 These meanings intertwine in the word "sensuality," which the *OED* defines as "physical necessities and appetites" (n. 1.b), "the lower or animal nature regarded as a source of evil; the lusts of the flesh" (n. 2), "the following of the lower nature in preference to the higher" (n. 3), and "excessive fondness for, or vicious indulgence in, the pleasures of the senses" (n. 4). OED Online. 12 June 2014. Oxford University Press. www.oed.com.library.smu.ca:2048/view/Entry/176017?redirectedFrom=sensuality#eid.
80 Sandys, *A Relation of a Journey begun An. Dom: 1610*, sig. A2v.
81 Ibid.
82 Robarts, *Honovrs Conquest*, sig. H3r.
83 Dimmock, *New Turks*; Vitkus. *Turning Turk*; Burton, *Traffic and Turning*; Bartels, *Speaking of the Moor*.
84 Johnson, *The Seven Champions of Christendom*, II, 205.
85 Helgerson, *Forms of Nationhood*, 47.
86 "ouches," "the gold or silver setting of a precious stone," Obs. OED Online. 12 June 2014. Oxford University Press.

87 Eden's Epistle prefaces the second, 1577, edition of his translation of Pietro Martire d'Anghiera's *De orbe novo*. This edition was expanded and prepared for publication by Richard Willes. *The history of trauayle in the West and East Indies*, sig. K7[r].

4 Desire and Knightly Masculinity

1 The dating of *Urania* is a complex issue. The first part was published in 1621, but the second part exists only as a seventeenth-century manuscript in the Newberry Library in Chicago. This unique holograph was used in the first publication of the second part in 2000. See *The Second Part of the Countess Montgomery's Urania*.
2 Wright, *Middle-class Culture in Elizabethan England*, 7–13.
3 Halperin, *How to Do The History of Homosexuality*, 88.
4 Forde, *Ornatus and Artesia*, sig. O2[v].
5 Berlant, "Intimacy: A Special Issue," 281.
6 Skretkowicz, *European Erotic Romance*, 169.
7 DiGangi, *Sexual Types*, 5.
8 Ibid., 6.
9 Ibid.
10 Ibid., 7.
11 Goldberg and Menon, "Queering History," 1610.
12 Stockton and Bromley, "Introduction," 9.
13 Simons, *The Sex of Men in Premodern Europe*, 25.
14 Crawford, "Sexual Knowledge in England," 83.
15 Skretkowicz, *European*, 27–164.
16 See *Homosexuality in Renaissance and Enlightenment England*, ed. Summers; Hammond, *Figuring Sex Between Men*; Juan Gil, *Before Intimacy*; Freccero, *Queer/Early/Modern*; Guy-Bray, *Homoerotic Space*; *Sodomy in Early Modern Europe*, ed. Betteridge; Schwarz, *Tough Love*; Orgel, *Impersonations*; Goldberg, *Sodometries*; *Queering the Renaissance*, ed. Goldberg; Saslow, "Homosexuality in the Renaissance" in *Hidden from History*, ed. Duberman et al.
17 Greene, *The Spanish Masquerado*, sig. C1[r].
18 Foxe, *The Pope Confuted*. sig. Jr.[r]
19 This definition is adapted from the OED Online, 14 June 2014, Oxford University Press. www.oed.com.library.smu.ca:2048/view/Entry/50684?redirectedFrom=dervish#eid.
20 Georgeuiz, *The Offspring of the House of Ottomano*, sig. D1[r].
21 Ibid., sig. G6[v]–7[r].

22 Ibid., sig. J8r.
23 Brown, *The Body and Society*.
24 In his book, *Renegade Women* (ix), Dursteller adopts this term from Carlo Ginzburg, who uses it in his study *The Cheese and the Worms*.
25 Pettet, *Shakespeare and the Romance Tradition*, 32.
26 Painter's version of Boccaccio's story appeared in the 1567 second part, reprinted together with the first in 1580, just at the cusp of the rise of prose romances.
27 The history of this story is detailed in Collingwood, *The Decameron*, 343–8.
28 Hutson, "Liking Men."
29 Ibid., 1083. Hutson provides an excellent summary of this story on pp. 1083–4.
30 I borrowed this term from Richard Helgerson, *Forms of Nationhood*, 44.
31 Quoted from Painter, *The Palace of Pleasure*, 370.
32 Painter, *The Palace*, 377.
33 Ibid.
34 Ibid., 371.
35 "Nothing would have given me greater joy," says Saladine to Messer Torello who is leaving for Pavia (on a gem-covered magic bed provided by Saladine's magicians), "than for us to have spent the rest of our lives together here, ruling as equals over the kingdom I now govern." Messer Torello, grateful to Saladine for rescuing him from slavery in Alexandria and thankful for the gifts received from him, is nevertheless in a rush to leave the Sultan's court in order to arrive at Pavia before the waiting period before the marriage day has expired: "since my mind is made up on the subject [of leaving], I beg you to act quickly in the manner you have proposed, for after tomorrow I shall no longer be expected." But Saladine lingers: "before bidding you farewell, I implore you in the name of our love and our friendship to remember me. And before our lives are spent, I beg you if possible to settle your affairs in Lombardy and come once more to visit me." He wants Messer Torello to write him letters in the meantime. Quoted from Boccaccio, *The Decameron*, 777–8.
36 Painter, *The Palace of Pleasure*, 363.
37 Ibid., 375.
38 Mauss, *The Gift*, 10–45.
39 Juan Gil, *Before Intimacy*, 1.
40 Ibid., 1.
41 Fulke Greville, for instance, describes his life-long friendship and cohabitation with Sir Philip Sidney, until Sidney left England to become governor of Flushing in 1585: "I lived with him and knew him from a child." Cited from Bray, *The Friend*, 44.

42 Bray, "Homosexuality and the Signs of Male Friendship in Elizabethan England," 43.

43 Hutson, *The Usurer's Daughter*, 90.

44 I explore this topic in "'Knights in Armes'," 170–92.

45 Constance C. Relihan has interrogated Painter's stories in relation to a production of feminist discourses in Elizabethan fictions. Relihan, *Fashioning Authority*, 42–6.

46 For issues regarding the writing of the history of same-sex desires, see Fradenburg and Freccero, "The Pleasures of History."

47 Bredbeck, *Sodomy and Interpretation*, 99–108; Jordan, *Renaissance Feminism*, 220–40; and Levine, *Men in Women's Clothing*, 1.

48 This is explored in detail in Jordan, *Renaissance Feminism*, 224–5.

49 Ibid., 225.

50 Ibid., 225, 85n.

51 Levine, *Men in Women's Clothing*.

52 I borrowed the idea of anxious masculinity from Breitenberg, *Anxious Masculinity in Early Modern England*.

53 Skretkowicz, *European*, 271.

54 See Matar, *Turks, Moors & Englishmen in the Age of Discovery*, 199.

55 DiGangi, *The Homoerotics of Early Modern Drama*. Cambridge.

56 Stewart, *Close Readers*, 8–37.

57 Parry, *A New and large discourse of the Trauels of Sir Anthony Sherley Knight, by Sea, and ouer Land, to the Persian Empire*, sig. D2^{r}.

58 Ibid., sig. C1r.

59 Discursive and formal features of early modern ethnographic writing are the subject of Brettell, "Introduction: Travel Literature, Ethnography, and Ethnohistory"; Craponzano, "On The Writing of Ethnography"; Marcus and Cushman, "Ethnographies as Texts"; Webster, "Dialogue in Fiction and Ethnography"; and George, "The Civilized West Looks at Primitive Africa."

60 Couverte, *A trve and almost incredible report of an Engishman*, sig. I1r.

61 Moryson, *An Itinerary, written by Fynes Moryson*, sig. X2^{v}.

62 Nicolay, *The Nauigations, peregrinations and voyages, made into Turkey*, sig. B4^{r}.

63 Timberlake, *A Trve and strange discourse of the trauailes of two English Pilgrimes*, sig. E4^{r}.

64 El-Rouayheb, *Before Homosexuality in the Arab-Islamic World*, 153.

65 In his collection of travel accounts, William Lithgow reports that sodomy was "rife" in many cities in Italy and in the Mediterranean, where to what appears to a Western "a monstrous filthinesse" is to the Italians and other

Mediterranean people "a pleasant pastime." Lithgow, *The Totall Discourse of the Rare Adventures and Painfull Peregrinations*, fol. 38. The idea that men from the East were particularly prone to lewdness, effeminacy, and sodomy acquired much purchase at the time, when stories of such alleged behaviour were brought from the East and then found confirmation in myths, as when Thomas Beard pens a fiction about the Assyrian king "Sardanapalus" who dressed in women's clothes, behaved lasciviously, acted in the effeminate manner and was prone to sodomy. See Beard, *The Theatre of Gods Iudgements*, sig. Z7$^{r–v}$.

66 Rocke, *Forbidden Friendship*. Also, a city-state open to commercial contacts with Mediterranean traders and those coming from Continental Europe, and ready to accommodate within its walls merchants (factors) from across Europe and the Easter Mediterranean, and of different faiths, Ragusa (Dubrovnik) nevertheless imposed restrictions of movement and habitations to Muslims, who, when they arrived to Dubrovnik, were relegated to special areas on the city limits during their stay. The city authorities also imposed a limit on the duration of their stay within those restricted areas. On the social culture of early modern Dubrovnik, and on the status and traffic of foreigners in early modern Dubrovnik, see Römer. *Okvir slobode*; "Stranac u srednjovjekovnom Dubrovniku," 27–37. These and other restrictions which existed alongside various liberties that characterized the political, social, and urban life of this prosperous small republic gave the city the reputation, in the words of a critic, of being at once an open and closed city.

67 Krekić, "Abominandum Crimen."

68 Ibid., 345.

69 Ibid., 339.

70 Ruggiero, *The Boundaries of Eros*; Rocke, *Forbidden Friendship*.

71 On female same-sex desire in the early modern period, see Traub, *The Renaissance of Lesbianism in Early Modern England*; "The Psychomorphology of the Clitoris"; "The Perversion of 'Lesbian' Desire"; Bly, *Queer Virgins and Virgin Queens on the Early Modern Stage*; Whalen, *Constructions of Female Homoeroticism in Early Modern Drama*; Schleiner, "Le feu caché," 605–19.

72 *The most excellent and pleasaunt Booke, entituled: the treasurie of Amadis of Fraunce*, sig. Ff2^{v}.

73 For an extended analysis of "lesbianism" in *Amadis de Gaule* see Schleiner, "Le feu caché, 293–311.

74 *The third and last part of Palmerin of England*, sig. Gg4^{r}.

75 Stewart makes a similar claim about the Catholics, in "A Society of Sodomites," 88–109. See also Matz, "Slander, Renaissance Discourses of Sodomy, and *Othello*," 261–76.

5 Cruising the Eastern Mediterranean

1 Sidney, *The Countesse of Pembrokes Arcadia*, sig. L6r.
2 Lodge, *Wits miserie, and the worlds madness*, sig. H3r.
3 Sidney, *The Countesse of Pembrokes Arcadia*, sig. L6r.
4 Bray, *Homosexuality in Renaissance England*, 50–5.
5 The *OED* gives examples from George Gascoigne's *Hundreth Sundrie Flowers*, 1573, Shakespeare's *A Midsummer Night's Dream* (1600), the anonymous *Second Maiden's Tragedy* (1611), and Thomas Heywood, *The English Traveller* (1633). Accessed 16 June 2014.
6 Interestingly, one of the earliest meanings of the word "play," according to the *OED* (6C) is "amorous disport, dalliance, sexual indulgence." In this meaning it first occurred in 1425, in "Cursor Mundi," a narrative poem in manuscript, which describes a providential view ("course"/cursor) of the scriptural history, written in Middle English. The situation in which "play" is used erotically involves men, Mathan and Jacob, and the brothers, Jacob and Joseph, in the context of the Fifth Age of the World and the Family of Virgin Mary. Here is the poet of "Cursor Mundi" on the subject: "Mathan gat Iacob in pleye,/Iacob Ioseph soth to seye/Of that side is to telle no mo." Quoted from "Cursor Mundi," Trinity College, Cambridge, MS R.3.8 (588), ed. Morris, Early English Text Society (1875), lines 9247–8.
7 Shakespeare, *A Midsummer Night's Dream*, ed. Holland, 145.
8 *More's History of King Richard III*, ed. Lumby, 36. I thank Alan Stewart for drawing my attention to this passage.
9 Connoting affection which intersects with transgression, "playfellow," is also used in *The Winter's Tale* (Polixenes to Hermione: "Your precious self had then not crossed the eyes / Of my young playfellow," 1.2.81–2), *Pericles* (Gower: "The beauty of this sinful dame … / In marriage pleasures playfellow, / Which to prevent he made a law / To keep her still," Sc. 1, 31, 34–6), and in *Cymbeline* (Innogen to Cymbeline: "It is your fault that I have loved Posthumus. / You bred him as my playfellow," 1.1.145–6). In the same context it also appears in Christopher Marlowe's *Dido, Queen of Carthage* (Venus, holding Cupid, says to Ascanius: "this young prince shall be thy playfellow," 2.1.307).
10 Traub, *The Renaissance of Lesbianism in Early Modern England*, 37.
11 Sidney, *The Countesse of Pembrokes Arcadia*, sig. L5r.
12 Pyrocles's and Musidoros's friendship based on parity, moderation, and virtue counters the libertinism of male youth has engulfed city life: "[Y]oung men [are] very fault-finding, but verie faultie: and so to newfanglenesse both of manner, apparel, and each thingels [*sic*], by

the custome of self-guiltie euill, glad to change though oft for worse; merchandise abused, and to townes decaied for want of just and naturall libertie." Sidney, *The Countesse*, sig. L1^r^.

13 For a good brief account of it see Shrank, "'Slacking of the Main Career,'" 240–54.

14 Bredbeck, *Sodomy and Interpretation*, 99–108.

15 Jordan, *Renaissance Feminism*, 220–40.

16 Charles, "Heroes as Lovers," 467–96.

17 Ibid., 467.

18 Ibid., 472.

19 Shrank, *Writing the Nation in Reformation England*, 247.

20 The changing perspectives on love, desire, and marriage emerge in Renaissance England at a time when, as Christopher Hill suggests, "Marriage was delayed longer [in England] than in any other known [Renaissance] society." See "Sex, Marriage, and the Family in England," *Economic History Review*, 2nd series, 31 (1978), 445. Sheppard argues that in the early seventeenth century, "well over a fifth" of youth remained unmarried. See "Manhood, Credit and Patriarchy in Early Modern England, 99.

21 Karras, *From Boys to Men*, 51.

22 O'Hara, *Courtship and Constraint*, 1.

23 Karras, *From Boys to Men*, 51.

24 Whetstone, *Avrelia*, sig. U1^r^. Whetstone's argument against forced marriage is directed not only against paternal involvement but also against the crushing freedom in the young as a result of such marriages. He says: "I crie out vpon forcement in Marriage, as the extreamest bondage that is: for that the ransome of libertie is the death of the one of the other of the maried. The father thinks he hath a happie purchase if he get a rich yong Warde to match with his daughter: but God he knows, and the vnfortunate couple often feele, that he byeth sorrow to his Childe, slander to himselfe, and perchance the ruine of an ancient Gentlemans house, by the riot of the sonne in Lawe, not louing his wife … Pleasure yields no solace to the sorrowfull no more can forcement enforce the free to fancie, sig. E3^r^–E4^v^.

25 With explicit sexual connotations, "bedfellow" appears in Shakespeare's *The Merchant of Venice* (Portia: "if I be left alone … / I'll have that doctor for my bedfellow," 5.1.230, 232) and *The Taming of the Shrew* (Katherine: "Happier the man whom favourable stars / Allots thee for his lovely bedfellow," 4.6.41–2), and, with homoerotic connotations, in Christopher Marlowe's *The Massacre at Paris* (Retes to Gonzago: "'Tis Talaeus, Ramus' bedfellow,'" 1.7.13).

26 Gouge, *Of domesticall duties*, 233.

27 *The second part of the historie of Palmerin d'Oliva*, sig. X1^r^.

28 Ibid., sig. J3r.
29 *The Honorable, pleasant and rare conceited Historie of Palmendos*, sig. K4v.
30 Hutson, "Chivalry for Merchants," 29–59.
31 Bray, "Homosexuality and the Signs of Male Friendship," 4.
32 Stewart, *Closet Readers*, 148–63. Epp has made a point that Montaigne's famous essay on friendship implies "the crucial and dangerous option of sexual relations between men who are social equals." See, "John Foxe and the Circumcised Stage," 281–313.
33 Masten, *Textual Intercourse*, 27–62.
34 Shannon, "Nature's Bias," 183–210, and *Sovereign Amity*; MacFaul, *Male Friendship in Shakespeare and his Contemporaries*, 18.
35 Bray and Rey, "The Body of the Friend," 65–84.
36 Traub, "Friendship's Loss," 17.
37 Cicero, "On Friendship," 19.
38 Robarts, *Phaender*, sig. M1v.
39 [Greene?], *A Paire of Tvrtle Doves*. This book is very rare, and in the catalogue of the rare book collection in The Harry Ransom Humanities Research Centre at University of Texas at Austin, the English translation of this book is described as "dubiously assigned to Robert Greene."
40 Ibid., sig. B3v–B4v.
41 For instance, it also happens to Narbonus and Phemocles, the two main characters in Austen Sackers's Euphuistic fiction, *Narbonus* (1580).
42 Ortúñez de Calahorra, *The second part of the first booke of the myrrour of knighthood*, sig. L1r.
43 Ibid., sig. L1r.
44 Ibid., sig. K8r.
45 Stewart, "The Early Modern Closet Discovered," 84.
46 Ibid., 83–7.
47 I provide an extended discussion of this episode in "'Knights in Armes'," 170–92 and "Cruising the Mediterranean," 59–74.
48 Ortuñez de Calahorra, *The second part of the first booke of the myrrour of knighthood*, Sig P5r.
49 Ibid., sig. P6r.
50 Bray and Rey, "The Body of a Friend," 70–2.
51 Stewart, *Closet Readers*, 125–47.
52 Parry, *Moderatus*, sig. C1r.
53 Foucault, "Friendship as a Way of Life," 204.
54 Bray, *Homosexuality in Renaissance England*, 43.
55 Parry, *Moderatus*, sig. K1r.
56 Ibid., sig. C2r.

57 E.C. Pettet makes an excellent point about cautioning us not to read emotions and characters as anything more than presentations of ideas about how romance produces and complicates narratives of idealized love. See *Shakespeare and the Romance Tradition*, 67–100.
58 Ibid., 80.
59 *The second part of the honourable historie of Palmerin d'Oliva*, sig. F1^{v}.
60 Ibid., sig. G1^{r}.
61 Ibid., sig. G2^{v}.
62 Ibid., sig. G3^{r}.
63 de Scudéry, *Ibrahim* (1652). The title page of this edition lists "Monsieur de Scudery" as the author of the French original.
64 The other two editions appeared in 1674 and 1677. The tragedy based on the prose romance was written by Elkanah Settle (1648–1724) under the title of *Ibrahim the Illustrious Bassa*. London: Tho[mas] Chapman, 1694. On the title page we read that this "tragedy" was "acted by Their Majesties servants."
65 de Scudéry, *Ibrahim*, sig. A2^{r}.
66 Ibid.
67 Ibid.
68 Ibid.
69 Ibid., sig. A2^{v}.
70 Shakespeare and Wilkins, *A Reconstructed Text of Pericles*, 14.
71 Twyne, *The patterne of paineful aduentures*, fol. 19.
72 Smith, *Homosexual Desire in Shakespeare's England*, 120–57.
73 Twyne, *The patterne of paineful aduentures*, fol. 19.
74 Ibid.
75 Ibid.
76 Ibid., fol. 20.
77 Ibid.
78 On prose romances as conduct books for young men see Stanivukovic, "English Renaissance Romances as Conduct Books for Young Men," 61–78.
79 Pires, "Persia," *Suma Oriental*, 23.
80 This term, coined by James Davidson, is quoted in Edwards's review, "Grades for boys," 12.
81 Khaled El-Rouayheb, *Before Homosexuality in the Arab-Islamic World*, 42.
82 Ibid.
83 Andrews and Kalpaklı, *The Age of Beloveds*, 40.
84 Ibid., 42.
85 Barthes, *The Rustle of Language*, 39 (emphasis in the original).
86 Barthes, *The Pleasure of the Text*.
87 Sandys, *A Relation of a Journey begun An: Dom: 1610*, sig. G5^{r}.

88 Traub has written about the fiction of female homoeroticism in a very similar narrative scenario in Nichoal de Nicolay's *The Navigations, Peregrinations, and Voyages, Made into Turkey* (1585) and Thomas Glover's account of Turkish baths published in the second volume of Samuel Purchas's collection of travel narratives, *Purchas His Pilgrimes,* which appeared in 1615, the same years as Sandy's account. See Traub, *The Renaissance,* 200–1.The date of Sandy's and Purchas's collections is not a coincidence because it was not uncommon for the same story to circulate between a number of different published texts.

89 Sandys, *A Relation of a Journey begun An: Dom: 1610*, sig. H1^{r}.

90 I borrow this phrase from Green, *The Chains of Eros.*

91 Green, *On Private Madness,* 323.

92 Sandys, *A Relation of a Journey begun An: Dom: 1616*, sig. K2^{r-v}.

93 A map of Morea ("Morea Penisvla" [*sic*]) shows the Pelopones Peninsula in the 1570s as a densely populated land (The Newberry Library, Novacco 2F 195).

94 Perry, *Literature and Favoritism in Early Modern England,* 131. Perry provides a detailed political context of the relationship between Carr and James, and the erotic aspect of favouritism on James's court.

95 I quote *Urania* from *The First Part*, ed. Roberts, 34.

96 Wroth, *Urania*, 35.

97 Ibid.

98 Ibid.

99 The male version of melancholia engenders an affect that mixes erotic and political demise, while female melancholia in *Urania,* as Helen Hackett shows, articulates romantic feeling from within a woman's private space. See "'A book, and solitariness': Melancholia, Gender and Literary Subjectivity in Mary Wroth's *Urania,*" 64–85.

100 Ortuñez de Calahorra, *The first part of the mirrour of princely deedes and knighthood*, sig. Aiii^{r}.

101 See Hutson, *The Usurer's Daughter.*

102 Roberts, ed. "Social Context," lxvii.

103 Hanson, "Sodomy and Kingcraft in *Urania* and *Antony and Cleopatra,*" 138.

104 Bromley, *Intimacy and Sexuality in the Age of Shakespeare*, 145.

105 *Xenophons Treatise of Householde*, fol. 24.

106 Pigeon, "Prose Fiction Adaptations of Sidney's *Arcadia,*" 118.

107 For example, in Barnabe Riche's Euphuistic fiction, *Don Simonides* (I, 1581; II, 1584), in a theologically intoned prophecy about the Fall of Rome, we find the following association between Catholics and sodomy, and between sodomy and the fall of civilization: "in time, proude *Celestine,*

I wishe thee mend thy misse or *Rome* shall fall, where now thy pompe, and greatest glorie is Thy *Sodomites*, thy *Baales* Priestes, shall be consum'd with fire Th foule escapes, shall opened be, and Princes hatefull yre Shall turne the walles, of *Sodom* doune." Riche, *The straunge and wonderfull aduentures of Do*[n] *Simonides*, sig. E4[r].

Afterword

1 Tatius, THE MOST DELECT-table and plasaunt History of Clitiphon and Leucippe.
2 Skretkowicz, *European Erotic Romance*; Katherine Duncan-Jones offers a brief discussion of Burton's dedication of his translation to his dedicatee, Henry Wriothesley, Earl of Southampton and Baron of Titchfield, as a text, that by celebrating the love of boys over the love of women is also revealing the kind of desire that Southampton himself would not have rejected. See Katherine Duncan-Jones, *Ungentle Shakespeare*, 79–81.
3 My argument here follows the theoretical discussion about geography as a field of knowledge through which power is disseminated. Foucault, "Questions of Geography," 65.
4 Harris, *Untimely Matter in the Time of Shakespeare*, 189.
5 Charles, "Heroes as Lovers, 468.
6 Timberlake, *A Trve and strange discourse of the trauailes of two English Pilgrimes*, sig. E4[r–v].
7 Bray, *Homosexuality in Renaissance England*, 28.
8 Lithgow, *The Totall Discourse of The Rare Adventures and Painefull Peregrinations of long Nineteene Yeares Travayles from Scotland to the most famous Kingdomes in Europe, Asia and Affrica*, 153.
9 *The third and last part of Palmerin of England*, sig. Ppp4[v].
10 Ibid., sig. Qqq1[r].
11 Ortuñez de Calahorra, *The second part of the first booke of the myrrour of knighthood*, sig. P5[r].
12 Munday, ZELAVTO, sig. O1[r].
13 Parker, *Inescapable Romance*; Skretkowicz, *European Erotic Romance*; Werth, *The Fabulous Dark Cloister*, 3.
14 Ballaster, *Fabulous Orients*.
15 Holden and Purcell, *The Corrupting Sea*, 20.
16 Ibid., 39.
17 Abulafia, *The Great Sea*, 453.
18 Ibid.

Bibliography

Manuscript Sources

London, The British Library

Additional 10,049.
Additional 15,212.
Additional 16,441.
Additional 17,299.
Additional 18,638.
Additional 22,283.
Additional 31,042.
Additional 37,024.
Additional 61,745.
Cotton A.ii.
Harley 326.
Harley 463.
Harley 7334.
Harley 2253.
Harley 6758.
Lansdowne 766.
Royal 15E.vi.
Sloane 457.

Oxford, The Bodleian Library

Additional C.126.
Douce 326.
Lat. misc. E.114.
MS 911.

Lincoln, Lincoln Cathedral Library

MS 91 (A.5.2)

Chicago, The Newberry Library

Case fY 1565.R52.

Washington, DC, The Folger Shakespeare Library

MS V.a.259.

Abbreviations

Arcadia (Old) Sir Philip Sidney. *The Countess of Pembroke's Arcadia (The Old Arcadia).* Edited by Jean Robertson. Oxford: The Clarendon Press, 1973.

Arcadia (New) Sir Philip Sidney. *The Countess of Pembroke's Arcadia (The New Arcadia).* Edited byVictor Skretkowicz. Oxford: Clarendon Press, 1987.

Catalogue *Catalogue of Romances in the Department of Manuscripts in the British Museum*, Vol. I and II, Edited by H.L.D. Ward (1883–93); Vol. III, Edited by J.A. Herbert (1910). London: Published by Order of the Trustees of The British Museum.

Greene *The Life and Complete Works in Prose and Verse of Robert Greene*, ed. Alexander B. Grossart, 15 vols. New York: Russell & Russell, 1964.

Hakluyt *The Hakluyt Handbook*, Vols. 104. Edited by D.B. Quinn. London: The Hakluyt Society, 1974.

Marlowe *The Complete Plays*, ed. J.B. Steane. London: Penguin, 1986.

OED *Oxford English Dictionary* Online. Oxford University Press, 2014.

Ovid *Ovid's Metamorphoses*, translated by Arthur Golding, edited by. Madeleine Forey. Baltimore: Johns Hopkins University Press, 2001.

State Papers Venice

– (1869). *1595–1597*. Edited by Mary Anne Everett Green. London: Her Majesty's Stationery Office, 1869. Repr. Nendeln, Liechtenstein: Kraus Reprint, 1967.

– (1897). *Calendar of State Papers and Manuscripts, Relating to English Affairs, Existing in the Archives and Collections of Venice, and in Other Libraries of Northern Italy*, Vol. IX, 1592–1603. Edited by Horatio F. Brown. London: Printed for Her Majesty's Stationery Office by Eyre and Spottiswoode, 1897.

– (1905). *Calendar of State Papers and Manuscripts, Relating to English Affairs, Existing in the Archives and Collections of Venice, and in other Libraries of Northern Italy*, Vol. XII, 1610–1613. Edited by Horatio F. Brown. London: Printed for His Majesty's Stationery Office, by Mackie and Co. Ltd, 1905.

– (1913). *Calendar of State Papers and Manuscripts, Relating to English Affairs, Existing in the Archives and Collections of Venice and in Other Libraries of Northern Italy*, Vol. XIX, 1625–1626. Edited by Allen B. Hinds. London: Hereford Times Limited, 1913.

– (1921). *Calendar of State Papers and Manuscripts, Relating to English Affairs, Existing in the Archives and Collections of Venice, and in Other Libraries of Northern Italy*, Vol. XXIII, 1632–1636. Edited by Allen B. Hinds. London: Published by His Majesty's Stationery Office, 1921.

STC *A Short-Title Catalogue of Books Printed in England and Ireland, 1475–1640*, 3 vols. Edited by A.W. Pollard and G.R. Redgrave, 2nd ed., revised and enlarged by Katherine F. Pantzer. London: The Bibliographical Society, 1986.

Wing *Short-Title Catalogue of Books Printed in England, Scotland, Ireland, Wales, and British America and the English Books Printed In Other Countries, 1641–1700*. Compiled by Donald Wing. New York: Printed for the Index Society of Columbia University Press, 1945–51.

Primary Sources

Acosta, Ioseph [José de Acosta], *The Naturall and Morall Historie of the East and West Indies*. Translated by E[dward] G[rimaston]. London: Edward Blount and William Aspley, 1604. STC 94.

Amadis de Gaule, Anon. (1619). Translated by Anthony Munday. Edited by Helen Moore. Aldershot: Ashgate, 2004.

– *The Second Booke of "Amadis de Gaule": Containing the description, wonders, and conquests of the Firme-Island, Englished by L*[azarus] *P*[yot]. London: C. Burbie, 1595. STC 542.

Amadis of France. The moste excellent and pleasaunt Booke, entituled: The treasurie of Amadis of Fraunce. London: Thomas Hacket, (?1572). STC 545.

– *The Treasurie of Amadis of Fraunce*. Translated by Thomas Pannell. London: H. Bynneman for T[homas] Hacket, (?1567). STC 12924.

Ascham, Roger. *The Scholemaster* (1570). Rpt. London: Bell and Daldy, 1863. Reissue New York: AMS Press, 1967.

Batman, Stephen. *The trauayled Pylgrime, bringing newes from all parts of the worlde, such like scarce harde of before.* London: Henry Denham, 1569. STC 1585.

Beard, Thomas. *The Theatre of Gods Iudgements.* London: Adam Islip, 1597. STC 1659.

Bevis of Hampton. *Syr Bevis of Hampton.* London: Thomas East, 1585. STC 1990.

Bible. *The Holy Bible, conteyning the Olde Testament and the Newe.* London: Christopher Barker, 1595. STC 2167.

Blount, Sir Henry. *A voyage into the Levant. A briefe relation of a iourney, lately performed by Master H.B. Gentleman, from England by the way of Venice, into Dalmatia, Sclavonia, Bosnah, Hungary, Macedonia, Thessaly, Thrace, Rhodes and unto Gran Cairo.* London: Andrew Crooke, 1636. STC 2095.

Boccaccio, Giovanni. *The Decameron.* Translated by G.H. McWilliam. London: Penguin Books, 1995.

Bodin, Jean. *The six bookes of a common-weale. Written by I. Bodin a famous lawyer, and a man of great experience in matters of state, but of the French and Latine copies, done into English by Richard Knolles.* London: Adam Islip, 1606. STC 3193.

Boemus, Ioannes. *The Manners, Lawes, and Customes of All Nations,* tr. Ed[ward] Aston. London: George Eld, 1611. STC 3198.5.

Botero, Giovanni [John Botero]. *The Worlde, or an historicall description of the most famous kingdomes and common-weales therein, Relating their situations, manners, customes, ciuill gouernment, and other memorable matters.* Translated by I.R. London: Iohn Iaggard, 1601. STC 3399.

– *A treatise, concerning the causes of the magnificence and greatnesse of cities, done into English by R*[obert]. *Peterson.* London: T.P. Purfoot, R. Ockould and H. Towes, 1606. STC 3405.

– *The Cause of the Greatnesse of Cities, with Certaine Observations concerning the Sea.* Translated by T.H. London: E.P. for Henry Seile, 1635. STC 3396.

– *Relations of the most famous kingdoms and Common-wealths thorowout the world; Discoursing of their Situations, Religions, Languages, Manners, Customes, Strengths, Greatnesse and Policies.* Translated by R.I. London: Iohn Haviland, 1630. STC 3404.

– *The Mirrour of Policie.* London: Adam Islip, 1598. STC 15228.5.

Breton, Nicholas. *The strange fortunes of two excellent Princes: in their liues and loues, to their equall Ladies in all the titles of true honour.* London: Nicholas Ling, 1600. STC 3702.

– *An Oldemans Lesson, and Youngmans Love.* London: Edward White, 1605. STC 3674.

– *Strange Newes out of divers Countries.* London: W. Iones for George Fayerbard, 1622. STC 3704.

Carr, Ralph. *The Mahumetane or Turkish Historie, translated from the French & Italian tongues by R*[alph] *Carr*. London: Thomas Este, 1600. STC 17997.

Cartigny, Jean de. *The voyage of the wandering knight, Shewing the whole course of mans life, how apt hee is to follow vanitie, and how hard it is for him to attaine to vertue / duised by Iohn Carheny, and translated out of French into Engl[i]sh.* Translated by W.G. of Southampton. London: William Stansby (?1626). STC 4703.

Cartwright, John. *The Preachers Travels.* London: Thomas Thorpe by Walter Burre, 1611. STC 4705.

Caussin, Nicholas. *A Saxon Historie of the Admirable Adventures of Clodoaldvs and his three Children.* Translated from French by Thomas Hawkins. London: Elizabeth Purslowe for Henry Seile, 1634. STC 4294.

Caxton, William. *The moste pleasant historye of Blanchardine, sonne to the King of Friz, & the faire lady Eglantine Queene of Tormaday, (surnamed) the proud Ladye in Loue.* London: William Blakewell, 1595. STC 522.

Cicero, Marcus Tullius. *Marcvs Tullius Ciceroes three bookes of duties to Marcus his sonne, tourned out of Latine into English, by Nicholas Grimald.* London: Thomas Este, 1596. STC 5286.

– "On Friendship," *The Letters of Marcus Tullius Cicero With his Treatises on Friendship and Old Age.* Translated by E.S. Shuckburgh. New York: P.F. Collier & Son, 1909.

– *De partitione oratoria.* Translated by H. Rackham, The Loeb Classical Library. Cambridge, Massachusetts and London: Harvard University Press, 1942.

– *De oratore.* Translated by E.W. Sutton and H. Rackham, 2 vols., The Loeb Classical Library. Cambridge, Massachusetts: Harvard University Press and London: Heinemann, 1942.

Cleveland, James. ΗΡΩΠΑΙΔΕΙΑ. *The Institution of a Young Noble Man.* Oxford: Ioseph Barnes, 1607. STC 5393.

Colet, Claude [*Florando de Inglaterra*]. *Palladine. The Famous, pleasant, and variable Historie, of Palladine of England. Discoursing of honourable Aduentures, of Knightly deedes of Armes and Chiuarlier: enterlaced likewise with the loue of sundrie noble personages, as time and affection limited their desires.* Translated by Anthony Munday. London: Edward Alde for John Perin, 1588. STC 5541.

Contarini, Gasparo. *The Commonwealth and Gouernment of Venice.* Translated by Lewes Lewkenor. London: John Windet for Edmund Mattes, 1599. STC 5642.

Cooper, Thomas. *Thesaurus linguae Romane & Britannicae.* London: Henrici Bynnemani [Henry Denham], 1578. STC 5688.

Cooper, Thomas. *Dictionarium Historicum & Poeticum propria locorum & Personarum vocabula breuiter* complectens, published with *Thesaurus linguae*

Romanae & Britannicae. Londini [London]: Henricum Wykes [Henry Wykes], 1565. STC 5686.

Coryate, Thomas. *Coryats Crudities*. London: W[illiam] S[tansby], 1611. STC 5808.

Couverte, Robert. *A trve and almost incredible report of an Englishman, that (being cast away in the good Ship called the Assention in Cambaya the farthest part of East Indies) Trauelled by Land through many vnknowne Kingdomes, and great Cities*. London: Thomas Archer and Richard Redmer, 1612. STC 5859.

Curio, Caellius Augustus. *A Notable Historie of the Saracens. As also of Turkes*. Translated by Thomas Newton. London: Abraham Veale, 1575. STC 6129.

Daborn, Robert. *The trauellers breuiat, or, An historical description of the most famous kingdomes in the world*. London: Iohn Iaggard, 1601. STC 3398.

d'Anghiera, Pietro Martire. *The decades of the newe worlde of west India conteynyng the nauigations and conquests of the Spanyardes, with the particular description of the moste ryche and large lands and ilandes lately founde in the west ocean perteynyng to the inheritaunce of the kings of Spayne … Wryten in the Latine tounge by Peter Martyr of Angleria, and translated into Englysshe by Rycharde Eden*. London: John Powell for Robert Toy, 1555. STC 648.

– *The history of trauayle in the West and East Indies, and other countreys lying eyther way, towards the fruitfull and ryche Moluccaes As Moscouia, Persia, Arabia, Syria, Aegypte, Ethiopia, Guinea, China in Cathayo, and Giapan: with a discourse of the Northwest passage. Gathered in parte, and done into Englyshe by Richarde Eden. Newly set in order, augmented, and finished by Richarde Willes*. London: Richarde Iugge, 1577. STC 649.

Daniel, Samuel. *The first part of the historie of England*. London: Nicholas Oakes, 1612. STC 6246.

Davis, John. *The voyages and works of John Davis, the navigator* (1595). Edited by Hastings Markham. London: Hakluyt Society, 1880.

d'Avity, Pierre. *The Estates, Empires & Principalities of the World*. London: Matthew Lawnes and John Bill, 1615. STC 988.

Day, Angel. *Daphnis and Chloe excellently describing the weight of affection, in a pastorall, and within the same pastorall. The shepheards holidaie*. Translated by Angell Daye. London: Robert Waldegraue, 1587. STC 6400.

Digby, Kenelm Sir. *Journal of a voyage into the Mediterranean* (1628). Edited from an autograph manuscript in the possession of William Watkin E. Wynne by John Bruce. Westminster: Camden Society, 1868.

Eden, Richard. *The History of Trauayle in the West and East Indies, and other countreys lying eyther way, towards fruitfull and ryche Moullaes. Gathered in parte, and done in Englyshe by Richarde Eden, newly set in order, augmented, and finished by Richarde Willes*. London: Richard Kugge, 1577. STC 649.

Favine, Andrew. *The Theater of Honour and Knighthood*. London: William Iaggard, 1623. STC 10717.

Fletcher, Giles. *The Policy of the Turkish Empire*. London: W[illiam] S[tansby], 1597. STC 24335.

Flores, Juan de. *Histoire de Aurelio et Isabelle* (1556). Translated by [?Robert Greene], *A Paire of Tvrtle, or, the Tragicall History of Bellora and Fidelio Seconded with the tragicall end of Agamio, wherein (besides other matters pleasing to the reader) by way of dispute betweene a knight and a lady, is described this neuer before debated question to wit: whether man to woman, or woman to man offer the greater temptations and allurements vnto vnbridled lust*. London: W[illiam] Jaggard for Francis Burton, 1606. STC 11094.

Forde, Emanuel. *Parismus, the Renowned Prince of Bohemia. His most famous, delectable, and pleasant Historie. Conteining His Noble Battailes fought against the Persians. His loue to Laurana, the Kings Daughter of Thessaly. And his straunge Aduentures in the Desolate Land*. London: Thomas Creede for Richard Oliue, 1598. STC 11171.

– *Parismenos: the Second Part of the most famous, delectable, and pleasant Histories of Parismus, the renowned Prince of Bohemia. The aduenturous trauels and Noble Chivalrie of Parismenos, the Knight of Fame, in diuers Countries* London: Thomas Creed, 1599. STC 11171.2.

– *The most pleasant historie of Ornatus and Artesia / Wherein is contained the vniust raigne of Thaeon King of Phrygia. Who with his sonne Lenon, (intending Ornatus death), right heire to the crowne, was afterwards slaine by his owne seruants, and Ornatus after many extreame miseries, crowned King*. London: Thomas Creede, 1607. STC 11169.

– *The Most Pleasant History of Ornatus and Artesia*. Edited by Goran Stanivukovic. Ottawa: Dovehouse, 2003.

– *The famovs historie of Montelyon, Knight of the Oracle, and Sonne to the Renowned Persicles King of Assyria Shewing, his strange birth, vnfortunate love, perilous adventures in armes, and how he came to the knowledge of his parents*. London: B. Alsop and T. Fawcet, 1633. STC 11167.

– *Montelyon, Knight of the Oracle*. Edited by Anne Falke. Salzburg Studies in English Literature, Vol. 99. Salzburg: Institut für Anglistik und Amerikanistik, Universität Salzburg, 1981.

Foxe, John. *The Pope confuted / The wholy and apostolique Church confuting the Pope*. The first action. Translated out of Latine into English, by Iames Bell. London: Thomas Dawson for Richard Sergier, 1580. STC 11241.

Gainsford, Thomas. *The glory of England, or A true description of many excellent prerogatiues and remarkeable blessings, whereby she triumpheth ouer all nations of the world with a iustifiable comparison betweene the eminent kingdomes of the earth, and herselfe*. London: Thomas Norton, 1618. STC 11517.

Georgeuiz, Bartholomeus [Bartolomej Georgijevic]. *The offspring of the house of Ottomano and officers pertaining to the greate Turkes court. Whereunto is added Bartholomeus Georgieuiz Epitome, of the customes rytes, ceremonies, and religion of the Turkes: with the miserable affliction of those Christians, whiche liue vnder their captiuities and bondage. In the ende also is adioyned the maner how Mustapha, oldest sonne of Soltan Soliman, twelfth Emperour of the Turkes, was murthered by his father, in the yere of our Lorde 1553. al Englished by Hugh Goughe*. London: Thomas Marshe, 1569. STC 11746.

Gervase, Markham. *The most famous and renowned historie, of that woorthie and illustrious knight Meruine, sonne to that rare and excellent mirror of princely prowesse, Oger the Dane, and one of that royall bond of unmatchable knighthoode, the twelfe peerers of France Wherein is declared, his rare birth, and stranger bringing up with his most honorable conquest of Ierusalem, Babilon, and diuers other cities from the pagan infidels: with many other memorable accidents of wonderous consequence*. London: R. Blower and Val[entine] Sims, 1612. STC 17884.

Gosson, Stephen. *Playes confuted in five actions proving that they are not to be suffred in a Christian commonweale, by the way both the cavils of Thomas Lodge, and the play of playes, written in their defence, and other objections of players frendes, are truly set downe and directlye aunsweared*. London: Thomas Gosson, 1582. STC 12095.

Gouge, William. *Of domesticall duties eight treatises. An exposition of that part of Scripture out of which domesticall duties are raised*. London: William Bladen, 1622. STC 12119.

– *The Dignitie of Chivalrie; Set forth in A Sermon Preached Before the Artillery Company of London*. London: George Miller, 1626. STC 12111.

Greene, Robert. *Arbasto, The Anatomie of Fortune. Wherein is discovered by pithie and pleasant Discourse, that the highest state of prosperities, is oftimes the first step to mishap, and that to stay vpon Fortunes lotte, is to treade on brittle Glasse*. London: H. Iackson, 1584. STC 12233.

– *The Spanish Masquerado / Wherein vnder a pleasant deuise, is disouered effectuallie, in certaine breefe sentences and mottos, the pride and insolencie of the Spanish state: with the disgrace conceiued by their losse, and the dismayed confusion of their troubled thoughtes. Whereunto by the author, for the better vnderstanding of his deuice, is added a brieefe glosse*. London: R. Ward for T. Cadman, 1589. STC 12309.

– *The Famous Historie of Albions Queene*. London: T. Pavier, 1600. STC 11502.

– *Gwydonius, or The Card of Fancy* (1584). Edited by Carmine G. Di Biase. Ottawa: Dovehouse, 2001.

Guicciordini, Franceso. *The Historie of Gvicciardin: Containing the Warres of Italia and other parts, continued for many yeares vnder sundrive Kings and Princes, together with the variations and accidents of the same. Reduced into English by Geffrey Fenton*. London: Richard Field, 1618. STC 12460.

Hakluyt, Richard, Younger and Elder. *The Principal Navigations*. Vol. 1 of *The Original Writings & Correspondence of the Two Richard Hakluyts*, 2 vols. The Hakluyt Society, 1935. Repr. Nendeln, Liechtenstein: Kraus Reprint, 1967.

– *The principall nauiations, voiages and disoueries of the English nation made by sea or ouer land, to the most remote and farthest distant quarters of the earth at any time within the compasse of these 1500. Yeeres: deuided into three seuerall parts, according to the positions of the regions whereunto they were directed. Whereunto is added the last most renow[n]ed English nauigation, round about the whole globe of the earth*. London: George Bishop and Ralph Newberie, 1589. STC 12625.

Hasleton, Richard. *Strange and wonderfull things Happened to Richard Hasleton … in his ten yeares trauailes in many forraine countries*. London: William Barley, 1595. STC 12925.

Heliodorus. *An Aethiopian Historie, written in Greeke by Heliodorus, Englished by Thomas Vnderdowne*. London: Frauncis Coldocke, 1587. STC 13043.

Heylyn, Peter. *The historie of that most famous saint and souldier of Christ Iesus; St. George of Cappadocia asserted from the fictions, in the middle ages of the Church; and opposition, of the present. The institution of the most noble Order of St. George, named the Garter. A catalogue of all the knights thereof until this present*. London: Bernard Alsop and Thomas Fawcet for Henry Seyle. 1631. STC 13272.

Horace. *Horace his arte of poetrie, pistles, and satyrs Englished and to the Earte of Ormounte by Tho*[mas] *Drant addressed*. Translated by Thomas Drant. London: Thomas Marshe, 1567. STC 13797.

– *Satires, Epistles and Ars Poetica*. Translated by H. Rushton Fairclough. Cambridge, Mass. and London: Harvard University Press, 1929.

Johnson, Richard. *The Seven Champions of Christendom* (1596/7). Edited by Jennifer Fellows. Aldershot: Ashgate, 2003.

– *The renowned history of the seven champions of Christendom, St. George of England, St. Denis of France, St. James of Spain, St. Anthony of Italy, St. Andrew of Scotland, St. Patrick of Ireland, and St. David of Wales, epitomized shewing their valiant exploits both by sea and land, their combating with giants, monsters, lions, and dragons … to which is added the true manner of their deaths*. London: Thomas Norris, [17700?], Wing J809B.

– *History of the Seven Champions of Christendom*. London: Tho[mas] Norris, [n.d.]. The Newberry Library, Case Y 1565.J.623.

Johnson, Samuel. *The Yale Edition of the Works of Samuel Johnson*. Edited by Arthur Sherbo. 18 vols., vol. 7, *Johnson on Shakespeare*. New Haven, CT: Yale University Press, 1958.

Joode, Gerard de [Cornelius de Iudacis]. *Speculum orbis terrarium*. Antwerp: A. Coninx, 1613.

Kirkman, John. *History of the Seven Champions of Christendome Acted at the Cocke-pit, and at the Red-Bull in St. Iohns streete, with a general liking. And never printed till this yere 1638. Written by I.K.* London: J. Okes, 1638. STC 15014.

Knolles, Richard. *The general historie of the Turkes from the first beginning of that nation to the rising of the Ottoman familie: with all the notable expeditions of the Christian princes against them. Together with the liues and conquests of the Othoman kings and emperours faithfullie collected out of the-/best histories, both auntient and modern, and digested into one continuat historie vntill this present yeare 1603.* London: Adam Islip, 1603. STC 15051.

Lithgow, William. *A most delectable and true discourse, of an admired and paineful peregrination from Scotland, to the most famous kingdomes in Europe, Asia and Affricke. With the particular descriptions (more exactly set downe then hath beene heretofore in English) of Italy, Sicilia, Dalmatia, Ilyria, Epire, Peloponnesus, Macedonia, Thessalia, and the whole continent of Greece, Crete, Rhodes, the Iles Cyclades and the chiefest countries of Asia Minor. From thence, to Cyprus, Phaenicia, Syria ... and the sacred citie Ierusalem.* London: Nicholas Okes, 1614. STC 15711.

– *The Totall Discourse of the Rare Adventures and Painefull Peregrinations of long Nineteene Yeares Travayles from Scotland to the most famous Kingdomes in Europe, Asia and Affrica.* London: Nicholas Oakes, 1632. STC 15713.

Lodge, Thomas. *A Margarite of America.* Edited by Donald Beecher. Toronto: Center for Reformation and Renaissance Studies, 2005.

– *Wits miserie, and the worlds madness: discouering the deuils incarnate of this age.* London: Adam Islip, 1596. STC 16677.

Maissoneuve, Estienne de [Steuen De Maison Neufe Bordeliois]. *The gallant delectrable and pleasavnt hystorie of Gerileon of Englande,* tr. Thomas Newton. London: Myles Ienninges, 1578. STC 17203.

Malynes, George de. *Saint George for England, allegorically described.* London: Richard Field for William Tymme, 1601. STC 17226a.

Mandeville, Sir John. *Mandeville's Travels, Texts and Translations,* 2 vols. Edited by Malcolm Letts. London: The Hakluyt Society, 1953.

– *The voiag*[e] *and trauayle, of syr John Mandeuile knight, which treateth of the way toward Hierusalem, and of maruayles of Inde with other ilands and countryes.* London: Thomas East, 1568. STC 17250.

Mercator, Gerhard. *Historia mundi: or Mercator's atlas containing his cosmographical description of the fabricke and figure of the world. Lately rectified in divers places, as also beautified and enlarged with new mappes and tables; by the studious industry of Iudocus Hondy.* Translated by W[ye] S[altonstall]. London: T. Cotes for Michael Sparke, 1635. STC 17824.5.

– *Gerardi Merc*[atoris] *Hondii atlas, or, A geographicke description of the regions, countries and kingdomes of the world, through Europe, Asia, Africa, and America, represented by new & exact maps*. Translated by Henry Hexham Amsterdam: 1638. STC 17828.

Meres, Francis. "Sketch of English literature, painting, and music, up to September 1598." *An English Garner: A Critical Essays and Literary Fragments*. Edited by Edward Arber and Thomas Seccombe. Westminster: Archibald Constable, 1903, 3–25.

Meyer, Albrecht. *Certaine briefe, and special instruction for gentlemen, merchants, students, soldiers, mariners and employed services abroade, or anie way occasioned to conuerse in the kingdoms, and gouernments of forren princes* London: Iohn Wolfe, 1589. STC 17784.

Milton, John. *The Major Works*. Edited by Stephen Orgel and Jonathan Goldberg. Oxford: Oxford University Press, 2003.

Minadoi, Giovanni Tommaso. *The history of the warres betweene the Turkes and the Persians. Written in Italian by Iohn-Thomas Minadoi, and translated into English by Abraham Hartwell. Containing the description of all such matters, as pertaine to religion, to the forces to the gouernment, and to the countries of the kingdome of the Persians. Together with the argument of every booke, & a new geographical mappe of all those territories*. London: [John Windet for] John Wolfe, 1595. STC 17943.

Misselden, Edward. *The center of the circle of commerce. Or, A refutation of a treatise, intituled The circle of commerce, or The ballance of trade, lately published by E.M. By Gerrard Mylines merchant*. London: William Jones, 1623. STC 17221.

– *The maintenance of free trade according to the three essentiall parts of traffique; namely commodities, moneys and exchange of moneys by fills of exchange for other countries, or, An answer to a treatise of free trade*. London: I. Leggatt for William Sheffard, 1622. STC 17226.

Moraes, Francisco de. *The honorable, pleasant and rare conceited historie of Palmendos, Son to the most Renowned Palmerin D'Oliva, Emperour of Constantinople, And the Heroick Queen of Tharsus*. Translated by Anthony Munday. London: J. C[harlewood] for S. Watersonne, 1589. STC 18064.

– *The famous History of Palmendos Son of the most Renowned Palmerin D'Oliva, Emperour of Constantinople, And the Heroick Queen of Tharsus*, tr. Anthony Munday. London: E. Alsop, 1653, Wing 377.

More, Thomas. *More's History of King Richard III*. Edited Rawson J. Lumby. Facsimile of the 1513 original. Cambridge: Cambridge University Press, 1883.

Morris, Richard, ed. "Cursor Mundi." Early English Text Society (1875), Pt. II, reprinted London, New York, Toronto: Oxford University Press, 1966.

Moryson, Fynes. *An Itinerary Written by Fyner Moryson Gent. First in the Latine Tongue, and then translated by him into English. Containing his Ten Yeeres Travell Through the Twelve Dominions of Germany, Bohmerland, Sweitzerland,*

Netherland, Denmarke, Poland, Italy, Turkey, France, England, Scotland, and Ireland. London: John Beale, 1617. STC 18205.

Munday, Anthony. *A Briefe Chronicle, of the Successe of Times from the Creation of the World, to this instant.* London: William Jaggard, 1608. STC 18258.

– *The admirable deliverance of 266. Christians by Iohn Reynard Englishman from the captiuitie of the Turkes, who had beene gally slaues many yeares in Alexandria.* London: Thomas Dawson, 1608. STC 18258.

Newes from Turkie and Poland, Anon. *Or A True and Compendious declaration of the proceedings betweene the great Turke, and his Maiestie of Poland, from the beginning of the Warres, until the latter end.* The Hague, 1622. STC 942.7.

Nicolay, Nicholas de. *The nauigations, peregrinations and voyages, made into Turkie by Nicholas Nicholay Daulphinois, Lord of Arfeuile, chamberlaine and geographer ordinarie to the King of Fraunce conteining sundry singularities which the author hath there seene and obserued: deuided into foure books, with threescore figures, naturally set forth as well of men as women, according to the diuersitie of nations, their port, intreatie, apparel, laws, religion and maner of liuing, aswel in time of warre as peace: with diuers faire and memorable histories, happened in our time.* Translated by T. Washington the younger. London: Thomas Dawson, 1585. STC 18574.

Oceander. The heroicall aduentures of the knight of the sea comprised in the most famous and renowned historie of the illustrious & excellently accomplished Prince Oceander, grand-sonne to the mightie and magnanimous Caranax, Emperour of Constantinople, and the Empresse Basilia; and sonne vnto the incomparable Olbiocles Prince of Grecia, by the beauteous Princesse Almidiana, daughter vnto the puissant King Rubaldo of Hungaria. London: R. Bradock for William Leake, 1600. STC 18763.

Ortelius, Abraham. *An Epitome of Ortelius, his Theater of the world, wherein the principal regions of the earth are described in smalle mappes. With a brief declaration annexed to each mappe. And done in more exact manner, then lyke declaration in Latin, French, or other language. It is also amplified with new mappes wanting in the Latin editions.* London [Antwerp]: H. Swingenij for Iohn Norton, 1601. STC 18857.

Ortúñez de Calahorra, Diego. *The first part of the mirrour of princely deedes and knighthood wherein is shewed the worthinesse of the Knight of the Sunne, and his brother Rosicleer, sonnes to the great Emperous Trebatio, with the straunge loue of the beautifull Princesse Briana,* [and] *the valiant actes of other noble princes and knights. Now newly translated out of Spanish into our vulgar English by M[argaret] T[yler].* London: Thomas East, 1580. STC 18860.

– *The second part of the first booke of the myrrour of knighthood in which is prosecuted the illustrious deedes of the knight of the Sunne, and his brother Rosicleer, sonnes vnto the Emperour Trebatio of Greece: with the valiant deedes of armes of sundrie worthie knightes, verie delightfull to bee read, and nothing *hurtfull to bee regarded. Now newly translated out of Spanish into our vulgar tongue by R*[obert] *P*[arry]. London: Thomas Este, 1585. STC 18862.

– *The mirrour of princeely deedes and knighthood wherein is shewed the worthinesse of the Knight of the Sunne, and his brother Rosicleer, sonnes to the great Emperour Trebatio: with the strange loue of the beautifull and excellent princesse Briana, and the valiant actes of other princes and knightes. Now newly translated out of Spanish into our vulgar English tongue, by M.*[argaret] *T*[yler]. London: Thomas Este. (?1587). STC 18859.

Painter, William. *The Palace of Pleasure*. Edited by Joseph Jacobs, 3 vols. Hildersheim: Georg Olms Verlagsbuchandlung, 1968.

– "Of Master Thorello and Saladine," "The Twentieth Nouell," in *The Palace of Pleasure* (1567). Edited by Joseph Jacobs, Vol. 2 of 3 vols. Hildersheim: Georg Olms Verlagsbuchandlung, 1968.

Palladine. The famous, pleasant and variable historie, of Palladine of England, Discoursing of honorable adventures, of knightly deeds of arms and chivalrie: enterlaced likewise with the loue of sundrie noble personages as time and affection limited their desires. Translated by *A*[nthony] *M*[unday]. London: J. Perin, 1588. STC 5541.

Palmendos. The honorable, pleasant and rare conceited historie of Palmendos, sonne to the famous and fortunate Prince Palmerin d'Oliua, Emperour of Constantinople and the Queene of Tharsus. Translated by A[nthony] *M*[unday]. London: J[ohn] C[harlewood] for Simon Watersonne, 1589. STC 18064.

Palmerin, of England. The second part, of the no lesse rare, historie of Palmerin of England (by F. de Moraes). Translated by A[nthony] M[unday]. London: T[homas]. Creede, 1596. STC 19161.

– *The third and last part of Palmerin of England. Enterlaced with the loues and fortunes of many gallant Knights and Ladies: A historie full of most choise and sweet varietie. Written in Spanish, Italian, and French.* Translated by A[nthony] M[unday] London: by I.R. for William Leake, 1602. STC 19165.

Palmerin, de Oliva. Palmerin D'Oliua, The Mirrour of nobilitie, mappe of honor, anotamie of rare fortunes, heroycall president of Loue: Wonder of chiualrie, and most accomplished knight in all perfections. Presenting to noble minds, theyr courtlie desire, to gentles, theyr choise expectations, and to the inferior sorte, bowe to imitate theyr vertues: handled with modestie to shun offense, yet all delightfull, for retreation. Written in the Spanish, Italian, and French; and from them turned into English by A[nthony] *M*[unday], one of the messengers of her Maiesties chamber. London: I. Charlewood for William Wright, 1588. STC 19157.

– *The second part of the historie of Palmerin d'Oliva, the Mirrour of Nobilitie, Mappe of Honor, anatomie of rare fortunes, heroicall president of Loue: Wonder of chiualrie.* Translated by A[nthony] M[unday]. London: Thomas Creede, 1597. STC 19158.

– *Palmerin D'Oliva. The first part shewing the mirour of nobilitie, the map of honour, anatomie of rare fortunes, heroicall presidents of love, wonder of chivalrie, and the most accomplished knight in all perfection. Presenting to noble minds, their courtly desire, to gentiles their expectations, and to the inferior sort, how to imitate their vertues: handled with modestie to shun offence, yet delightfull for recreation. Written in Spanish, Italian, and French, and from them turned into English, by A*[nthony] *M*[unday], *one of the messengers of his Majesties chamber*. London: T. Fawcet, 1637. STC 19160.

Primaleon of Greece. The famous and renowned historie of Primaleon of Greece, sonne to the great and mighty Prince Palmerion d'Oliua, Emperour of Constantinople Describing knightly deedes of armes, as also the memorable aduentures of Prince Edward of England: and continuing the former history of Palmendos, brother to the fortunate Prince Primaleou, &c. The first booke. Translated out of French and Italian, into English by A[nthony] *M*[unday]. London: Thomas Snodham, 1619. STC 20367.

Parry, Robert. *Moderatus, the most delectable & famous historie of the black knight*. London: R. Johnes, 1595. STC 19337.

Parry, William. *A new and large discourse of the trauels of sir Anthony Sherley Knight, by sea, and ouer land, to the Persian Empire, Wherein are related many straunge and wonderfull accidents: and also, the description and conditions of those countries and people he passed by: with his returne into Christendome. Written by William Parry gentleman, who accompanied Sir Anthony in his trauells*. London: Felix Norton, 1601. STC 19343.

Pires, Tomé. *The Suma Oriental of Tomé Pires: An Account of the East, from the Red Sea to Japan, written in Malacca and India in 1512–1515*. Translated from the Portuguese and edited by Armando Cortesão, The Hakluyt Society, 1944. Repr. Nendeln, Liechtenstein: Kraus Repring Limited, 1967.

Pliny, the Elder. *The Historie of the World, Commonly called, THE NATVRALL HISTORIE OF C. PLINY SECUNDVS*. Translated by Philemon Holland. London: Adam Islip, 1601. STC 20629.

Riche, Barnabe. *The straunge and wondefull aduentures of Do*[n] *Simonides, a gentilman Spaniarde: Conteuyning verie pleasaunte discourse: Gathered for the recreation aswell of our noble young gentilmen, as our honourable courtly Ladies*. London: Robart [*sic*] Walley, 1581. STC 21002.

Robarts, Henry. *A Defiance to Fortune: Proclaimed by Andrugio, noble Duke of Saxony, declaring his miseries, and continually crossed with vnconstant Fortune, the banishment of himselfe, his wife and children*. London: John Proctor, 1590. STC 21078.

– *The Historie of Pheander The Mayden Knight. Describing his Honorable Travailes and haughty attempts in Armes, with his successe in loue: enterlaced with many pleasant discourses, wherein the gauer may take delight, and the valiant youthfull, be encouraged by honourable and worthie aduenturing, to gaine fame*. London: Tho[mas] Creede, 1595. STC 21086.

– *Honovrs conquest / Wherein is conteined the famous hystorie of Edward of Lancaster recounting his honourable trauailes to Ierusalem, his heroic adventures and honours, in sundrie countries gained: his resolutions, and attempts in armes. With the famous victories performed by the knight, of the vnconquered castel, a gallant English knight, his admirable forces, and sundrie conquests obtained, with his passions and sucesse in loue: full of pleasant discourses, and much varietie*. London: Thomas Creede, 1598. STC 21082.

Roberts, Lewes. *The merchants mappe of commerce wherein, the universall manner and matter of trade, is compendiously handled. The standard and currant coines of sundry princes, observed. The reall and imaginary coines of accompts and exchanges, expressed. The natural and artificiall commodities of all countries for transportation declared. The weights and measures of all eminent cities and townes of traffique, collected and reduced one into another; and all to the meridian of commerce practiced in the famous citie of London*. London: R.O[ulton] for Ralphe Mabb, 1638. STC 21094.

– *The treasure of traffike, or, A discourse of forraigne trade*. London: Nicholas Bourne, 1641, Wing R1602.

Roe, Sir Thomas. *The Negotiations of Sir Thomas Roe, in His Embassy to the Ottoman Porte*. London: Samuel Richardson and Society for the Encouragement of Learning, 1740.

Romance of King Alexander, Anon. London: R. Faques, (?1525). STC 321.

Rowland, Smith, ed. *The Greek Romances of Heliodorus, Longus, and Achilles Tatius*. London: Henry G. Bohn, 1855.

Rosaccio, Giuseppe. *Viaggio da Venetia, a Constantinopoli Per Mare, e per Terra, & insieme quello di Terra Santa*. Venetia: Giacomo Franco, 1598.

Sanderson, John. *The Travels of John Sanderson in the Levant, 1584–1602*. Edited by Sir William Forster. London: Printed for the Hakluyt Society, 1931.

Sandys, George. *A Relation of a Iourney begun An. Dom: 1610. Foure bookes Containing a description of the Turkish Empire, of AEgypt, of the Holy Land, of the remote parts of Italy, and illands adioyning*. London: W[illiam]. Barrett, 1621. STC 21726.

Saunders, Thomas. *A true description and breefe discourse, of a most lamentable voiage, made latelie to Tripolie in Barbarie, in a ship named the IESVS wherein is not onely shewed the great miserie, that then happened the aucthor hereof and his whole companie, aswell the marchants as the marriners in that voyage, according to the cursed custome of those barbarous and cruell tyrants, in their terrible vsage of Christian captiues: but also, the great vnfaithfulnesse of those heathenish infidels, in not regarding their promise. Together, with the most wonderful iudgement of God, vpon the king of Tripolie and his sonne, and a great number of his people, being all the tormentors of those English captiue. Set foorth by Thomas Saunders, one of those captiues there at the same time.* London: Edward White, 1587. STC 21778.

Scudéry, Madeleine de. *Ibrahim, or the Illustrious Bassa an excellent new romance the whole work in four parts / written in French by Monsieur de Scudery and now Englished by Henry Cogan, Gent.* London: Humphrey Moseley, 1652. Wing 52161.

Shakespeare, William. *A Midsummer Night's Dream.* Edited by Peter Holland. Oxford: Oxford University Press, 1995.

Shakespeare, William and George Wilkins. *A Reconstructed Text of Pericles, Prince of Tyre.* Edited by Roger Warren on the basis of a text prepared by Gary Taylor and Macd. P. Jackson. Oxford: Oxford University Press, 2003.

Sidney, Sir Philip. *A Defence of Poetry, English Renaissance Literary Criticism.* Edited by Brian Vickers. Oxford: Oxford University Press, 2003, 336–91.

– *The Countesse of Pembrokes Arcadia.* London: [R. Field] for William Ponsonbie, 1598. STC 22541.

Spenser, Edmund. *The Faerie Queene.* Edited by Thomas P. Roche. London: Penguin Books, 1978.

Stafforde, Robert. *A geographicall and anthological description of all the empires and kingdomes, both of continent and ilands in this terrestrial globe / Relating their scituations, manners, customes, prouinces, and gouernments.* London: Nicholas Oakes, 1618. STC 23136.

Tatius, Achilles. *THE MOST DELECT-able and plasaunt History of* Clitophon and *Leucippe, newly translated into English, By W*[illiam] *B*[aldwin]. London: Thomas Creede for William Mattes, 1597. STC 1370.

Thomas, William. *The History of Italye / a booke excedying profitable to be redde: because it intreateth of the astate of many and diuers common weales, how their haue ben,* [and] *now be gouerned.* London: Thomas Marshe, (1549),1621. STC 24018.

Thorie, John. *The theatre of the earth, Containing very short and compendious descriptions of all countries, gathered out of the cheefest cosmographers, both ancient and moderne, and disposed in alphabeticall order. For the benefit of all such delight to e acquainted with the knowledge of strange countries, and the situation thereof, and especially for travellers, to whom the portability of this small volume will not be little commodious. What is performed in this booke is more at large set downe to the reader view in the next leafe.* London: Willian Iones, 1601. STC 23932.

Timberlake, Henry. *A trve and strange discourse of the trauailes of two English pilgrimes what admirable accidents befell them in their iourney to Ierusalem, Gaza, Grand Cayro, Alexandria, and other places. Also what rare antiquities, monuments, & notable memories (concording with the ancient reme*[m]*brances in the holy Scriptures) they saw in Terran Sancta, with a perfect description of the old and new Ierusalem, and situation of the countries about them. A discourse of no lesse admiration, the*[n] *well worth the regarding, written by one of them, on the behalf of himself, and his fellow pilgrime*. London: Thomas Archer, 1608. STC 24080.

Torkington, Richard. *The oldest diarie of Englysshe Travell*. London: [n.p.], 1517, Not in STC.

Twyne, Laurence. *The patterne of paineful aduentures: containing the most excellent, pleasant and variable historie of the strange accidents that befell vnto Prince Apollonius, the Lady Lucina his wife, and Tharsia his daughter. Gathered into English by Laurence Twine*. London: Valentine Simmes for E. N., 1594. STC 709.5.

Watson, Henry. *Valentine and Orson, the Two Sonnes of the Emperous of Greece. Newly Corrected and amended, with new Pictures lively expressing the Historie*. London: Thomas Purfoot, (1565) 1637. STC 24573.

Webbe, William. *The Rare and most wonderfull things which Edw*[ard] *Webbe an Englishman borne, hath seene and passed in his troublesome trauailes, in the Cities of Iarusalem, Damasko, Bethlehem and Galely: and in the landes of Iewrie, Egypt, Grecia, Russia, and Prestor Iohn. Wherein is set forth his extreame slauery sustained many yeeres together in the Gallies and warres of the great Turke, against the landes of Persia, Tartaria, Spaine, and Portugale, with the maner of his relasement and coming into England in May last*. London: William Wright, 1590. Not in STC.

– *The rare and most wonderfull thinges which Edward Webbe an Englishman borne, hath seene ane passed in his troublesome trauailes, in the citties of Ierusalem, Dammasko, Bethelem and Galely: and the lands of Iewrie, Egipt, Grecia, Russia, and in the land of Prester Iohn*. London: Ralph Blower for Thomas Pauier, 1600. Not in STC.

Whetstone, George. *Avrelia: The Paragon of Pleasures and Princely Delights*. London: Richard Iohnes, 1593. STC 25338.

Wroth, Mary. *The First Part of The Countess of Montgomery's Urania*. Edited by Josephine A. Roberts. Binghampton, NY: Center for Medieval and Early Renaissance Studies, 1995.

– *The Second Part of the Countess of Montgomery's Urania*. Edited by Josephine A. Roberts; completed by Suzanne Gossett and Janel Mueller. Tempe, AZ: Renaissance English Texts Society in conjunction with Arizona Center for Medieval and Renaissance Studies, 1999.

Xenophon. *The VIII. Bookes of Xenophon, Containinge the Institutio[n], schole, and education of Cyrus, the noble Kynge of Persye: and also his ciuill and princelye estate, his expedition into Babylon, Syria and Aegypt, and his exhortation before his death, to his children. Translated out of Greeke into English by M. William Bercker*. n.p., 1567. STC 26067.

– *Xenophons Treatise of Hovseholde*. Translated by Gentian Hervet. London: [W. Copland] for Abraham Vele, 1557. STC 26074.

– *Xenophons Treatise of Householde*. Translated by Gentian Hervet. London: John Alde, 1573. STC 26075.
– *Memorabilia and Oeconomicus*, Vol. 4 of 7. Translated by E.C. Merchant. Cambridge, Mass: Harvard University Press and London: William Heineman, [1923], 1968.

Secondary Sources

Abulafia, David. *The Great Sea: A Human History of the Mediterranean*. London: Penguin, 2012.
– "What is the Mediterranean?." In *The Mediterranean in History*. Edited by David Abulafia. Los Angeles: The Paul Getty Museum, 2003, 11–30.
Adams, Robert. "Bold Bawdy and Open Manslaughter: The English New Humanist Attack on Medieval Romance." *The Huntington Library Quarterly* 33 (1959): 33–48.
Adelman, Janet. "Making Defect Perfection: Shakespeare and the One-Sex Model." In *Enacting Gender on the English Renaissance Stage*. Edited by Viviana Comensolli and Anne Russell. Urbana and Chicago: University of Illinois Press, 1999, 23–52.
Andrea, Bernadette. *Women and Islam in Early Modern English Literature*. Cambridge: Cambridge University Press, 2007.
Andrews, Walter, and Mehmet Kalpakli. *The Age of Beloveds: Love and the Beloved in Early-Modern Ottoman and European Culture and Society*. Durham: Duke University Press, 2005.
Aerke, Kristian Paul Guido. "Theatrical Technique in Seventeenth-Century Prose Fiction." PhD dissertation, University of Georgia, 1989.
Aksan, Virginia H., and Daniel Goffman, ed. *The Early Modern Ottomans: Remapping the Empire*. Cambridge: Cambridge University Press, 2007.
Amussen, Susan Dwyer. "Punishment, Discipline, and Power: The Social Meanings of Violence in Early Modern England." *Journal of British Studies* 34 (1995): 1–34.
Aldrich, Robert. *The Seduction of the Mediterranean: Writing, Art and Homosexual Fantasy*. London: Routledge, 1993.
Arber, Edward. *Transcript of the Registers of the Company of Stationers of London, 1554–1640*, 2 vols. New York: P. Smith, 1950.
Archer, John Michael. *Old Worlds: Egypt, Southwest Asia, India, and Russia in Early Modern English Writing*. Stanford: Stanford University Press, 2001.
Arikan, Zeki. "The Ban on the Export of Certain Articles from the Levant to the Mediterranean Ports during the Fifteenth and Sixteenth Centuries." In *The Silk Roads: Highways of Culture and Commerce*. Edited by Vadim Eliiseeff.

New York and Oxford: Berghahn Books and UNESCO Publishing, 2000, 199–208.

Armitage, David. *The Ideological Origins of the British Empire*. Cambridge: Cambridge University Press, 2000.

– "Literature and Empire." In *The Origins of Empire*. Edited by Nicholas Canny. Oxford: Oxford University Press, 2001, 98–123.

Artemel, Süheylâ. "'Turkish' Imagery in Elizabethan Drama." *Review of National Literatures* 4:1 (1973): 82–98.

Aslanian, Sebouh David. *From the Indian Ocean to the Mediterranean: The Global Trade Networks of Armenian Merchants from New Julfa*. Berkeley, New York, and London: University of California Press, 2011.

Babinger, Franz. *Mehmed the Conqueror and His Time*. Translated by Ralph Manheim. Princeton: Princeton University Press, 1978.

Baker, Ernst A. *The History of the English Novel*. Vol. 2: *The Elizabethan Age and After*. London: H.F. and G. Witherby, 1937.

Bakhtin, Mikhail M. *The Dialogic Imagination: Four Essays*. Edited by Michael Holquist. Translated by Caryl Emerson and Michael Holquist. Austin: University of Texas Press. 1981.

Ballaster, Ros. *Fabulous Orients: Fictions of the East in England, 1662–1785*. Oxford: Oxford University Press, 2007.

Barber, Giles. *Daphnis and Chloe: The Markets and Metamorphoses of an Unknown Bestseller*. London: The British Library, 1989.

Barber, Peter. "The Christian Knight, the Most Christian King and the Rules of Darkness." *The Map Collector* 52 (1990): 8–13.

Barbour, Reid. *Deciphering Elizabethan Fiction*. Newark: University of Delaware Press and London and Toronto: Associated University Press, 1993.

Barbour, Richmond. *Before Orientalism: London's Theatre of the East, 1576–1626*. Cambridge: Cambridge University Press, 2003.

Bartels, Emily C. *Speaking of the Moor: From Alcazar to Othello*. Philadelphia: University of Pennsylvania Press, 2008.

– *Spectacles of Strangeness: Imperialism, Alienation, and Marlowe*. Philadelphia: University of Pennsylvania Press, 1993.

– "The Double Vision of the East: Imperialist Self-Construction in Marlowe's *Tamburlaine*, Part One." *Renaissance Drama* 23 (1992): 3–24.

Barthes, Roland. *The Rustle of Language*. Translated by Richard Howard. Berkeley and Los Angeles: University of California Press, 1984.

– *The Pleasure of the Text*. Translated by Richard Howard. New York: Hill and Wang and The Noonday Press, 1975.

Bearden, Elizabeth. *The Emblematics of the Self: Ekphrasis and Identity in Renaissance Imitations of Greek Romance*. Toronto: University of Toronto Press, 2012.

– "Painting Counterfeit Canvases: American Memory *Lienzos* and European Imaginings of the Barbaria in Cervantes's *Los trabajos de Persiles y Sigismunda*." PMLA 121:3 (2006): 735–52.

Bennett, Josephine Waters. *The Rediscovery of Sir John Mandeville*. New York: Kraus, 1971.

Berlant, Lauren. "Intimacy: A Special Issue." *Critical Inquiry* 24 (1998): 281– 8.

Betteridge, Tom, ed. *Sodomy in Early Modern Europe*. Manchester and New York: Manchester University Press, 2002.

Birchwood, Matthew. *Staging Islam in England: Drama and Culture, 1640–1685*. Cambridge: D.S. Brewer, 2007.

Blayney, W.M. Peter. "The Alleged Popularity of Playbooks." *Shakespeare Quarterly* 56:1 (2005): 33–50.

Blažević, Zrinka. *Ilirizam prije ilirizma*. Zagreb: Golden marketing-Tehnička knjiga, 2008.

Blunt, Wilfred. *The Golden Road to Samarkand*. London: Hamish Hamilton, 1973.

Bly, Mary. *Queer Virgins and Virgin Queens on the Early Modern Stage*. Oxford: Oxford University Press, 2000.

Bolgar, Robert Ralph. "Hero and Anti-Hero: the Genesis and Development of *Miles Christianus*." In *Concepts of the Hero in the Middle Ages and the Renaissance*. Edited by Norman T. Burns and Christopher Reagan. London: Hodder and Stoughton, 1971, 120–45.

Bonheim, Helmut. "Emanuel Forde: *Ornatus and Artesia*," *Anglia* 90: 1–2 (1972): 43–59.

– ed. *The English Novel Before Richardson: A Checklist of Texts and Criticism to 1970*. Metuchen, NJ: Scarecrow Press, 1971.

Bosworth, Clifford Edmund. *An Intrepid Scot: Willian Lithgow of Lanark's Travels in the Ottoman Lands, North Africa and Central Europe 1609–21*. Aldershot: Ashgate, 2006.

Boulnois, Luce. *The Silk Road*. Translated by Dennis Chamberlin. London: George Allen & Unwin, 1966.

Bovill, E.W. *The Golden Trade of the Moors*. London: Oxford University Press, 1958.

Bracewell, Wendy Catherine. *The Uskoks of Senj: Piracy, Banditry, And Holy War in the Sixteenth-Century Adriatic*. Ithaca, NY and London: Cornell University Press, 1992.

Braudel, Fernand. *The Mediterranean and the Mediterranean World in the Age of Philip II*. Translated by Sîan Reynolds. 2 vols. New York: Harper & Row, 1976.

– *Capitalism and Material Life 1400–1800*. Translated by Miriam Kochan. London: Weidenfeld and Nicolson, 1973.

– "La Terre" and "La Mer." In *La Méditerranée: l'espace et l'historie*. Edited by Fernand Braudel. Paris: Flammarion, 1985. 1–80.

– "Personal Testimony." *The Journal of Modern History* 44:4 (1972): 448–67.

Bray, Alan. *Homosexuality in Renaissance England.* London: Gay Men's Press, 1982.

– "Homosexuality and the Signs of Male Friendship in Elizabethan England." *History Workshop Journal* 29 (1990): 1–19.

– "To Be a Man in Early Modern Society: The Curious Case of Michael Wigglesworth." *History Workshop Journal* 41 (1996): 155–65.

– *The Friend.* Chicago: University of Chicago Press, 2003.

Bray, Alan, and Michel Rey. "The Body of the Friend: Continuity and Change in Masculine Friendship in the Seventeenth Century." In *English Masculinities 1660–1800.* Edited by Tim Hitchcock and Michèle Cohen. London and New York: Longman, 1999, 65–84.

Bredbeck, Gregory W. *Sodomy and Interpretation: Marlowe to Milton.* Ithaca and London: Cornell University Press, 1991.

Breitenberg, Mark. *Anxious Masculinity in Early Modern England.* Cambridge: Cambridge University Press, 1996.

Brennan, Michael G. "The Literature of Travel." In *The Cambridge History of the Book in Britain*, Vol. 4. Edited by John Barnard and D.F. McKenzie. Cambridge: Cambridge University Press, 2002, 246–73.

Brettell, Caroline B. "Introduction: Travel Literature, Ethnography, and Ethnohistory." *Ethnohistory* 33:2 (1986): 127–38.

British Museum. *Manuscript Maps, Charts, and Plans, and Topographical Drawings in the British Museum*, 3 vols. London: Published by the Trustees of the British Museum, 1844 (facsimile 1962).

Britton, Dennis Austin. *Becoming Christian: Race, Reformation, and Early Modern English Renaissance.* New York: Fordham University Press, 2014.

Bromley, James M. *Intimacy and Sexuality in the Age of Shakespeare.* Cambridge: Cambridge University Press, 2012.

Bromley, James M., and Will Stockton, ed. *Sex Before Sex: Figuring the Act in Early Modern England.* Minneapolis and London: University of Minnesota Press, 2013.

Brotton, Jerry. *A History of the World in Twelve Maps.* London: Allen Lane, 2012.

– *The Renaissance Bazaar: From the Silk Road to Michelangelo.* Oxford: Oxford University Press, 2002.

– *Trading Territories: Mapping the Early Modern World.* Ithaca, NY: Cornell University Press, 1998.

– "'This Tunis, sir, was Carthage': Contesting Colonialism in *The Tempest.*" In *Post-Colonial Shakespeares.* Edited by Ania Loomba and Martin Orkin. London and New York: Routledge, 1998, 23–42.

– "Terrestrial Globalism: Mapping the Globe in Early Modern Europe." In *Mappings.* Edited by Denis Cosgrove. London: Reaktion Books, 1999, 71–89.

Brown, Peter. *The Body and Society: Men, Women and Sexual Renunciation in Early Christianity*. New York: Columbia University Press, 1988.

Brummett, Palmira. *Ottoman Seapower and Levantine Diplomacy in the Age of Discovery*. Albany, NY: SUNY Press, 1994.

Burke, Peter. *Popular Culture in Early Modern Europe*. New York: New York University Press, 1978.

Burlin, Robert B. "Middle English Romance: The Structure of Genre." *The Chaucer Review* 30:1 (1995), 1–14.

Burton, Jonathan. *Traffic and Turning: Islam and English Drama, 1579–1624*. Newark, Delaware: University of Delaware Press, 2005.

Bushnell, Rebecca. "Tyranny and Effeminacy in Early Modern England." In *Reconsidering the Renaissance*. Edited by Mario Di Cesare. Binghampton, NY: Medieval and Renaissance Texts and Studies, 1992, 339–54.

Calbi, Maurizio. "'Unshap't Bodies': Masculinity Travels East." In *Cultural Encounters Between East and West, 1453–1699*. Edited by Matthew Birchwood and Matthew Dimmock. Newcastle-upon-Tyne: Cambridge Scholars Press, 2005, 132–141.

Capp, Bernard. "Popular Literature." In *Popular Culture in Seventeenth-Century England*. Edited by Barry Reay. New York: St Martin's Press, 1985, 198–243.

Carey, John. "Structure and Rhetoric in Sidney's *Arcadia*." In *Sir Philip Sidney: An Anthology of Modern Criticism*. Edited by Dennis Kay. Oxford: Clarendon Press, 1987, 245–64.

Carnicelli, D.D. "The Widow and the Phoenix: Dido, Carthage, and Tunis in *The Tempest*." *Harvard Library Bulletin* 27:4 (1979): 389–433.

Casey, Charles. "Heroes as Lovers: Erotic Attraction Between Men in Sidney's *New Arcadia*." *Criticism* 34:4 (1992): 467–96.

Cavanagh, Sheila T. *Cherished Torment: The Emotional Geography of Lady Mary Wroth's Urania*. Pittsburgh: Duquesne University Press, 2001.

Cave, Terence. "Locating the Early Modern." *Paragraph* 29:1 (2006): 12–26.

Chambers, Iain. *Mediterranean Crossings: The Politics of An Interrupted Modernity*. Durham, NC and London: Duke University Press, 2008.

Charbonneau, Joanne, and Désirée Cromwell. "Gender and Identity in the Popular Romance." In *A Companion to Medieval Popular Romance*. Edited by Raluca L. Radulescu and Cory James Rushton. Cambridge: D.S. Brewer, 2009, 96–110.

Chew, Samuel Claggett. *The Crescent and the Rose: Islam and England During the Renaissance*. New York: Oxford University Press, 1937.

Clare, Patricia Ingham. *Sovereign Fantasies: Arthurian Romance and the Making of Britain*. Philadelphia: University of Pennsylvania Press, 2001.

Cohn, Jan. *Romance and the Erotics of Property: Mass-Market Fiction for Women*. Durham, NC and London: Duke University Press, 1988.

Collingwood, A. Lee. *The Decameron, Its Sources and Analogues*. New York: Haskell House, 1966.

Conley, Tom. "Pierre Boaistuau's Cosmographic Stage: Theater, Text, and Map." *Renaissance Drama*, n.s., 23 (1992): 59–86.

Conway, Eustace. *Anthony Munday and Other Essays*. New York: privately printed, 1927.

Cooper, Helen. "Introduction." In *Christianity and Romance in Medieval England*. Edited by Rosalind Field, Phillipa Hardman, and Michelle Sweeney. Cambridge: D.S. Brewer, 2010, xiii–xxi.

– "Shakespeare and the Middle Ages," Inaugural lecture delivered at the University of Cambridge, 29 April 2005, 1–38.

– *The English Romance in Time: Transforming Motifs* from *Geoffrey of Monmouth* to the *Death* of *Shakespeare*. Oxford: Oxford University Press, 2004.

– "'This worthy olde writer:' *Pericles* and other Gowers, 1592–1640." In *A Companion to Gower*. Edited by Sîan Echard. Cambridge: D.S. Brewer, 2004, 99–114.

– "Counter-Romance: Civil Strife and Father Killing in the Prose Romances." In *The Long Fifteenth Century, Essays for Douglas Gray*. Edited by Helen Cooper and Sally Mapstone. Oxford: Clarendon Press, 1997, 142–62.

Corbett, Julian S. *England in the Mediterranean: A Study of the Rise and Influence of British Power Within the Straits, 1603–1713*, 2 vols. London: Longmans Green, 1904.

– "Marginal Waters: *Pericles* and the idea of jurisdiction." In *Literature, Mapping, and the Politics of Space in Early Modern Britain*. Edited by Andrew Gordon and Bernhard Klein. Cambridge: Cambridge University Press, 2001, 155–80.

Cormack, Bradin. *A Power to do Justice: Jurisdiction, English Literature, and the Rise of Common Law, 1509–1625*. Chicago and London: University of Chicago Press, 2007.

Cormack, Leslie B. *Charting and Empire: Geography and the English Universities, 1580–1620*. Chicago and London: University of Chicago Press, 1997.

Crane, Ronald Salmon. *The Vogue of Medieval Chivalric Romance During the English Renaissance*. Monasha: George Banta Publishing, 1919.

Crane, Susan. *Gender and Romance in Chaucer's Canterbury Tales*. Princeton, NJ: Princeton University Press, 1994.

Craponzano, Vincent. "On the Writing of Ethnography." *Dialectical Anthropology* 2 (1977): 69–73.

Crawford, Patricia. "Sexual Knowledge in England, 1500–1750." In *Sexual Knowledge, Sexual Science: The History of Attitudes to Sexuality*. Edited by Roy Porter and Mikuláš Teich. Cambridge: Cambridge University Press, 1994, 82–106.

Cressy, David. "Gender Trouble and Cross-Dressing in Early Modern England." *Journal of British Studies* 35:4 (1996): 438–65.

– *Literacy and the Social Order: Reading and Writing in Tudor and Stuart England.* Cambridge: Cambridge University Press, 1980.

Daileader, Celia R. *Racism, Misogyny, and the Othello Myth: Inter-racial Couples from Shakespeare to Spike Lee.* Cambridge: Cambridge University Press, 2005.

D'Amico, Jack. *The Moor in English Renaissance Drama.* Tampa: University of South Florida Press, 1991.

Das, Nandini. *Renaissance Romance: The Transformation of English Prose Fiction, 1570–1620.* Farnham, Surrey and Burlington, VT: Ashgate, 2011.

Davies, C.S.L. *Peace, Print and Protestantism 1450–1558.* London: Hart-Davis, Macgibbon, 1976.

Davis, Alex. *Renaissance Historical Fiction: Sidney, Deloney, Nashe.* Cambridge: D.S. Brewer, 2011.

Davis, Ralph. "England and the Mediterranean." In *Essays in the Economic and Social History of Tudor and Stuart England in Honour of R.H. Tawney.* Edited by F.J. Fisher Cambridge: Cambridge University Press, 1961, 117–37.

Davis, Walter. *Idea and Act in Elizabethan Fiction.* Princeton: Princeton University Press, 1969.

de Grazia, Margreta. "Anachronism." In *Cultural Reformations: Medieval and Renaissance in Literary History.* Edited by Brian Cummings and James Simpson. Oxford: Oxford University Press, 2010, 13–32.

Delumeau, Jean. *La Peur en Occident (XIVe–XVIIIe): Une cite assiégée.* Paris: Librarie Arthème Fagard, 1978.

DiGangi, Mario. *Sexual Types: Embodiment, Agency, and Dramatic Character from Shakespeare to Shirley.* Philadelphia: University of Pennsylvania Press, 2011.

– *The Homoerotics of Early Modern Drama.* Cambridge: Cambridge University Press, 1997.

Dimmock, Matthew. *Mythologies of the Prophet Muhammad in Early Modern English Culture.* Cambridge: Cambridge University Press, 2013.

– *New Turks: Dramatizing Islam and the Ottomans in Early Modern England.* Aldershot: Ashgate, 2005.

– "'Captive to the Turke': Responses to the Anglo-Ottoman Capitulations of 1580." In *Cultural Encounters Between East and West, 1453–1699.* Edited by Matthew Dimmock and Matthew Birchwood. Newcastle-upon-Tyne: Cambridge Scholars Press, 2005, 43–63.

Dimmock, Matthew, and Andrew Hadfield, ed. *The Religions of the Book: Christian Perceptions, 1400–1660.* New York and Basingstoke: Palgrave-Macmillan, 2008.

Dolan, Frances E. "Re-reading Rape in *The Changeling.*" *The Journal of Early Modern Cultural Studies* 11:1 (2011), 4–29.

Doñabeitia, María Luisa. "The Inevitable Death of Desdemona: Shakespeare and the Mediterranean Tradition." *Proceedings of the II Conference of the Spanish Society for Renaissance Studies (SEDERI)*. Edited by S. G. Fernández-Corugedo. Oviedo: Universidad Oviedo Servicio de Publicationes, 1992, 83–93.

Dolven, Jeff. *Scenes of Instruction in Renaissance Romance*. Chicago and London: University of Chicago Press, 2007.

Doody, Margaret Anne. *The True Story of the Novel*. New Brunswick, NJ: Rutgers University Press, 1996.

Doroszlaï, Alexandre. *Ptolémée et l'hippogriffe: La géographie de l'Arioste soumise à l'épreuve des cartes*. Turin: Edizione dell'Orso, 1988.

Duncan-Jones, Katherine. *Ungentle Shakespeare: Scenes from His Life*. London: Methuen Drama, 2010.

Durham, Charles W. III. "Character and Characterization in Elizabethan Prose Fiction," PhD dissertation, Ohio University, 1969.

Dursteller, Eric R. *Renegade Women: Gender, Identity, and Boundaries in the Early Modern Mediterranean*. Baltimore: Johns Hopkins University Press, 2011.

Đurić, Ivan. *Sumrak Vizantije: Vreme Jovana VIII Paleologa, 1392–1448*. Zagreb: Naprijed, 1989.

Echevería, Roberto Gonzáles. *Myth and Archive: A Theory of Latin American Narrative*. Cambridge: Cambridge University Press, 1990.

Edwards, Catherine. "Grades for Boys." In review of James Davidson, *The Greeks and Greek Love*. London: Weidenfeld and Nicolson, 2007. *Times Literary Supplement* 5476. 14 March 2008, 12.

El-Rouayheb, Khaled. *Before Homosexuality in the Arab-Islamic World, 1500–1800*. Chicago and London: University of Chicago Press, 2005.

Eldem, Edhem, Daniel Goffman, and Bruce Masters. *The Ottoman City between East and West: Aleppo, Izmir, and Istanbul*. Cambridge: Cambridge University Press, 1999.

Elk, Martine Van. "'This sympathized one day's error:' Genre, Representation, and Subjectivity in *The Comedy of Errors*." *Shakespeare Quarterly* 60:1 (2009): 47–72.

Epp, Garrett P.J. "John Foxe and the Circumcised Stage." *Exemplaria* 9:2 (1997): 281–313.

Epstein, Mordecai. *The English Levant Company: Its Foundation and Its History to 1640* (1908). New York: Burt Franklin, 1968.

Esdaile, Arundell, compiler. *A List of English Tales and Prose Romances Printed Before 1740*. London: The Bibliographical Society, 1912.

Evans, Murray. *Reading Middle English Romance: Manuscript Layout, Decoration, and the Rhetoric of Composite Structure*. Montreal & Kingston: McGill-Queen's University Press, 1995.

Everett, Barbara. "Making and Breaking in Shakespeare's Romances." *London Review of Books*, 22 March 2007, 19–22.

– "'Spanish' Othello: The Making of Shakespeare's Moor." *Shakespeare Survey* 35 (1982): 101–12.

Everett, Dorothy. "A Characterization of the English Medieval Romances." In *Essays on Middle English Literature* by Dorothy Everett. Edited by Patricia Kean. Oxford: Clarendon Press, 1959, 1–22.

Falke, Anne. "The Work Well Done that Pleaseth All": Emanuel Forde and the Seventeenth-Century Popular Chivalric Romance." *Studies in Philology* 78 (1981): 241–54.

– "Medieval and Popular Elements in the Romances of Emanuel Forde," PhD dissertation, Michigan State University, 1974.

Farmer, Alan B., and Zachary Lesser, "The Popularity of Playbooks Revisited." *Shakespeare Quarterly* 56:1 (2005): 1–32.

Fellows, Jennifer. "Printed Romance in the Sixteenth Century." In *A Companion to Medieval Popular Romance*. Edited by Raluca L. Radulescu and Cory James Rushton Cambridge: D.S. Brewer, 2009, 67–78.

Ferguson, Arthur B. *The Indian Summer of English Chivalry: Studies in the Decline and Transformation of Chivalric Idealism*. Durham, NC: Duke University Press, 1960.

– *Chivalric Tradition in Renaissance England*. Washington, DC: The Folger Shakespeare Library, 1986.

Ferguson, Frances. "Rape and the Rise of the Novel." *Representations* 20 (Fall 1987): 88–112.

Fernández-Armesto, Felipe. "Imperial Measures: Grand Delusions in Defining the Dominators of the World." *Times Literary Supplement*, 24 September 2010, 8–9.

Finkelstein, Andrea. *Harmony and Balance: An Intellectual History of Seventeenth-Century English Economic Thought*. Ann Arbor: University of Michigan Press, 2000.

Finlayson, John. "Definitions of Middle English Romance." *Chaucer Review* 15 (1980): 43–62.

Foster, William. *England's Quest of Eastern Trade*. London: A&C Black, 1933.

Foucault, Michel. "Friendship as a Way of Life." In *Foucault Live (Interviews, 1961–84)*. Translated by Lysa Hochroth and John Johnston. Edited by Sylvère Lotringer. New York: Semiotext(e), 1989, 201–9.

– "Of Other Spaces." *Diacritics* 16 (1986): 22–7.

– "Questions on Geography." In *Power/Knowledge: Selected Interviews & Other Writings, 1972–1977*. Edited by Colin Gordon. New York: Pantheon Books, 1977, 63–77.

Foulkes-Roberts A. "Robert Parry's Diary." In *Archaeologica Cambriensis*, 6th series, 15 (1915): 109–39.

Fowler, Alastair. *Kinds of Literature: An Introduction to the Theory of Genres and Modes*. Oxford: Clarendon Press, 1985.

Fowler, Elizabeth and Roland Greene, ed. *The Project of Prose in Early Modern Europe and the New World*. Cambridge: Cambridge University Press, 1997.

Foyster, Elizabeth A. *Manhood in Early Modern England: Honour, Sex and Marriage*. London and New York: Longman, 1999.

France, John. *The Crusades and the Expansion of Catholic Christendom, 1000–1714*. London and New York: Routledge, 2005.

Freccero, Carla. *Queer/Early/Modern*. Durham, NC and London: Duke University Press, 2006.

Fredenburg, Louise O., and Carla Freccero. "The Pleasures of History." *GLQ* 1 (1995): 371–84.

Frye, Northrop. *The Secular Scripture: A Study of the Structure of Romance*. Cambridge, MA and London: Harvard University Press, 1976.

Fuchs, Barbara. *The Poetics of Piracy: Emulating Spain in English Literature*. Philadelphia: University of Pennsylvania Press, 2013.

– *Romance*. New York and London: Routledge, 2004.

– *Passing for Spain: Cervantes and the Fictions of Identity*. Urbana and Chicago: University of Illinois Press, 2003.

– *Mimesis and Empire: The New World, Islam, and European Identities*. Cambridge: Cambridge University Press, 2001.

– "Faithless Empires: Pirates, Renegadoes, and The English Nation." *ELH* 67 (2000): 45–69.

Fumerton, Patricia. *Cultural Aesthetics: Renaissance Literature and the Practice of Social Ornament*. Chicago and London: University of Chicago Press, 1991.

Gallagher, Catherine, and Stephen Greenblatt. *Practicing New Historicism*. Chicago and London: University of Chicago Press, 2000.

Gaunt, J.L. "*The Most Excellent History of Ornatus and Artesia*: An Unusual Restoration Abridgement." *Studies in Short Fiction* 14 (1977): 399–401.

George, Katherine. "The Civilized West Looks at Primitive Africa, 1400–1800: A Study in Ethnocentricism." *Isis* 46 (1958): 62–72.

Giddens, Anthony. *The Consequences of Modernity*. Cambridge: Cambridge University Press, 1990.

Gillies, John. "Introduction: Elizabethan Drama and the Cartographizations of Space." In *Playing the Globe: Genre and Geography in English Renaissance Drama*. Edited by John Gillies and Virginia Mason Vaughan. Madison, Teaneck: Fairleigh Dickinson University Press, Associated University Press, 1998, 19–45.

Ginzburg, Carlo. *The Cheese and the Worms: The Cosmos of a Sixteenth-Century Miller*. Baltimore: Johns Hopkins University Press, 1992.

Goffman, Daniel. *The Ottoman Empire and Early Modern Europe*. Cambridge: Cambridge University Press, 2002.

– *Britons in the Ottoman Empire 1642–1660*. Seattle and London: University of Washington Press, 1998.

– *Izmir and the Levantine World, 1550–1650*. Seattle and London: University of Washington Press, 1990.

Goldberg, Jonathan. *The Seeds of Things: Theorizing Sexuality and Materiality in Renaissance Representations*. New York: Fordham University Press, 2009.

– ed. *Queering the Renaissance*. Durham, NC and London: Duke University Press, 1994.

– *Sodometries: Renaissance Texts, Modern Sexualities*. Stanford: Stanford University Press, 1992.

– "Sodomy in the New World: Anthropologies of Old and New." *Social Text* 29 (Fall 1991): 46–56.

– *James I and the Politics of Literature: Jonson, Shakespeare, Donne and Their Contemporaries*. Stanford: Stanford University Press, 1989.

Goldberg, Jonathan, and Madhavi Menon. "Queering History." *PMLA* 120:5 (2005): 1608–17.

Goody, Jack. *Renaissances: The One or the Many?* Cambridge: Cambridge University Press, 2010.

Gordon, Andrew, and Bernhard Klein, ed. *Literature, Mapping, and the Politics of Space in Early Modern Britain*. Cambridge: Cambridge University Press, 2001.

Grafton, Anthony. *What Was History: The Art of History in Early Modern Europe*. Cambridge: Cambridge University Press, 2007.

Green, André. *The Chains of Eros: The Sexual in Psychoanalysis*. Translated by Luke Thurston. London and New York: Karnac, 2001.

– *On Private Madness*. London and New York: Karnac, 2005.

Green, Lawrence D. *John Rainold's Oxford Lectures on Aristotle's Rhetoric*. Newark, NJ: Associated University Press, 1986.

Greenblatt, Stephen. "Shakespeare and the Exorcists." In *Shakespeare and the Question of Theory*. Edited by Patricia Parker and Geoffrey Hartman. London: Methuen, 1985, 163–87.

Greene, Molly. "Beyond the Northern Invasion: The Mediterranean in the Seventeenth Century." *Past and Present* 174 (February 2002): 42–71.

– *A Shared World: Christians and Moslems in the Early Modern Mediterranean*. Princeton: Princeton University Press, 2000.

Grenfell, Joanne Woolway. "Do Real Knights Need Maps? Charting Moral, Geographical and Representational Uncertainty in Edmund Spenser's

The Faerie Queene." In *Literature, Mapping, and the Politics of Space in Early Modern Britain*. Edited by Andrew Gordon and Bernard Klein. Cambridge: Cambridge University Press, 2001, 224–38.

Griffin, Nathaniel E. "The Definition of Romance." *PMLA* 37:1 (March 1923): 50–70.

Grogan, Jane. "'Headless Rome' and Hungry Goths: Herodotus and *Titus Andronicus*." *English Literary Renaissance* 43:1 (Winter 2013), 30–61.

Gurr, Andrew. *Playgoing in Shakespeare's London*. Cambridge: Cambridge University Press, 1988.

Guy-Bray, Stephen. *Homoerotic Space: The Poetics of Loss in Renaissance Literature* Toronto: University of Toronto Press, 2002.

Hackel, Heidi Brayman, and Peter C. Mancall. "Richard Hakluyt the Younger's Notes for the East India Company in 1601: A Transcription of Huntington Library Manuscript EL 2360." *Huntington Library Quarterly* 67:3 (2004): 423–36.

Hackett, Helen. *Women and Romance Fiction in the English Renaissance*. Cambridge: Cambridge University Press, 2000.

– "'A book, and solitariness': Melancholia, Gender and Literary Subjectivity in Mary Wroth's *Urania*." In *Renaissance Configurations: Voices, Bodies, Spaces, 1580–1690*. Edited by Gordon McMullan. Houndmills and New York: Palgrave, 1998, 64–85.

– "The Torture of Limena: Sex and Violence in Lady Mary Wroth's *Urania*." In *Voicing Women: Gender and Sexuality in Early Modern Writing*. Edited by Kate Chedgzoy, Melanie Hansen, and Suzanne Trill. Edinburgh: Edinburgh University Press, 1996, 93–110.

– "'Yet Tell me Some Such Fiction': Lady Mary Wroth's *Urania* and the 'Femininity' of Romance." In *Women, Texts, and Histories 1575–1760*. Edited by Clare Brant and Diane Purkiss. London and New York: Routledge, 1992, 39–68.

Hadfield, Andrew. "Travel." In *Cultural Reformations: Medieval and Renaissance in Literary History*. Edited by Brian Cummings and James Simpson. Oxford: Oxford University Press, 2010, 134–49.

– *Literature, Travel and Colonialism in the English Renaissance, 1540–1625*. Oxford: Clarendon Press, 1998.

Halperin, David M. *How to Do the History of Homosexuality*. Chicago and London: University of Chicago Press, 2002.

Hamilton, A.C. "Elizabethan Prose Fiction and Some Trends in Recent Criticism." *Renaissance Quarterly* 37 (1984): 21–33.

Hammond, Paul. *Figuring Sex Between Men from Shakespeare to Rochester*. Oxford: Clarendon Press, 2002.

Hamilton, Paul. *Historicism*. London and New York: Routledge, 2002.

Hanning, Robert W. *The Individual in Twelfth-Century Romance*. New Haven and London: Yale University Press, 1977.

Hanson, Ellis. "Sodomy and Kingcraft in *Urania* and *Anatomy and Cleopatra*." In *Homosexuality and Renaissance and Enlightenment England*. Edited by Claude Summers. New York: The Hawath Press, 1992, 135–152.

Hardman, Phillipa, and Marianne Ailes. "Crusading, Chivalry and the Saracen World in Insular Romance." In *Christianity and Romance in Medieval England*. Cambridge: D.S. Brewer, 2010, 45–65.

Harley, J.B. "Silences and Secrecy: The Hidden Agenda of Cartography in Early Modern Europe." *Imago Mundi* 40 (1988): 57–76.

Harris, Jonathan. *Untimely Matter in the Time of Shakespeare*. Philadelphia: University of Pennsylvania Press, 2009.

– "Usurers of Color: The Taint of Jewish Transnationality in Mercantilist Literature and *The Merchant of Venice*." Edited by Helen Ostovich, Mary Vilcox, and Graham Roebuck. Newark: University of Delaware Press, 2008, 124–38.

Hasluck, F.W. "Notes on manuscripts in the British Museum Relating to Levant Geography and Travel." British School of Athens, British School of Archaeology, *Annual* 12 (1905–6): 197–215.

Helgerson, Richard. "The Folly of Maps and Modernity." In *Literature, Mapping, and the Politics of Space in Early Modern Britain*. Edited by Andrew Gordon and Bernhard Klein. Cambridge: Cambridge University Press, 2001, 241–62.

– *Forms of Nationhood: The Elizabethan Writing of England*. Chicago and London: University of Chicago Press, 1992.

– *The Elizabethan Prodigals*. Berkeley: University of California Press, 1976.

Henderson, Philip, ed. *Shorter Novels: Seventeenth Century*. London: J.M. Dent and New York: E.P. Dutton, 1930.

Heng, Geraldine. *Empire of Magic: Medieval Romance and the Politics of Cultural Fantasy*. New York: Columbia University Press, 2003.

Hess, Andrew. "The Battle of Lepanto and Its Place in Mediterranean History." *Past and Present* 57 (1972): 53–73.

– *The Forgotten Frontier: A History of the Sixteenth-Century Ibero-African Frontier*. Chicago and London: The University of Chicago Press, 1978.

Heyworth, Gregory. *Desiring Bodies: Ovidian Romance and the Cult of Form*. Notre Dame: University of Notre Dame, Press, 2009.

Hill, Christopher. "Sex, Marriage, and the Family in England." *Economic History Review*, 2nd series, 31 (1978): 450–63.

Hill, Rosalind. "The Christian View of the Muslim at the Time of the First Crusade." In *The Eastern Mediterranean Lands in the Period of the Crusades*. Edited by P.M. Hott. Westminster, England: Aris and Phillips, 1977, 1–8.

Holden, Peregrine, and Nicholas Purcell. *The Corrupting Sea: A Study of Mediterranean History*. Oxford: Blackwell Publishing, 2000.

Houlbrooke, Ralph A. *The English Family 1450–1700*. London and New York: Longman, 1984.

Hsy, Jonathan. *Trading Tongues: Merchants, Multilingualism, and Medieval Literature*. Columbus, OH: Ohio State University Press, 2013.

Hunter, G.K. "The Making of *Sententiae* in Elizabethan Printed Plays, Poems, and Romances." In *The Library*, 5th ser., 6 (1951): 171–88.

Hurd, Richard [Bishop]. *Moral and Political Dialogues; with Letters on Chivalry and Romance*. 3 vols. London: W. Bowyer and J. Nichols for T. Cadell, 1771.

Hutcheon, Linda. *A Theory of Adaptation*. New York and London: Routledge, 2006.

Hutson, Lorna. *The Invention of Suspicion: Law and Mimesis in Shakespeare and Renaissance Drama*. Oxford: Oxford University Press, 2007.

– "Liking Men: Ben Jonson's Closet Opened." *ELH* 71 (2004):1065–96.

– "Chivalry for Merchants; or Knights of Temperance in the Realms of Gold." *Journal of Medieval and Early Modern Studies* 26:1 (1996): 29–59.

– "Fortunate Travelers: Reading for the Plot in Sixteenth-Century England." *Representations* 41 (Winter 1993): 83–103.

– *Thomas Nashe in Context*. Oxford: Clarendon Press, 1989.

– *The Usurer's Daughter: Male Friendship and Fictions of Women in Sixteenth-Century England*. London and New York: Routledge, 1994.

Imber, Colin. *The Ottoman Empire, 1300–1650: Structure of Power*. New York and Houndmills: Palgrave-Macmillan, 2002.

– "The Crusade of Varna, 1443–1445: What Motivated the Crusades?." In *The Religions of the Book: Christian Perceptions, 1400–1660*. Edited by Matthew Dimmock and Andrew Hadfield. Basingstoke and New York: Palgrave-Macmillan, 2008, 45–65.

Ingham, Patricia Clare. *Sovereign Fantasies: Arthurian Romance and the Making of Britain*. Philadelphia: University of Pennsylvania Press, 2001.

İnalcik, Halįl. "The Heyday and Decline of the Ottoman Empire." In *The Cambridge History of Islam*, Vol. 1 of 2 vols. Cambridge: Cambridge University Press, 1970, 324–53.

Ingram, Martin. "The Reform of Popular Culture? Sex and Marriage in Early Modern England." In *Popular Culture in Seventeenth-Century England*. Edited by Barry Reay. New York: St Martin's Press, 1985, 129–65.

Iyengar, Sujata. *Shades of Difference: Mythologies of Skin Color in Early Modern England*. Philadelphia: University of Pennsylvania Press, 2005.

Jackson, W.T.H. "The Nature of Romance." *Yale French Studies* 51 (1974): 12–25.

Jameson, Fredric. "Magical Narratives: Romance as Genre." *New Literary History* 7 (1975–76): 135–63.

Jardine, Lisa. *Worldly Goods: A New History of the Renaissance.* New York and London: Doubleday, 1996.

Jardine, Lisa, and Jerry Brotton. *Global Interests: Renaissance Art Between East and West.* London: Reaktion Books, 2005.

– "Companionate Marriage Versus Male Friendship: Anxiety for the Lineal Family in Jacobean Drama." In *Political Culture and Cultural Politics in Seventeen-Century England.* Edited by Susan D. Amussen and Mark A. Kishlansky. Manchester: Manchester University Press, 1995, 234–54.

Jardine, Lisa, and William Sherman. "Pragmatic Readers: Knowledge Transactions and Scholarly Services in Late Elizabethan England." In *Religion, Culture and Society in Early Modern Britain: Essays in Honour of Patrick Collinson.* Edited by Anthony Fletcher and Peter Roberts. Cambridge: Cambridge University Press, 1994, 102–24.

Jed, Stephanie. *Chaste Thinking: The Rape of Lucrece and the Birth of Humanism* Bloomington: Indiana University Press, 1989.

Jewkes, W.T. "The Literature of Travel and the Mode of Romance in the Renaissance." *Bulletin of the New York Public Library* 67 (1963): 219–36.

Jocelyn, Catty. *Writing Rape, Writing Women in Early Modern England: Unbridled Speech.* New York: St Martin's Press, 1999.

Jones, Eldred D. *The Elizabethan Image of Africa.* n.p.: Published for the Folger Shakespeare Library by the University of Virginia Press, 1971.

Jones, Norman L. "The Adaptation of Tradition: The Image of the Turk in Protestant England." *East European Quarterly* 12:2 (1978): 161–75.

Jordan, Constance. *Renaissance Feminism: Literary Texts and Political Models.* Ithaca and London: Cornell University Press, 1990.

Juan Gil, Daniel. *Before Intimacy: Asocial Sexuality in Early Modern England* Minneapolis and London: University of Minnesota Press, 2006.

Kabbani, Rana. *Imperial Fictions: Europe's Myths of Orient.* London: Pandora, 1988.

Kahn, Victoria. *Wayward Contracts: The Crisis of Political Obligation in England, 1640–1674.* Princeton and Oxford: Princeton University Press, 2004.

– "Margaret Cavendish and the Romance of Contract." *Renaissance Quarterly* 50:2 (Summer 1997): 526–66.

– *Rhetoric, Prudence, and Skepticism in the Renaissance.* Ithaca and London: Cornell University Press, 1985.

Kamps, Ivo, and Jyotsna G. Singh. *Travel Knowledge: European "Discoveries" in the Early Modern Period.* Houndmills, Basingstoke, and New York: Palgrave, 2001.

Karras, Ruth Mazzo. *From Boys to Men: Formations of Masculinity in Late Medieval Europe.* Philadelphia: University of Pennsylvania Press, 2003.

Keay, John. *The Honourable Company: A History of the English East India Company.* London: Harper Collins, 1991.

Keen, Maurice. "Brotherhood in Arms." *History* 47 (1962): 1–17.

Keene, Derek. "Material London in Time and Space." In *Material London, ca. 1600*. Edited by Lena Cowen Orlin. Philadelphia: University of Pennsylvania Press, 2000, 55–74.

Keiser, Elizabeth B. *Courtly Desire and Medieval Homophobia: The Legitimation of Sexual Pleasure in* Cleanness *and Its Contexts*. New Haven and London: Yale University Press, 1997.

Kelly, Henry Ansgar. "The Varieties of Love in Medieval Literature According to Gaston Paris." *Romance Philology* 40:3 (1987): 302–27.

Ker, W.P. "Romance." In *Collected Essays of W.P. Ker*. Edited by Charles Whibley, Vol. 2 of 2 vols. London: Macmillan, 1925, 310–26.

– "The Elizabethan Voyagers." In *Collected Essays of W.P. Ker*. Edited by Charles Whibley, Vol. 1 of 2 vols. London: Macmillan, 1925, 1–9.

– *Epic and Romance*. New York and London: The Macmillan Company, 1897.

Kerrigan, John. *Archipelagic English: Literature, History, and Politics, 1603–1707*. Oxford: Oxford University Press, 2008.

King, Thomas A. *The Gendering of Men, 1600–1750: The English Phallus*. Madison, WI: University of Wisconsin Press, 2004.

Koenigsberger, H.G. *The Government of Sicily under Phillip II of Spain*. Ithaca, NY: Cornell University Press, 1969.

Kostić, Veselin. *Dubrovnik i Engleska, 1300–1650*. Beograd: Srpska Akademija Nauka, 1975.

– "Ragusa and the Spanish Armada." *Balcanica* 3 (1972): 195–235.

Krekić, Bariša. "Adominandum Crimen: Punishment of Homosexuals in Renaissance Dubrovnik." *Viator: Medieval and Renaissance Studies* 18 (1987): 337–45.

– *Dubrovnik: A Mediterranean Urban Society, 1300–1600*. Aldershot: Variorum, 1997.

– "Developed Autonomy: The Patricians in Dubrovnik and Dalmatian Cities." In *Urban Society of Eastern Europe in Premodern Times*. Edited by Bariša Krekić. Los Angeles and London: University of California Press, 1987, 185–215.

Krueger, Robert L. *Women Readers and the Ideology of Gender in Old French Verse Romance*. Cambridge: Cambridge University Press, 1993.

Lach, Donald F. *Asia in the Making of Europe*. Vol. 1, *The Century of Discovery*. Chicago: University of Chicago Press, 1965.

Letts, Malcolm. *Sir John Mandeville: Travels, Texts and Translations*, 2nd series, Vol. 2. no. 101–2. London: Hakluyt Society, 1953.

– *Sir John Mandeville: The Man and His Book*. London: Bachworth Press, 1949.

Levine, Laura. *Men in Women's Clothing: Anti-theatricality and Effeminization, 1579–1642*. Cambridge: Cambridge University Press, 1994.

Liebler, Naomi Conn. "Bully St. George: Richard Johnson's *Seven Champions of Christendom* and the Creation of the Bourgeois National Hero." In *Early Modern Prose Fiction: The Cultural Politics of Reading*. Edited by Naomi Conn Liebler. New York and London: Routledge, 2007, 115–29.

Linton, Joan Pong. *The Romance of the New World: Gender and the Literary Formations of English Colonialism*. Cambridge: Cambridge University Press, 1998.

Little, Jr, Arthur. *Shakespeare Jungle Feaver: National Imperial Re-visions of Race, Rape, and Sacrifice*. Stanford: Stanford University Press, 2000.

Lockey, Brian C. *Law and Empire in English Renaissance Literature*. Cambridge: Cambridge University Press, 2006.

Lovett, Morss Robert, and Helen Sard Hughes. *The History of the Novel in England*. Boston: Houghton Mifflin, 1932.

Lucas, Caroline. *Writing for Women: The Example of Woman as Reader in Elizabethan Romance*. Milton Keynes: Open University Press, 1989.

Luckyj, Christina. "The Politics of Genre in Early Modern Women's Writing: The Case of Lady Mary Wroth." *English Studies in Canada* 27 (2001): 253–82.

Lučić, Josip. "The Earliest Contacts Between Dubrovnik and England." In *Dubrovnik Relations with England: A Symposium*, April 1976. Edited by Rudolf Filipović and Monica Partridge. Zagreb: University of Zagreb, 1976, 9–29.

Macfarlane, Alan. *Marriage and Love in England 1300–1840*. Oxford and New York: Basil Blackwell, 1987.

MacFaul, Tom. *Male Friendship in Shakespeare and his Contemporaries*. Cambridge: Cambridge University Press, 2007.

Mack, Peter. *Elizabethan Rhetoric: Theory and Practice*. Cambridge: Cambridge University Press, 2002.

MacLean, Gerald. *The Rise of Oriental Travel: English Visitors to the Ottoman Empire, 1580–1720*. New York and Houndmills: Palgrave Macmillan, 2004.

MacLean, Gerald, and William Dalrymple, ed. *Re-Orienting the Renaissance: Cultural Exchanges with the East*. New York and Houndmills: Palgrave Macmillan, 2005.

MacLean, Gerald, and Nabil Matar. *Britain and the Islamic World, 1558–1713*. Oxford: Oxford University Press, 2011.

Manners, Ian. *European Cartographers and the Ottoman World, 1500–1750: Maps from the Collection of O. J. Sopranos*. Chicago: The Oriental Institute Museum of The University of Chicago, 2007.

Marchitello, Howard. *Narrative and Meaning in Early Modern England: Browne's Skull and Other Histories*. Cambridge: Cambridge University Press, 1997.

Marcus, George, and Dick Cushman. "Ethnographies as Texts." *Annual Review of Anthropology* 11 (1982): 25–70.

Margolies, David. *Novel and Society in Elizabethan England.* London and Sydney: Croom Helm, 1985.

Maslen, R.W. "Sidneian Geographies." *Sidney Journal* 20:2 (2002): 45–65.

Masten, Jeffrey. *Textual intercourse: Collaboration, authorship, and sexualities in Renaissance drama.* Cambridge: Cambridge University Press, 1997.

Matar, Nabil. *Islam in Britain 1558–1685.* Cambridge: Cambridge University Press, 1998.

– *Britain and Barbary, 1589–1689.* Gainesville: University Press of Florida, 2005.

– "The Anglo-Muslim Disputation in the Early Modern Period." In *Cultural Encounters Between East and West, 1453–1699.* Edited by Matthew Dimmock and Matthew Birchwood. Newcastle-upon-Tyne: Cambridge Scholars Press, 2005, 29–42.

– "Introduction: England and Mediterranean Captivity, 1577–1704." In *Piracy, Slavery, and Redemption: Barbary Captivity Narratives from Early Modern England.* Edited by Daniel J. Vitkus. New York: Columbia University Press, 2001, 1–52.

– *Turks, Moors, and the Englishmen in the Age of Discovery.* New York: Columbia University Press, 1999.

– "'Turning Turk': Conversion to Islam in English Renaissance Thought." *The Durham University Journal* 86 (1994): 33–43.

Matchinske, Megan. *Writing, Gender and State in Early Modern England: Identity Formation and the Female Subject.* Cambridge: Cambridge University Press, 1998.

Matvejevic, Predrag. *Mediterranean: A Cultural Landscape.* Translated by Michael Henry Heim. Berkeley, Los Angeles, London: University of California Press, 1999.

Matz, Robert. "Slander, Renaissance Discourse of Sodomy, and *Othello.*" *ELH* 66:2 (1999): 261–76.

Mauss, Marcel. *The Gift: Forms and Functions of Exchange in Archaic Societies.* Translated by Ian Cunnison. New York: Norton, 1967.

McBurney, William H., ed. *English Prose Fiction 1700–1800 in the University of Illinois Library.* Urbana: University of Illinois Press, 1965.

McCoy, Richard C. *The Rites of Knighthood: The Literature and Politics of Elizabethan Chivalry.* Berkeley, Los Angeles, and London: University of California Press, 1989.

– *Sir Philip Sidney: Rebellion in Arcadia.* Hassocks, Sussex: Harvester Press, 1979.

McCulloch, J.R., ed. *Early English Tracts on Commerce.* Cambridge: Printed for the Economic History Society, 1952.

McDonald, Russ. *Shakespeare's Late Style.* Cambridge: Cambridge University Press, 2006.

McJanet, Linda. "'History Written by The Enemy': Eastern Sources About the Ottomans on the Continent and in England." *English Literary Renaissance* 36:3 (2006): 396–429.

– "Genre and Geography: The Eastern Mediterranean in *Pericles* and *The Comedy of Errors*." In *Playing the Globe: Genre and Geography in English Renaissance Drama*. Edited by John Gillies and Virginia Mason Vaughan. Madison, London: University Associated Press, 1998, 86–106.

McKeon, Michael. *The Origins of the English Novel, 1600–1740*. Baltimore: The Johns Hopkins University Press, 1988.

McLeod, Bruce. *The Geography of Empire in English Literature 1580–1745*. Cambridge: Cambridge University Press, 1999.

Mentz, Steve. *Romance for Sale in Early Modern England: The Rise of Prose Fiction*. Aldershot and Burlington: Ashgate, 2006.

Meserve, Margaret. *Empires of Islam in Renaissance Historical Thought*. Cambridge, MA and London: Harvard University Press, 2008.

Miller, Naomi. *Mapping the City: The Language and Culture of Cartography in the Renaissance*. London and New York: Continuum, 2003.

Miner, Earl. "Some Issues of Literary 'Species, or Distinct Kind.'" In *Renaissance Genres*. Edited by Barbara Kiefer Lewalski. Cambridge, Mass. and London: Harvard University Press, 1986, 15–44.

Mish, Charles C., ed. *English Prose Fiction, 1600–1700*. Charlottesville: Bibliographical Society of the University of Virginia, 1967.

– "Best Sellers in Seventeenth-Century Fiction." *Papers of the Bibliographical Society of America* 47 (1953): 356–73.

– "Black Letter as a Social Discriminant in Seventeenth-Century Fiction." *Papers of the Bibliographical Society of America* 47 (1953): 627–30.

– "Comparative Popularity of Early Fiction and Drama." *Notes and Queries* 197 (1952): 269–70.

Montrose, Louis. *The Purpose of Playing: Shakespeare and the Cultural Politics of the Elizabethan Theatre*. Chicago and London: University of Chicago Press, 1996.

Moore, Helen. "The Eastern Mediterranean in the English *Amadis* Cycle, Book V." *Yearbook of English Studies* 41:1 (2011): 113–25.

Moretti, Franco. *Graphs, Maps, Trees: Abstract Models for Literary History*. London and New York: Verso, 2005.

– "The Slaughterhouse of Literature." *Modern Language Quarterly* 61:1 (2000): 207–27.

– "Conjectures on World Literature." *New Left Review* 1 (2000): 54–68.

Morgan, David. *Medieval Persia, 1040–1797*. Essex: Pearson Education Limited, 1988.

Morgan, E. Delmer, and C.H. Cooke. ed. *Early Voyages and Travels in Russia and Persia by Anthony Jenkins and Other Englishmen*. Vol. 1. London: Hakluyt Society, 1886.

Morse, Ruth. "Two Gentlemen and the Cult of Friendship," *Neuphilologische Mitteilungen* 84 (1983): 214–24.

Mosse, George L. "Friendship and Nationalism." In *Nationalism and Sexuality: Respectability and Abnormal Sexuality in Modern Europe*. New York: Howard Fertig, 1985, 66–89.

Murrin, Michael. *Trade and Romance*. Chicago: University of Chicago Press, 2014.

– *History and Warfare in Renaissance Epic*. Chicago and London: University of Chicago Press, 1997.

Neal, Derek G. *The Masculine Self in Late Medieval England*. Chicago and London: University of Chicago Press, 2008.

Newcomb, Lori Humphrey. *Reading Popular Romance in Early Modern England*. New York: Columbia University Press, 2002.

– "'Social Things': The Production of Popular Culture in the Reception of Robert Greene's *Pandosto*." *ELH* 61 (1994): 753–71.

– "The Sources of Romance, the Generation of Story, and the Patters of the Pericles Play." In *Staging Early Modern Romance: Prose Fiction, Dramatic Romance, and Shakespeare*. Edited by Mary Ellen Lamb and Valerie Wayne. New York and London: Routledge, 2008, 21–46.

Ng, Su Feng. "Global Renaissance: Alexander the Great and Early Modern Classicism from the British Isles to the Malay Archipelago." *Comparative Literature* 58:4 (2006): 293–312.

Norbrook, David. *Poetry and Politics in the English Renaissance*. Oxford: Oxford University Press, 2002.

O'Connell, Laura Stevenson. "The Elizabethan Bourgeois Hero-Tale: Aspects of an Adolescent Social Consciousness." In *After the Reformation: Essays in honor of J.H. Hexter*. Edited by Barbara C. Malamet. Philadelphia: University of Pennsylvania Press, 1980, 268–90.

O'Connor, John J. *Amadis de Gaule and Its Influence on Elizabethan Literature*. New Brunswick, NJ: Rutgers University Press, 1970.

O'Hara, Diana. *Courtship and Constraint: Rethinking the Making of Marriage in Tudor England*. Manchester: Manchester University Press, 2000.

Ord, Melanie. *Travel and Experience in Early Modern Literature*. New York and Houndmills: Palgrave Macmillan, 2008.

Orgel, Stephen. *Impersonations: The Performance of Gender in Shakespeare's England*. Cambridge: Cambridge University Press, 1996.

– *The Illusion of Power: Political Theater in the Renaissance*. Berkeley, Los Angeles, London: University of California Press, 1975.

Pamuk, Şevket. "Braudel's Eastern Mediterranean Revisited." In *Braudel Revisited: The Mediterranean World, 1600–1800*. Edited by Gabriel Piterburg, Teofilo F. Ruiz, and Geoffrey Symcox. Toronto: University of Toronto Press, in association with the UCLA Center for Seventeenth and Eighteenth-Century Studies, and the William Andrews Clark Memorial Library, 2010, 99–126.

Parker, Patricia A. *Inescapable Romance: Studies in the Poetics of a Mode*. Princeton: Princeton University Press, 1979.

Patchell, Mary. *The 'Palmerin' Romances in Elizabethan Prose Fiction* (1947). New York: AMS Press, 1966.

Perry, Curtis. *Literature and Favoritism in Early Modern England*. Cambridge: Cambridge University Press, 2006.

Pettet, E.C. *Shakespeare and Romance Tradition*. London and New York: Staple Press, 1949.

Phillips, Joshua. "Chronicles of Wasted Time: Anthony Munday, Tudor Romances, and Literature of Labor." *ELH* 73 (2006): 781–803.

– "Dangerous Sea and Unvalued Jewels: Some Notes on Shakespeare's Consciousness of the Sea," *English* 10:60 (1955): 215–20.

Pigeon, Renée Marie. "Prose Fiction Adaptations of Sidney's *Arcadia*." PhD dissertation, University of California at Los Angeles, 1988.

Potter, Lois. *Secret Rites and Secret Writing: Royalist Literature, 1641–1660*. Cambridge: Cambridge University Press, 1989.

Prendergast, Christopher. "Across the 'Between.'" *New Left Review*. 86 (2014): 151–8.

Prendergast, Maria Teresa Micaela. *Renaissance Fantasies: The Gendering of Aesthetics in Early Modern Fiction*. Kent, OH and London: Kent State University Press, 2000.

Pruvost, René. *Matteo Bandello and Elizabethan Fiction*. Paris: Librarie Ancienne Honoré Champion, 1937.

Quint, David. *Epic and Empire: Politics and Generic Form from Virgil to Milton*. Princeton, NJ: Princeton University Press, 1993.

Radway, Janice A. *Reading the Romance: Women, Patriarchy, and Popular Literature*. Chapel Hill and London: University of North Carolina Press, 1984.

Ramsay, G.D. *English Overseas Trade During the Centuries of Emergence: Studies in Some Modern Origins of the English-Speaking World*. London: Macmillan; New York: St Martin's Press, 1957.

Randall, Dale B.J. *The Golden Tapestry: A Critical Survey of Non-Chivalric Spanish Fiction in English Translation, 1543–1637*. Durham: Duke University Press, 1963.

Relihan, Constance C. *Cosmographical Glasses: Geographical Discourse, Gender, and Elizabethan Fiction*. Kent, Ohio and London: Kent State University Press, 2004.

– *Fashioning Authority: The Development of Elizabethan Novelistic Discourse*. Kent, Ohio and London: Kent State University Press, 1994.

Rice, Warner. "Early English Travelers to Greece and the Levant." In *Essays and Studies in English and Comparative Literature*, University of Michigan

Publications, Language and Literature, Vol. 10. Ann Arbor: University of Michigan Press, 1933, 205–60.

Richardson, Brenda E. "Two English Francophiles: Some French Influences on Fashionable Elizabethan Fiction." *Proceedings of the Royal Irish Academy* 84:6 (1984): 225–35.

Rigolot, François. "The Renaissance Crisis of Exemplarity." *Journal of the History of Ideas* 59:4 (1998): 557–63.

Robertson, Jean, and D.J. Gordon, ed., *A Calendar of Dramatic Records in the Books of the Livery Companies of London, 1485–1640*, Vol. 3. London: The Malone Society, 1954.

Robbins, Bruce. "Commodity Histories." *PMLA* 120:2 (March 2005): 454–63.

Robinson, Benedict S. *Islam and Early Modern English Literature: The Politics of Romance from Spenser to Milton*. New York and Houndmills: Palgrave-Macmillan, 2007.

Rocke, Michael. *Forbidden Friendships: Homosexuality and Male Culture in Renaissance Florence*. New York and Oxford: Oxford University Press, 1996.

Römer, Zdenka Janeković. *Okvir slobode: dubrovačka vlastela između srednjovjekovlja i humanizma. Zagreb-Dubrovnik: Zavod za povjesne znanosti HAZU, 1999.*

– "Stranac u srednjovjekovnom Dubrovniku i između prihvaćenosti i odbačenosti." *Radovi Zavoda za hrvatsku povjest* 26 (1993): 27–37.

Rothman, E. Natalie. "Becoming Venetian: Conversion and Transformation in the Seventeenth-Century Mediterranean." *Mediterranean Historical Review* 21:1 (2006): 39–75.

Rothstein, Natalie. "Silk in the Early Modern Period, c. 1500–1780." In *The Cambridge History of Western Textiles*, Vol. 1 of 2 vols. Cambridge: Cambridge University Press, 2003, 528–61.

Rowe, John Howard. "Ethnography and Ethnology in the Sixteenth Century." *Kroeber Anthropological Society Papers* 30 (1964): 1–19.

Royster, Salibelle. "From Athens to Istanbul: Background for Literature." *Education* 91:4 (1971): 333–6.

Ruggiero, Guido. *The Boundaries of Eros: Sex Crime and Sexuality in Renaissance Venice*. New York and Oxford: Oxford University Press, 1985.

Said, Edward. *Orientalism*. New York: Vintage Books, 1979.

Salzman, Paul. *English Prose Fiction: 1558–1700. A Critical History*. Oxford: Clarendon Press, 1985.

Sanchez, Melissa E. *Erotic Subjects: The Sexuality of Politics in Early Modern English Literature*. Oxford: Oxford University Press, 2011.

Sanford, Rhonda Lemke. *Maps and Memory in Early Modern England*. New York and Houndmills: Palgrave-Macmillan, 2002.

Saunders, Corinne. *Rape and Ravishment in the Literature of Medieval England*. Cambridge and Rochester, NY: D.S. Brewer, 2001.

Scanlon, Paul A. "A Checklist of Prose Romances in English: 1474–1603." *The Library*, 5th series, 33:2 (1978): 143–52.

Schlauch, Margaret. "English Short Fiction in the 15th and 16th Centuries." *Studies in Short Fiction* 3:4 (1966): 393–434.

Schleck, Julia. "'Plain Broad Narrative of Substantial Facts': Credibility, Narrative, and Hakluyt's *Principall Navigations*." *Renaissance Quarterly* 59 (2006): 768–94.

Schleiner, Louise. "Ladies and Gentlemen in Two Genres of Elizabethan Fiction." *Studies in English Literature, 1500–1900* 29 (1989): 1–20.

Schleiner, Winfried. "Male Cross-Dressing and Trasvestism in Renaissance Romance." *Sixteenth-Century Journal* 19 (1988): 605–19.

– "Le feu caché: Homosocial Bonds Between Women in a Renaissance Romance." *Renaissance Quarterly* 45: 2 (1992): 293–311.

Schmidgall, Gary. "*The Tempest* and *Primaleon*: A New Source." *Shakespeare Quarterly* 37:4 (1986): 423–39.

Schwarz, Kathryn. *Tough Love: Amazon Encounters in the English Renaissance*. Durham and London: Duke University Press, 2000.

Schwoebel, Robert. *The Shadow and the Crescent: The Renaissance Image of the Turk 1453–1517*. Nieuwkoop: B. De Graaf, 1967.

Sedgwick, Eve Kosofsky. *Between Men: English Literature and Male Homosocial Desire*. New York: Columbia University Press, 1985.

Shannon, Laurie. *Sovereign Amity: Figures of Friendship in Shakespearean Contexts*. Chicago and London: University of Chicago Press, 2002.

– "Nature's Bias: Renaissance Homonormativity and Elizabethan Comic Likeness." *Modern Philology* 98:2 (2000): 183–210.

Shepard, Alexandra. *Meanings of Manhood in Early Modern England*. Oxford: Oxford University Press, 2003.

– "Manhood, Credit and Patriarchy in Early Modern England, c. 1580–1640." *Past and Present* 167 (2000): 75–106.

Sherman, William H. *Used Books: Marking Readers in Renaissance England*. Philadelphia: University of Pennsylvania Press, 2008.

Shrank, Cathy. *Writing the Nation in Reformation England, 1530–1580*. Oxford University Press, 2004.

Shuger, Debora Kuller. *The Renaissance Bible: Scholarship, Sacrifice and Subjectivity* Berkeley, Los Angeles, London: University of California Press, 1998.

Simons, Patricia. *The Sex of Men in Premodern Europe: A Cultural History*. Cambridge: Cambridge University Press, 2011.

Simpson, James. *Reform and Cultural Revolution*. Vol. 2, *1350–1547*, of *The Oxford English Literary History*. Oxford: Oxford University Press, 2002.

Skilliter, S.R. *William Harborne and the Trade with Turkey 1578–1582: A Documentary Study of the First Anglo-Ottoman Relations*. Oxford: Oxford University Press, 1977.

Skinner, Quentin. *The Foundations of Modern Political Thought*. Vol. 1, *The Renaissance*. Cambridge: Cambridge University Press, 1978.

Skretkowicz, Victor. *European Erotic Romance: Philhellene Protestantism, Renaissance Translation and English Literary Politics*. Manchester: Manchester University Press, 2010.

Sloan, Kim. *A New World: England's First View of America*. London: The British Library, 2007.

Smith, Alan G.R. *The Emergence of a Nation State: The Commonwealth of England, 1529–1660*. London and New York: Longman, 1984.

Smith, Clara A., comp. *List of Manuscript Maps in the Edward E. Ayer Collection*. Chicago: The Newberry Library, 1927.

Smith, Nigel. *Literature and Revolution in England, 1640–1660*. New Haven and London: Yale University Press, 1994.

Smith, R. Bruce. *Shakespeare and Masculinity*. Oxford: Oxford University Press, 2000.

Solga, Kim. "Rape's Metatheatrical Return: Rehearsing Sexual Violence Among the Early Moderns." *Theatre Journal* 58.1 (2006): 53–72.

Sphyroeras, Vasilis, Anna Avramea, and Spyros Asdrahas. *Maps and Mapmakers of the Aegean*. Translated by G. Cox and J. Solman. Athens: Olkos Ltd., 1985.

Spufford, Margaret. *Small Books and Pleasant Histories: Popular Fiction and Its Readership in Seventeenth-Century England*. London: Methuen, 1981.

Stallybrass, Peter. "Marginal England: The View from Aleppo." *Center or Margin: Revisions of the English Renaissance In Honour of Leeds Barroll*. Edited by Lena Cowen Orlin. Salinsgrove, PA: Susquehana University Press, 2006.

Stanford Encyclopedia of Philosophy. "Madeleine de Scudéry." http://plato.stanford.edu/entries/madeleine-scudery./ Accessed 8 August 2013.

Stanivukovic, Goran. "The Prenovel: Theory in the Archive." In *Narrative Developments from Chaucer to Defoe*. Edited by Gerd Bayer and Ebbe Klitgård. New York and Abington: Routledge, 2011. 178–98.

– "English Renaissance Romances as Conduct Books for Young Men." In *Early Modern Prose Fiction: The Cultural Politics of Reading*. Edited by Naomi Conn Liebler. New York and London: Routledge, 2007, 60–78.

– "'Knights in Armes': The Homoerotics of the English Renaissance Prose Romances." In *Prose Fiction and Early Modern Sexualities in England, 1570–1640*. Edited by Constance C. Relihan and Goran V. Stanivukovic. New York and Houndmills: Palgrave-Macmillan, 2003, 171–92.

– "Cruising the Mediterranean: Narratives of Sexuality and Geographies of the Eastern Mediterranean in Early Modern English Prose Romances."

In *Remapping the Mediterranean World in Early Modern English Writings*. Edited by Goran Stanivukovic. New York and Houndmills: Pagrave-Macmillan, 2007, 59–74.

– "Recent Studies of English Renaissance Literature of the Mediterranean." *English Literary Renaissance* 32:1 (2002): 168–86.

Starkey, David, et al. *The English Court from the Wars of the Roses to the Civil War*. London and New York: Longman, 1987.

Stevens, Paul. "Heterogenizing Imagination: Globalization, *The Merchant of Venice*, and the Work of Literary Criticism." *English Literary History* 36 (2005): 425–37.

Stevenson, Laura Caroline. *Praise and Paradox: Merchants and Craftsmen in Elizabethan Popular Literature*. Cambridge: Cambridge University Press, 1984.

Stewart, Alan. "A Society of Sodomoties: Religion and Homosexuality in Renaissance England." In *Love, Friendship and Faith, 1300–1800*. Edited by Laura Gowing, Michael Hunter, and Miri Rubin. New York and Basingstoke: Palgrave-Macmillan, 2005, 88–109.

– *Close Readers: Humanism and Sodomy in Early Modern England*. Princeton: Princeton University Press, 1997.

– "The Early Modern Closet Discovered, *Representations* 50 (1995): 76–100.

– "'Come from Turkie': Mediterranean Trade in Late Elizabethan London," In *Remapping*. Edited by G. Stanivukovic, 157–77.

Stockton, Will, and James M. Bromley. *Sex Before Sex: Figuring the Act in Early Modern England*. Minneapolis and London: University of Minnesota Press, 2013.

Strohm, Paul. "The Middle English Narrative Genres." *Genre* 13 (1980), 379–88.

– "The Origins and Meaning of Middle English *Romaunce*." *Genre* 10 (1977), 1–28.

Suárez-Navaz, Liliana. *Rebordering the Mediterranean: Boundaries and Citizenship in Southern Europe*. New York and Oxford: Berghahn Books, 2004.

Subrahmanyam, Sanjay. *Three Ways to Be Alien: Travails & Encounters in the Early Modern World*. Waltham, Mass.: Brandeis University Press, 2011.

Sullivan, Ceri. *The Rhetoric of Credit: Merchants in Early Modern Writing*. Madison: Fairleigh Dickinson University Press; London: Associated University Press, 2002.

Summers, Claude, ed. *Homosexuality in Renaissance and Enlightenment England*. Binghampton, NY: Harrington Press, 1992.

Summers, David A. "Re-fashioning Arthur in the Tudor Era." *Exemplaria* 9:2 (1997): 371–92.

Swarth, Ana. *Rape and Religion in English Renaissance Literature: A Topical Study of Four Texts by Shakespeare, Drayton, and Middleton*. Uppsala: Acta Universitatis Upsaliensis, 2003.

Taylor, Barry. "Academic Exchange: Text, Politics, and the Construction of English and American Identities in Contemporary Renaissance Criticism." In *Discontinuities: New Essays on Renaissance Literature and Criticism*. Edited by Viviana Comensoli and Paul Stevens. Toronto: University of Toronto Press, 1998, 181–200.

Thirsk, Joan. *Alternative Agriculture: A History, from the Black Death to the Present Day* Oxford: Oxford University Press, 1997.

Thomas, Henry. *Spanish and Portuguese Romances of Chivalry: The Revival of the Romance of Chivalry in the Spanish Peninsula, and Its Extension and Influence Abroad*. Cambridge: The University Press, 1920.

– "The Romance of Amadis of Gaul." *Transactions of the Bibliographical Society* 11 (1913): 251–97.

– "The Palmerin Romances." *Transactions of the Bibliographical Society* 14 (1916): 98–144.

Traub, Valerie. "Friendship's Loss: Alan Bray's Making of History." In *Love, Friendship and Faith in Europe, 1300–1800*. Edited by Laura Gowing, Michael Hunter, and Miri Rubin. Houndmills and New York: Palgrave-Macmillan, 2005, 15–42.

– *The Renaissance of Lesbianism in Early Modern England*. Cambridge: Cambridge University Press, 2002.

– "Mapping the Global Body." In *Early Modern Visual Culture: Representation, Race, and Empire in Renaissance England*. Edited by Peter Erickson and Clark Hulse. Philadelphia: University of Pennsylvania, 2000, 44–97.

– "The Psychomorphology of the Clitoris." *GLQ: A Journal of Lesbian and Gay Studies* 2:1–2 (1995), 81–113.

– "The Perversion of 'Lesbian' Desire." *History Workshop Journal* 41 (1996), 19–49.

Van Elk, Martine. "'This sympathizèd one day's error': Genre, Representation, and Subjectivity in *The Comedy of Errors*." *Shakespeare Quarterly* 60:1 (2009): 47–72.

Vickers, Brian. *In Defence of Rhetoric*. Oxford: Clarendon Press, 1988.

Vinaver, Eugene. *The Rise of Romance*. Oxford: Clarendon Press, 1971.

Vitkus, Daniel. *Turning Turk: English Theater and the Multicultural Mediterranean, 1570–1630*. New York and Houndmills: Palgrave Macmillan, 2003.

– "Early Modern Orientalism: Representations of Islam in Sixteenth- and Seventeenth-Century Europe." In *Western Views of Islam in Medieval and Early Modern Europe: Reception of Other*. Edited by David R. Blanks and Michael Frassetto. London: Macmillan, 1999, 207–30.

Wakelin, Daniel. *Humanism, Reading and English Literature 1430–1530*. Oxford: Oxford University Press, 2008.

Wang, Yu-Chiao. "Caxton's Romances and their Early Tudor Readers." *Huntington Library Quarterly* 67 (2004): 173–88.

Warkentin, Germaine. Review of Franco Moretti, *Graphs, Maps, Trees*. London and New York: Verso, 2005. *The Library: The Transactions of the Bibliographical Society* 7:3 (2006): 342–4.

Warren, Roger, ed. "Introduction." William Shakespeare and Roger Wilkins. A Reconstructed Text of *Pericles, Prince of Tyre*. Oxford: Oxford University Press, 2003.

Watt, Tessa. *Cheap Print and Popular Piety, 1550–1640*. Cambridge: Cambridge University Press, 1991.

Weber, Max. *The Protestant Ethic and the Spirit of Capitalism*. London and New York: Routledge, 2001.

Webster, Steven. "Dialogue in Fiction and Ethnography." *Dialectical Anthropology* 7 (1982): 91–114.

Wells, Robin Headlam. *Shakespeare on Masculinity*. Cambridge: Cambridge University Press, 2000.

Wells, Stanley. "Shakespeare and Romance." In *Later Shakespeare*. Edited by John Russell Brown and Bernard Harris. London: Edward Arnold, 1966, 49–79.

Werth, Tiffany Jo. *The Fabulous Dark Cloister: Romance in England After the Reformation*. Baltimore: Johns Hopkins University Press, 2011.

Whalen, Denise A. *Construction of Female Homoeroticism in Early Modern Drama*. New York and Houndmills: Palgrave Macmillan, 2005.

White, Hayden. *Tropics of Discourse, Essays in Cultural Criticism*. Baltimore and London: The Johns Hopkins University Press, 1985.

White, R.S. "Metamorphosis by Love in Elizabethan Romance, Romantic Comedy, and Shakespeare's Early Comedies." *The Review of English Studies*, n.s. 35:137 (1984): 14–44.

Wolff, Samuel Lee. *The Greek Romances in Elizabethan Prose Fiction*. New York: Columbia University Press, 1912.

Wood, Frances. *The Silk Road. Two Thousand Years in the Heart of Asia*. Berkeley and Los Angeles: University of California Press, 2002.

Woodbridge, Linda, and Sharon Beehler, ed. *Women, Violence and English Renaissance Literature: Essays Honoring Paul Jorgensen*. Tempe: Arizona Center for Medieval and Renaissance Studies, 2003.

Worden, Blair. *The Sound of Virtue: Philip Sidney's* Arcadia *and Elizabethan Politics*. New Haven and London: Yale University Press, 1996.

Wrenn, C.L., ed. *Beowulf, with the Finnesburg Fragment*. London: George G. Harrup, 1958.

Wright, Celeste Turner. *Anthony Mundy: An Elizabethan Man of Letters.* Berkeley: University of California Publications in English, Vol. 2 (1928). Repr. Milwood, NY: Kraus Reprint, 1977.

Wright, Louis B. *Middle-Class Culture in Elizabethan England.* Ithaca, NY: Published for the Folger Shakespeare Library by Cornell University Press, 1958.

– "Henry Robarts: Patriotic Propagandist and Novelist." *Studies in Philology* 29 (1932): 176–99.

Wrightson, Keith. *English Society 1580–1680.* New Brunswick, NJ: Rutgers University Press, 1982.

Young, Michael B. *James VI and I and the History of Homosexuality.* New York and Basingstoke: Palgrave-Macmillan, 2000.

Ze'evi, Dror. *Producing Desire: Changing Sexual Discourse in the Ottoman Middle East, 1500–1900.* Berkeley: University of California Press, 2006.

Zurcher, Amelia A. *Seventeenth-Century English Romance: Allegory, Ethics, and Politics.* New York and Houndmills: Palgrave-Macmillan, 2007.

Index

www.ingramcontent.com/pod-product-compliance
Lightning Source LLC
LaVergne TN
LVHW041112090826
844660LV00061B/798/J
9781442648876